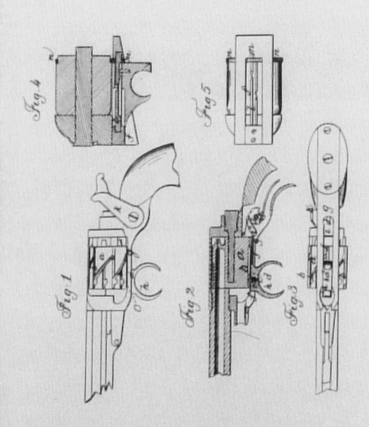

Fig. 4

Fig. 5

Fig. 1

Fig. 2

Fig. 3

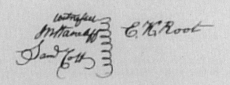

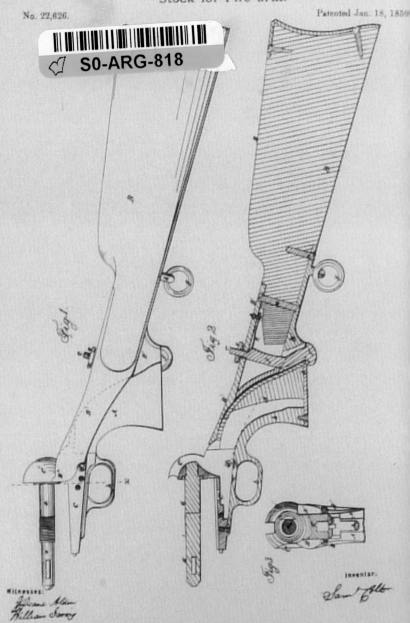

Fig. 1

Fig. 2

Fig. 3

Witnesses:

Inventor.

Pictured are two of the most important guns in Colt history, the 1847 Walker revolvers shipped to Capt. Samuel Hamilton Walker by Samuel Colt. Walker was killed on October 9, 1847 during the battle of Huamantla in

COLT SINGLE ACTION
From Patersons To Peacemakers

Written & Photographed By Dennis Adler

CHARTWELL
BOOKS, INC.

Featuring Guns From The Dr. Joseph A. Murphy,
Dennis LeVett, And Dow Heard Collections
Additional Photography Courtesy Of Greg Martin Auctions

This edition published in 2007 by
CHARTWELL BOOKS
A division of BOOK SALES, INC.
114 Northfield Avenue
Edison, New Jersey 08837

Published by arrangement with Dennis Adler who is represented by
International Transactions, Inc. of New York, USA

A special thank you to Colt's Manufacturing Company LLC and
New Colt Holding Corp. for granting us permission to use the
COLT trademark (Serpentine C).

Edited by R.L. Wilson

Designed by Keith Betterley

ISBN-13: 978-0-7858-2305-6
ISBN-10: 0-7858-2305-0

Printed in China

Vincit qui patitur, "He conquers who suffers."
— Samuel Colt

To all the engineers, craftsmen, and engravers
who helped make Colt something to write about,
and to Jeanne for sharing my enthusiasm of fine guns

The author is pictured with one of the most rare and unusual of early cartridge guns, a Colt 1860 Army long cylinder conversion.

Acknowledgements

When you write a book you need help. When you write a gun book, you need a lot of help – a cadre of collectors, a good gunsmith, engravers, holster makers, period clothiers, a prop house, and the list goes on. If it sounds more like making a movie than writing a book, there are quite a few similarities. If *Colt Single Action* was a movie, this book would be the storyboard. It is comprised of still images that paint a visual tale of America's preeminent 19th century gunmaker, Samuel Colt. Chapters are like scenes, each graphically detailing a period in Colt's early history, with one chapter flowing into the next as the story evolves. Characters are introduced, wars are fought, heroes and villains emerge; and all of it centered on Sam Colt and the guns produced in Hartford, Connecticut from the 1840s to the early 1880s.

This book would not have been possible without the contributions made by noted Colt collectors Dr. Joseph A. Murphy, Dennis LeVett, and Dow Heard, along with custom guns pictured in several chapters that were recreated for the book from the originals by master gunsmith Robert L. Millington of ArmSport LLC in Eastlake, Colorado, and master engraver John J. Adams, Sr. of Adams & Adams in Vershire, Vermont.

The backdrops designed for many of the photographic layouts are composed of original and reproduction period saddles, holsters, and western accessories. The clothing and hats seen in many of the layouts were supplied by Jim Boeke of River Junction Trade Company in McGregor, Iowa. Many guns are also depicted with period holsters, some of which were made by Jim Lockwood of Legends in Leather in Prescott, Arizona, Greg Doring of Ned Buckshot's Wild West, in Minneapolis, Minnesota, and Jim Barnard of Trailrider Products in Littleton, Colorado. All of these gentlemen are dedicated historians in their own right, who continue to handcraft historic American products in the tradition of the American West. A special note of thanks to James Hathaway and Orvis in Manchester Vermont (www.orvis.com) for supplying clothing from their Theodore Roosevelt Collection featured in *Colt Single Action* with a copy of Teddy Roosevelt's engraved and ivory stocked Single Action Army revolver.

There are many others in the background who contribute to a good book, individual collectors with perhaps only a handful of important guns, or just one, who made their prized possessions available. Our thanks to Texas Gun Collectors Association members Bobby Vance, Roger Muckerheide, and Calvin Patrick for their contributions to the chapters on Colt cartridge conversions, perhaps one of the most important periods in Colt's history.

A very special tip of the hat to my agent Peter Riva, without whose faith in this author there would be far fewer books bearing my name today. Thanks also to my friends Mark McNeely and Chuck Ahearn of Allegheny Trade Company in Duncansville, Pennsylvania for supplying original accessories and ammunition featured throughout the book, and the inimitable R. L. Wilson, for his editorial contributions and use of photographs from his personal collection.

No matter how many collectors you find, or how many guns you photograph, there are always the "unobtainable" – examples that are neither in collections at the time or are impossible to recreate. For this we often turn to one of the great auction houses in America, Greg Martin Auctions in San Francisco, California. Martin has compiled a photographic reference library of rare guns and memorabilia second to none, and thus the "unobtainable" became obtainable for this book. My thanks to Greg and his staff for providing Colt Single Action models and accessories that would have been impossible to acquire for the book. Other rare photos and historical information were supplied courtesy of authors and historians Herbert G. Houze and Stuart Mowbray, and the Wadsworth Atheneum Museum of Art in Hartford, Connecticut.

Our entire publishing group is also thankful to Kathy Hoyt and Joseph Dieso of Colt's Firearms Manufacturing Company for supplying additional historical data and allowing the use of the Colt, Peacemaker, and Single Action Army trademarks.

Last, but of great importance, is a publisher who believes in the book and is willing to go the extra distance to ensure a quality product. The best photographs are only as good as the paper on which they are printed, and Chartwell Books has spared no expense in providing the highest quality paper and printing in the industry, while at the same time bringing to market a quality book at a remarkably affordable price.

As George Peppard used to say on *The A Team*, "I love it when a plan comes together."

Dennis Adler

Contents

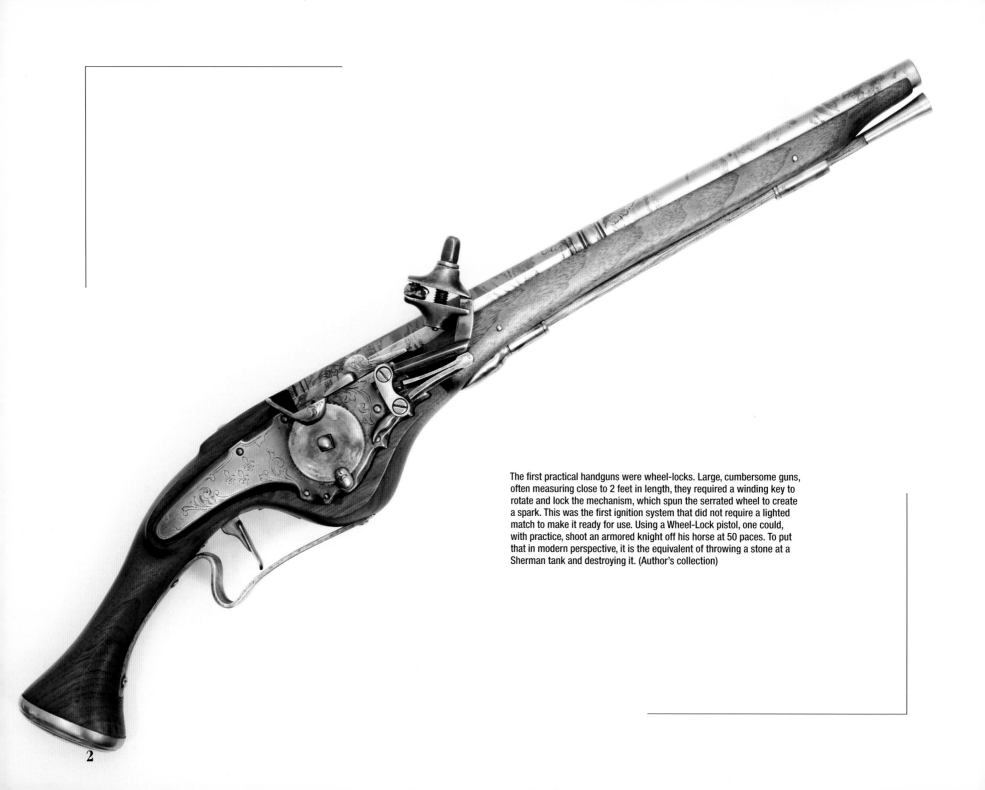

The first practical handguns were wheel-locks. Large, cumbersome guns, often measuring close to 2 feet in length, they required a winding key to rotate and lock the mechanism, which spun the serrated wheel to create a spark. This was the first ignition system that did not require a lighted match to make it ready for use. Using a Wheel-Lock pistol, one could, with practice, shoot an armored knight off his horse at 50 paces. To put that in modern perspective, it is the equivalent of throwing a stone at a Sherman tank and destroying it. (Author's collection)

Introduction
Colt and the American Frontier
Guns for a Generation of Heroes and Villains

Prior to the Paterson revolver handguns in America were, for the most part, variations of European flint and percussion lock models with single or double barrels, the latter being either of the swivel barrel, over-and-under (superposed), and shotgun (side-by-side) designs, also known as a Howdah Pistol.[1] This is not to say other types of "multiple shot" handguns weren't manufactured prior to the Paterson, particularly in Europe, which was always at least a decade ahead of America in the design of firearms. Ironically, it was a trio of Americans – Captain Artemas Wheeler, Elisha Haydon Collier, and Cornelius Coolidge – who patented the very first workable revolving pistol in 1818. Known as the Collier revolver it was patented in the United States on June 10, 1818, with subsequent patents filed in England and France. It was produced from 1819 by John Evans & Son of London, and used in quantity by British forces in India. Originally built as a flintlock, the Collier was not a rousing success in America as it was both costly to manufacture and the cylinder had to be rotated manually. The advent of the percussion lock and Collier's inability to quickly adapt their pistols to the newer, more practical ignition system spelled the end for America's first revolver, though hardly anyone noticed. Collier's greatest market was Great Britain. The last Collier pistols, fitted with percussion locks, were produced from 1824 through 1827, almost a decade before Samuel Colt filed his first patent.

When the American Frontier was being settled in the early 1800s, the revolver was little more than a fanciful idea; an idea that might have changed the course of one battle on the Texas-Mexico border in 1836 had Sam Colt already introduced the Paterson revolver by the time the Alamo fell. Texas was to become the strongest adherent of the Patent Firearms Manufacturing Company of Paterson, New Jersey by 1844. Colt's 5-shot,

The earliest flintlock designs appeared around 1615 but did not become widely accepted until the mid 17th century. The flintlock utilized a simpler, more robust firing mechanism actuated by the cock, which held a piece of flint between its jaws. The flintlock hammer simply fell against a metal leaf called a frizzen, creating a spark with the flint that ignited the powder in the flash pan and thus the charge within the barrel. Pictured is a rare c.1800-1840 swivel-barrel flintlock featuring iron furniture. Master gunsmith Leonard Day reproduced the early multiple-shot pistol design from an original gun. The swivel barrel design was used on both longrifles and pistols, allowing a quick follow up shot by rotating the second barrel and lock into battery. (Period knife and sheath by Steve and Sue Shroyer.)

[1] A Howdah was a seat or platform, commonly with a railing and a canopy, placed on the back of an elephant. A Howdah pistol was generally a large (usually .60 cal. and up) double barrel percussion or cartridge model intended for close-quarters use against tigers. These same style pistols also proved to be formidable close combat weapons in the hands of special British military units, and far across the Atlantic, on the American Frontier of the early 19th century, where single shot pistols were still the most common sidearm in use.

The .46 caliber Collier Patent Flintlock Revolver featured a 5-shot fluted cylinder. Originally intended to use a spring wound mechanism with which to automatically rotate the cylinder after each shot, production models required the cylinder be rotated by hand after each discharge. The one great failing of the Collier was that it began life in 1818 as a flintlock. It was soon made obsolete by the percussion lock, and it took Collier until 1824 to adopt a percussion lock mechanism. The Collier's design no doubt influenced young Sam Colt, who encountered the guns during a trip to India in 1830. Over 10,000 pounds sterling worth of Collier Arms were shipped to India in the 1820s. The Collier is regarded today as the first revolver. (Photo courtesy Greg Martin Auctions)

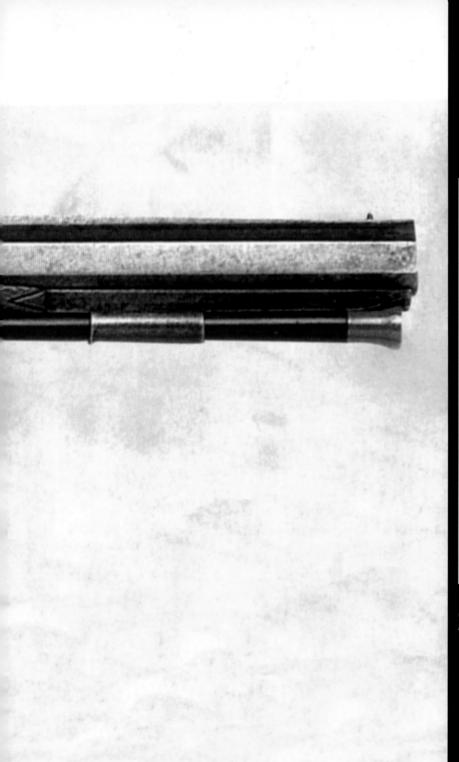

Later Collier models, such as the examples shown, were offered with a percussion lock beginning in 1824. The cylinders still had to be rotated by hand. (Photo from Little John's Auction Service, Ross Miller Estate auction August 2006 catalog)

The Colt Paterson was the first successful revolver with a mechanically rotated cylinder actuated by cocking the hammer.

.36 caliber Paterson Holster Model revolvers would become legendary in the hands of the United States Mounted Rifles led by Capt. Jack Hayes. The Republic of Texas (Texas did not become a state until 1845) had initially purchased a quantity of Paterson revolvers in 1842 for the territorial Navy, but many of the revolvers found their way into the hands of Hayes and his Texas Rangers. In 1844 the most famous battle involving Paterson revolvers was fought by less than two dozen Rangers led by Hayes, who engaged an estimated 80 Comanche warriors, killing or wounding half of them before the Indians withdrew. In a letter to Sam Colt, Walker praised the Patersons and voiced his hopes for Colt to build an even better revolver.

Although Colt had been unsuccessful in his first venture as an armsmaker, with his fledgling New Jersey enterprise going into receivership in 1842, five years later his arrangements to build 1,000 Colt "Whitneyville-Walker" .44 caliber revolvers for Capt. Samuel Walker and the U.S.M.R. put him on a road to prosperity that would last the rest of his life and make Colt's Fire Arms Manufacturing Company of Hartford, Connecticut the most successful and influential armsmaker in the United States.

By the early 1850s Colt would have far reaching influence across Europe through his foreign manufacturing and sales (particularly in London), and relationships with heads of state personally established by Sam Colt through his gifts of hand engraved, cased presentation guns.

By the beginning of the Gold Rush in 1848-49, there was barely a sodbuster, Argonaut, lawman, soldier, man or woman who had not heard of or laid hands on a Colt revolver. When the Gold Rush began, California was a peculiarly lawless place. On the actual discovery date of gold at Sutter's Mill, California was still technically part of Mexico and under American military occupation as the result of the Mexican-American War, a conflict where the Colt Whitneyville-Walker had played a priminent role. With the signing of the treaty between Mexico and the US on February 2, 1848, California became a part of the United States, but a unique part – it was neither a formal territory nor a state. California was in political limbo, a region under US military control but without the benefit of a civil legislature, executive or judicial body. Local citizens operated under a confusing and changing mixture of Mexican rules, American principles, and personal dictates. And more than a few disputes were settled at the end of a Colt barrel. This was *the* wild west.

At the start of the American Civil War in 1861 Colt's Patent Fire Arms Manufacturing Company was one of the largest and most successful business concerns in the country, regardless of one's political leanings, or at least until 11 Southern States seceded from the Union. By that time

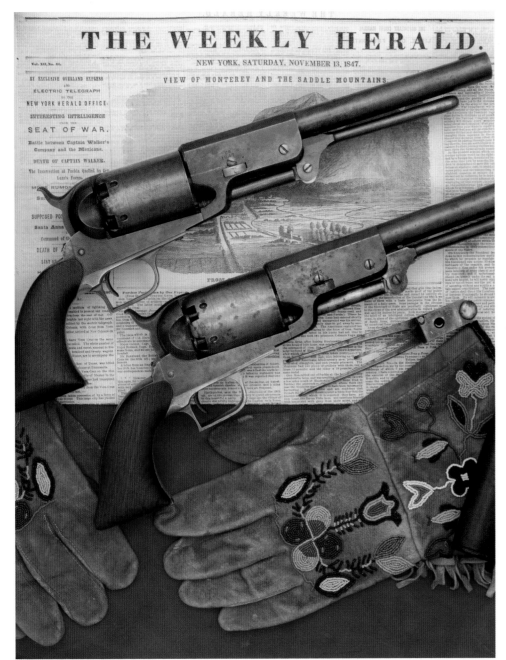

Beginning in 1847 Samuel Colt brought the percussion pistol into the fullness of its development. Colt's produced a wide variety of black powder revolvers between 1847 and 1873, which included the massive .44 caliber 1847 Walker (top left and going counter clockwise) .44 caliber First, Second and Third Model Dragoons, the .5-shot, 36 caliber 1862 Pocket Police, .31 caliber 1848 Baby Dragoon, and .36 caliber 1865 Pocket Navy, .44 caliber 1860 Army with rebated cylinder or fluted cylinder, and the .36 caliber 1861 Navy, and 1851 Navy, the latter four becoming the principal sidearms of the Union during the Civil War.

there was an entire range of Colt revolvers from small-caliber pocket-sized pistols to the mighty .44 caliber Dragoons (successors to the 1847 Walker), and the highly regarded .36 caliber 1851 Navy and .44 caliber 1860 Army, the latter two becoming the principal side arms of the US military throughout the War Between The States.

Sam Colt may have perfected and patented the design for the revolving cylinder pistol, but he wasn't alone in the American firearms business; he was instead the catalyst for an emerging industry that flourished throughout the early and middle half of the 19th century. Among Colt's most successful contemporaries was E. Remington & Sons in Ilion, New York. After the Colt's patent for the revolving cylinder expired, Remington introduced the revolutionary 1858 Army Model chambered for .44 caliber loads, and the lighter .36 caliber Navy version. The Remington revolvers featured a solid top strap and a fixed (threaded) barrel,

Colt's largest competitor was E. Remington & Sons, which introduced its first revolvers in 1858, immediately after the Colt's patent expired. Remington took an entirely different approach to the design of percussion revolvers using a fixed barrel and a frame with a top strap. Both ideas would be incorporated by Colt in their new 1873 Single Action Army. (Author's collection)

providing greater strength and ease of operation compared to Colt's wedge-pinned barrel and open top design, which by 1858 was now almost 20 years old. One could change out a Remington cylinder in seconds without having to remove the barrel. The top strap added strength to the frame, and above all, the threaded Remington barrels assured greater accuracy. In the heat of battle, a Colt barrel wedged too tightly could easily bind the cylinder. Colt nevertheless remained the dominant American pistol of the Civil War era, and well into the postwar expansion west in the late 1860s and early 1870s. For more than 35 years the percussion revolver, either manufac-

tured by Colt's, Remington, or others, both here and abroad, remained the prevailing design.

The handgun had come a long way from primitive single shot 16th century wheel-locks, but in many ways had remained much the same for nearly 300 years, requiring three individual elements in order to function: powder, ball, and a means of igniting the charge. The advent of the metallic cartridge prior to the Civil War, which combined all three components into one, hastened the beginning of a new era in American firearms manufacturing.

As the American frontier opened up in the post Civil War era, the cartridge pistol become a means by which one could

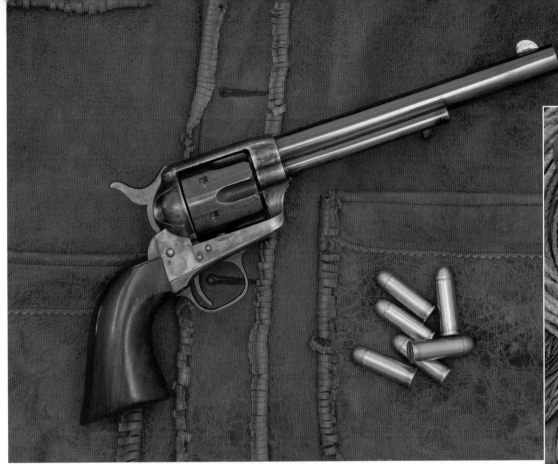

With Colt's introduction of the Peacemaker in 1873, the Hartford armsmaker created the most successful and longest lived handgun in history. (Model P Colt from the Dr. Joseph A. Murphy collection)

afford self protection through the concealment of a charged and readied sidearm, easily retrieved and in time of need the great equalizer of both man and beast.

There were a substantial variety of cartridge firing revolvers used by both sides during the Civil War, few of which, aside from the new, small caliber (.22 and .32 rimfire) Smith & Wesson models, that were manufactured in the United States. All of the larger caliber cartridge guns used by both Union and Confederate forces were imported from Europe, as was the ammunition. Despite the prolific number of cartridge firing revolvers in use throughout the Civil War, the loose powder, patch, cap-and-ball percussion revolver remained the standard military sidearm, and equally so among the majority of civilians on both sides of the conflict. By 1868, however, the true heirs were about to set foot upon the stage, and they were Colt, Remington, and Smith & Wesson. The future of American arms manufacturing was about to turn a corner and by 1873 Colt would once again rise to the occasion and reaffirm its place as the leader in handgun design for the remainder of the 19th century.

The interim period between the end of percussion revolvers and those designed for the new metallic cartridge provided Colt's clientele with some of the most interesting and elegant revolver designs of the mid 19th century. Pictured are a variety of factory converted percussion models rebuilt to fire metallic cartridges. (Dow Heard collection)

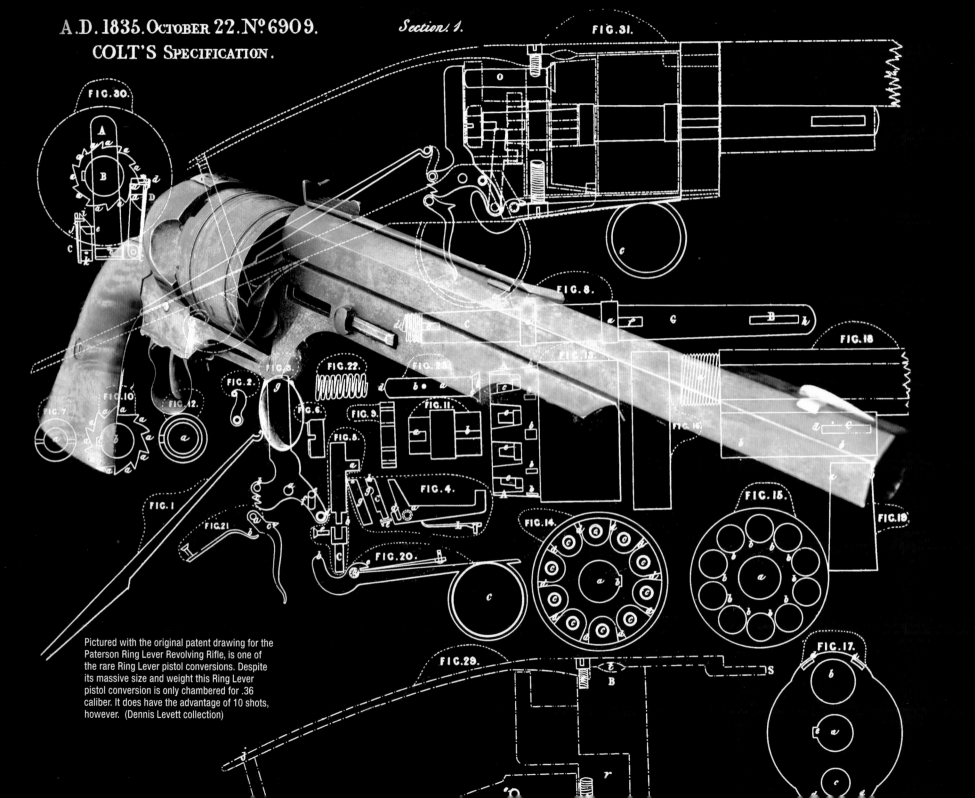

FIG. 31.

FIG. 30.

FIG. 8.

FIG. 18.

FIG. 3.

FIG. 22.

FIG. 2.

FIG. 23.

FIG. 13.

FIG. 6.

FIG. 9.

FIG. 11.

FIG. 16.

FIG. 10.

FIG. 12.

FIG. 7.

FIG. 5.

FIG. 4.

FIG. 15.

FIG. 1.

FIG. 14.

FIG. 19.

FIG. 21.

FIG. 20.

FIG. 17.

FIG. 29.

Pictured with the original patent drawing for the
Paterson Ring Lever Revolving Rifle, is one of
the rare Ring Lever pistol conversions. Despite
its massive size and weight this Ring Lever
pistol conversion is only chambered for .36
caliber. It does have the advantage of 10 shots,
however. (Dennis Levett collection)

Chapter One

Samuel Colt Invents
The Story Begins

Samuel Colt was just 21 years old when he filed his first patent for the design of a percussion revolver with a mechanically-rotated cylinder. What is interesting, is he filed this patent in Great Britain, and then in France, before applying for a patent in the United States. Colt knew that a U.S. patent would preclude the filing for patents in England and France, whereas no such stipulation prevented him from filing in the U.S. after he had secured his foreign patent rights.

Colt's British patent was issued on October 22, 1835, the French patent on November 16, 1836, and his U.S. patent on February 25, 1836, (followed by a letter of extension) thus providing him with the exclusive rights to build percussion revolvers based upon the fundamentals of his design through 1857.

The specific features of that patent read as follows:

1. *The application of the caps at the end of the cylinder.*
2. *The application of a partition between the caps.*
3. *The application of a shield over the caps as a security against moisture and the action of the smoke upon the works of the lock.*

Samuel Colt in his youth cut quite a striking figure and this rather imperious portrait was also indicative of his showman like personality, which not only helped establish his first enterprise but generate sales. Despite the failure of the Patent Fire Arms Manufacturing Company, Colt had secured his place in the industry and when he came back in 1847, he was there for the duration. (Photo courtesy R.L. Wilson archives)

4. *The principle of the connecting-rod between the hammer and the trigger.*
5. *The application of the shackle to connect the cylinder with the ratchet.*
6. *The principle of locking and turning the cylinder.*
7. *The principal of uniting the barrel with the cylinder by means of the arbor running through the plate and the projection under the barrel.*
8. *The principle of the adopter and the application of the lever, neither of which is used in pistols.*

The underlying principle of Colt's design was to enable the pawl, attached to the hammer of a percussion gun, to move as the gun was cocked, and through this movement turn the cylinder mechanically. Colt had covered every possible interpretation of his design, (and would in later years bring suit against other arms makers, specifically Massachusetts Arms Co., for patent infringement), ensuring that only Colt would be able to legally manufacture a revolver in the United States.

He had no doubt been influenced by the Collier flintlock revolver, which had proven more popular

At the age of 16 Sam Colt carved a wooden cylinder, hammer and arbor, the basic elements of his design for the revolver. Although initially the design was for a Pepperbox with barrels automatically rotated by cocking the gun, Colt decided the idea would work just as well if a cylinder could be rotated around a single stationary barrel. The rest as they say is history.

in England and India than the United States, despite its American design and patent. Where the Collier failed was in a practical means of rotating the cylinder each time the hammer was cocked. Thus the production guns relied on the individual to turn the cylinder after each shot. While this was far more efficient than having to reload entirely after the gun had been discharged, or swivel a second barrel and lock into battery, it was less than ideal.

Sam Colt was convinced there had to be a way to rotate the cylinder mechanically. The Collier method had been unsuccessful. Young Sam's solution was unique. At the time of his "inspiration" he was only 16 and serving as a seaman aboard the cargo ship Corvo[1] during its 1830 voyage to Calcutta. On the journey, as the story has been told, Colt sat and observed the action of the ship's wheel, or possibly the windlass (a cylinder or barrel turned by a crank), and imagined this could also be a practical way for making a pistol cylinder rotate mechanically. He spent his free time carving a wooden cylinder, cylinder arbor, and hammer, the fundamentals of his design. Originally it was to be a Pepperbox revolver, with one barrel for each chamber. After cocking the hammer, a ring lever was used to both actuate the rotation of the cylinder (or in this instance barrels) and upon further movement rearward, discharge the firearm. The Pepperbox design was cumbersome and there were already models with manually rotated cylinders on the market. After returning home he had prototypes built, one of which blew up upon testing. After further study of his design Colt concluded that the same components could be utilized to turn a multi-shot cylinder around a stationary barrel, which could be held by a metal wedge passing through

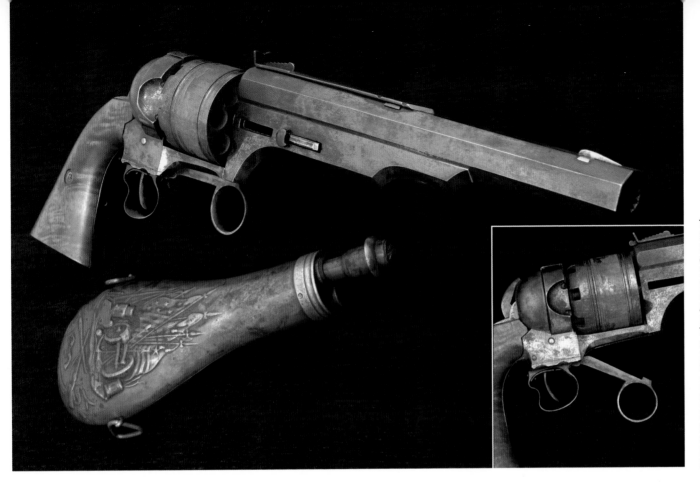

The No.2 Ring Lever Revolving Rifle featured a barrel lug mounted loading lever. The example shown was offered in the December 8, 2003 Greg Martin auction and valued at between $30,000 and $40,000. A similar model is also shown modified into a revolving pistol. The speed with which one could operate the Ring Lever as a handgun is questionable as the forward ring first had to be pulled down to cock the hammer. Nevertheless, such a massive handgun with 8-shots would have been a formidable weapon in the 1830s. (Ring Lever Rifle courtesy Greg Martin Auctions. Ring Lever Pistol from the Dennis Levett collection)

the barrel lug and an opening in the extension of the cylinder arbor. This became the basis for his second designs, a revolving rifle and pistol.

Some of Colt's earliest patent drawings, c.1835, were for a ring lever rifle (relating back to his first design for the Pepperbox action) and for a pistol design, which would evolve into the Paterson revolver by 1836. Both had been prototyped the previous year, as was a shotgun variation of the revolving rifle. Most of these examples, both early finger lever and ring lever variants, were handcrafted first by Anson Chase of Hartford (the original Pepperbox design and first revolving rifle), and then John Pearson, a talented Baltimore gunmaker who had perfected his skills in England.

By 1836, Sam Colt held U.S. and European patents covering his various designs and was ready to begin manufacturing. This was perhaps the first time that the reality of becoming an armsmaker had entered into his mind. Colt lacked the finances required to build a manufacturing plant. Up to this point in time he had relied solely upon Pearson to build guns one at a time.

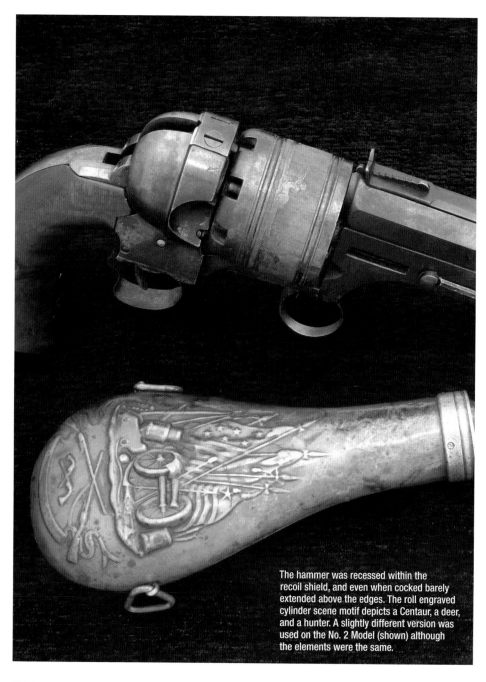

The hammer was recessed within the recoil shield, and even when cocked barely extended above the edges. The roll engraved cylinder scene motif depicts a Centaur, a deer, and a hunter. A slightly different version was used on the No. 2 Model (shown) although the elements were the same.

As noted by R.L. Wilson in *The Book of Colt Firearms*, Colt's innovative designs attracted the attention of several wealthy New York venture capitalists (one of who was a relative) and with their money behind him, Colt was able to establish the Patent Arms Manufacturing Company of Paterson, New Jersey, chartered by act of the Legislature of New Jersey on the 5th of March, 1836. Though Colt was "in business" he was hardly ready to begin manufacturing guns in 1836. Aside from the time necessary to set up machinery in the new facility, Colt's prototype designs needed refining. Although the prototype Paterson revolver had been a striking design, it was fraught with problems, specifically the complete enclosure of the cylinder, an idea which proved both impractical and dangerous. Tests had shown the Paterson was prone to chain fires (multiple chambers firing simultaneously) due to the enclosed cylinder design which potentially allowed sparks to ignite other chambers. It was necessary to redesign the frame and cylinder before production. Thus when the guns came to market their cylinders were free of the original encasements. (Interestingly, in 1872, a decade after Sam Colt had passed away, C.B. Richards patent for converting the Colt 1860 Army to fire metallic cartridges shrouded the back of the cylinder in a fashion reminiscent of the original Paterson prototypes).

The first production-built Paterson arms would not leave the New Jersey factory until late 1836, and then only in small numbers. To the dismay of his investors, the first products from Sam Colt would not be the anticipated revolving pistols, but rather revolving rifles based on the ring lever design.

Early production through the beginning of 1837 consisted of the Paterson Revolving Rifle, known as the No. 1, followed by the first Paterson Revolver, also designated No. 1. By the end of the year, Samuel Colt had four models in production (two rifles, two pistols) and the Patent Firearms Manufacturing Company closed the books on 1837 with nearly 1,000 rifles and pistols built. Sam Colt was finally "in business."

The No. 1 Ring Lever Revolving Rifle was Colt's first Paterson model and the first design put into production in New Jersey. Both the No.1 and No. 2 Models are fascinating designs, albeit complicated ones. The First Model was available in a wide variety of chamberings to include .34, .36, .38, .40, and .44 calibers, and in 8 or 10 shots. The No. 1 was generally offered with one barrel length, 32-inches, though shorter lengths were made, and of course, some longarms, usually of a later model, were restocked as pistols with barrels shortened

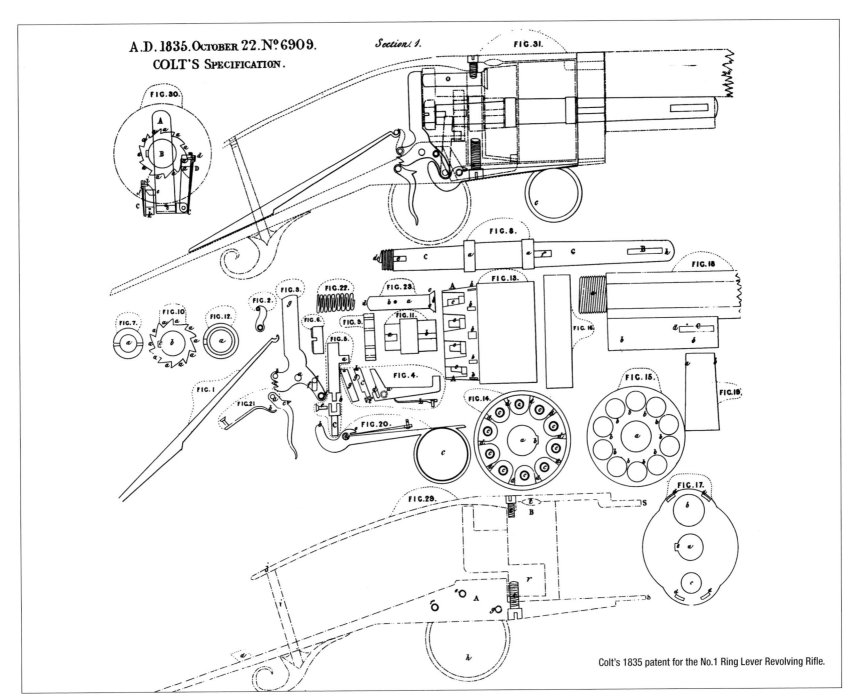

A.D. 1835. October 22. № 6909.
COLT'S Specification.

Section 1.

Colt's 1835 patent for the No.1 Ring Lever Revolving Rifle.

Renowned Paterson collector Dennis LeVett today and at age 11 when he purchased his first Colt Paterson Carbine. Levett is shown holding one of his rare Ring Lever Revolving Pistol conversions to give a sense of scale to this massive handgun.

to 10-$^7/_{16}$ inches. Within the First Model series it is estimated that no more than 200 were manufactured from 1837 through 1838. Replaced by the No. 2 Model, the Paterson was now available only in .44 caliber (8 shot) and in two standard barrel lengths, 28-inches and 32-inches. More popular than its predecessor, a total of approximately 500 were built between 1838 and 1841. The single most important feature of the No.2 was a loading lever attached to the right side of the barrel lug. No. 1 Models could also be fitted with a lever but did not come equipped with them. Loading was generally accomplished by removing the barrel and placing the supplied loading tool in the cylinder arbor notch, and then loading each chamber. The attached loading lever on the No. 2 facilitated much faster reloading and practicality for military use, as the barrel did not have to be removed to load.

During their production run numerous changes were made to the No. 1 and No. 2 designs regarding the cylinders, and particularly the removal of the topstrap from the No. 2 design effecting the "open top" appearance that would become standard Colt fare until 1873.

In 1839 the Army of the Republic of Texas placed two orders for the No.2 Paterson Revolving Rifles, two lots of 50 each in August and October. Examples of the No. 2 are also known to have been converted into large caliber revolvers, which begs the question, were these converted

Weighing over 80 ounces (more than five pounds), the Ring Lever Pistol Conversion with 10-7/16ths inch barrel was a handful for any man. The operation was cumbersome and to effectively shoot it required two hands, using the index finger of the off hand to cock the forward ring, and the trigger finger of the right hand to fire. The gun was, in that respect, quite ambidextrous. Note that the back of the triggerguard has been contoured to relieve the middle finger of the strong hand from being impacted upon firing. (Dennis Levett collection)

Colt devised a capper to expedite affixing percussion caps on the cylinder nipples. This device held an entire tin of percussion caps under spring tension, pushing the next cap into line as each was placed atop the nipple. (Dennis Levett collection)

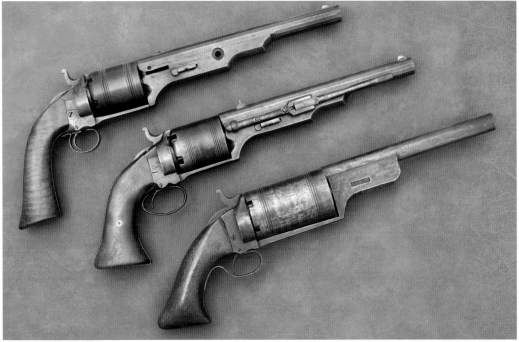

Pictured are three 1839 carbine pistol conversions. "It's hard to know the history of some of these early Paterson conversions," says noted Paterson collector Dennis Levett. "It is very clear that someone felt that the Paterson Carbine would make a better pistol. The examples in my collection are fitted with pistol grips and the barrels have been cut down to anywhere from 9-5/8ths inches to as long as 10-7/16 inches, creating a large caliber revolver and at a time when they did not otherwise exist." The two Carbine examples (with and without loading lever) are .525 and .50 caliber, respectively, with smoothbore barrels. The shotgun pistol conversion is chambered in 20 gauge. (Dennis Levett collection)

A Texas Paterson with 7-1/2 inch barrel looks more like a pocket pistol in comparison to these Paterson Carbine pistol conversions!

The Paterson Carbine Pistol made for one very imposing revolver in the early 1840s packing six .525 caliber rounds.

Left side barrel markings on the 1839 Carbine read: *Patent Arms Mfg. Co. Paterson, N.J. Colt's Pt.*

rifles the actual predecessors to the Walker? It is unlikely that the Ring Lever models had any serious impact on the development of the Walker because of their action; however, the Model 1839 Carbine presents a completely different design approach, one which immediately made obsolete the No.1 and No. 2 Revolving Rifles, and as a conversion to pistol, may have been the inspiration for the Walker.

The 1839 Carbine introduced the external hammer for cocking. The new "open top" models were chambered in .525 caliber (six shot) with squareback cylinders, attached loading levers, and either 24-inch, 28-inch, or 32-inch "smoothbore" barrels. This was to become the most popular of the Paterson Revolving Rifles, remaining in production through 1845 (under John Ehlers) surviving the Patent Fire Arms Manufacturing Company (which went into receivership in 1841) and by Samuel Colt as late as 1850 through his new Colt's Firearms Manufacturing Company. Total production is estimated to have been 950. Of the approximately 50 Carbines later sold by Sam Colt (c.1849-1853), all of these examples were purchased by Colt from the State of Rhode Island (which had ordered them through Ehlers c.1845). Colt had them refinished and most notably had the cylinders turned down leaving them "in the white" as were all Walker Colt cylinders. These examples are regarded today as 1839/1848 Paterson Revolving Carbines.

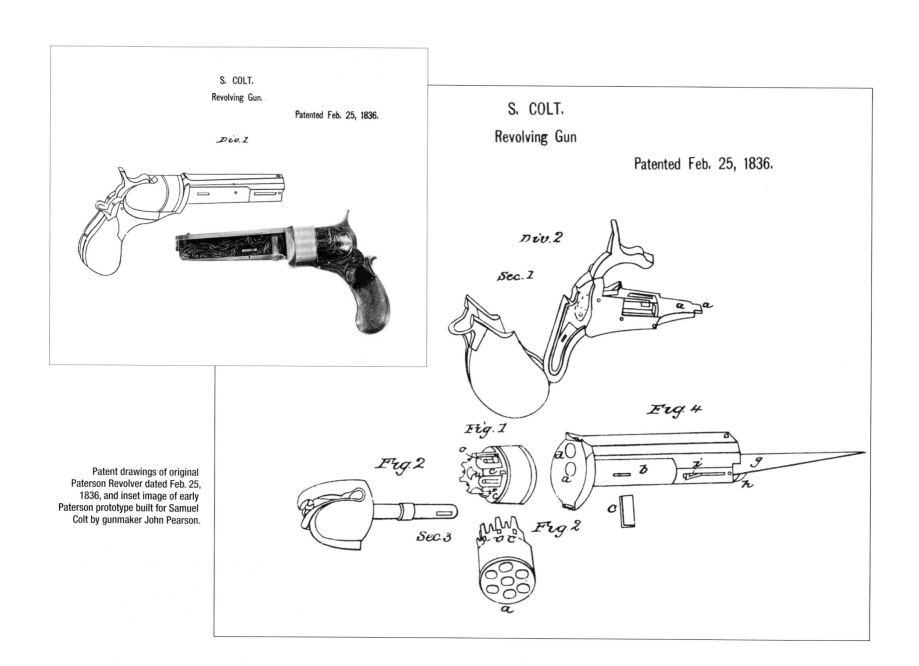

Patent drawings of original Paterson Revolver dated Feb. 25, 1836, and inset image of early Paterson prototype built for Samuel Colt by gunmaker John Pearson.

This deluxe, engraved Paterson prototype c.1835 was reputedly used as a promotional model in attracting investors for the Patent Fire Arms Manufacturing Co. Built by John Pearson, the six-shot .33 caliber revolver was inlaid with German silver. What is notable about this and several earlier designs for the Paterson is the complete enclosure of the cylinder, an idea which proved impractical and dangerous, as it was proven to contribute to chain fire (multiple chambers firing simultaneously), thus when the guns came to production the cylinder was free of any encasements. (photo courtesy R.L. Wilson archives)

The 1839 was essentially a very big Paterson pistol, far simpler and more rugged in design than the No.1 and No. 2. Lighter in weight than the Ring Lever Models, which averaged 8 pounds, 8 ounces, the Carbine tipped the scales at 7 pounds, 11 ounces. Most examples found today have the attached loading lever, although early Carbines were manufactured without the lever. These specimens came with the Paterson combination loading tool and barrel kick off tool (shaped like a large question mark). In addition, records show that approximately 50 Carbines were produced with rifled rather than smoothbore barrels.

The 1839 was an elegant evolution of the Colt Revolving Rifle and could also be ordered in a 16 gauge shotgun variation. This was the advantage of the smoothbore barrels, as the rifles could also double as six-shot scatterguns. This predates the six-shot Winchester Lever Action shotgun by nearly half a century.

The 1839 Carbines converted to large caliber pistols in the early 1840s by private gunsmiths can be regarded as true predecessors to the 1847 Walker Colt. Though these specimens are rare, they do exist. Far more massive than even the Walker, these rare Carbine conversions were for their time, the most powerful revolvers in the world.

Shown top center is a fine Ehlers No.2 Improved .31 caliber Pocket Model with loading lever. Below that another No. 2 Model with vine scroll engraving. To the right, a rare flat bottom grip No. 2 Model. At [f]ar right a No. 3 Model with 5-1/2 inch barrel. Across the bottom, at top a very rare No. 5 Texas Paterson with 12-inch barrel, center a First Model New Improved Ehlers with loading lever, and a No 5 Holster

Chapter Two

The Paterson Colts
Success and Failure

Around 1517 AD the first wheel-lock pistols were seen in southern Germany, and the cities of Nuremberg, Augsburg, Munich, and Dresden, along with neighboring countries, such as the Netherlands and Denmark. Although a design with the complexity of a clockworks the wheel-lock offered one the ability, for the very first time, to carry a loaded firearm on their person, primed and ready to discharge. It did, however, have some rather vexing problems, the greatest of which was reliability. Not so much with the gun, as with the shooter. If, in the heat of battle, one wound the wheel in the wrong direction, the chain that operated the wheel often broke or became dislodged, rendering the gun inoperable. And if one lost the spanner key, there was no way in which to wind the clockwork-like mechanism – once more rendering the gun useless, except as a rather elaborate truncheon. And in that respect, most were built with large, rounded hardwood grips capped by a solid brass grotesque mask. Good for whacking.

Despite its shortcomings the wheel-lock pistol design flourished for more than a century,

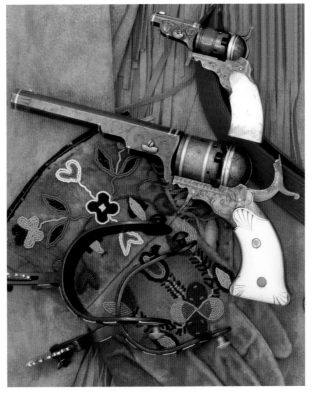

Samuel Colt's No. 5 Holster Model and the earliest known engraved Baby Paterson. (Dr. Joseph A. Murphy Collection)

though mostly among the aristocracy which preferred pistols not be permitted into the hands of commoners. That changed in the latter half of the 17th century when the first flintlock pistols began to appear. Sturdier, simpler to build, and far less costly to manufacture, the flintlock could be regarded as the firearms equivalent of Henry Ford's Model T, bringing the pistol within reach of almost anyone regardless of caste. The flintlock utilized a simpler, more robust firing mechanism actuated by the cock (so named for its shape resembling a rooster's neck and head), which held a piece of flint between its jaws. Unlike the wheel-lock, which spun the serrated wheel to create a spark, the flintlock hammer simply fell against a metal leaf called a frizzen, creating a spark with the flint that ignited the powder in the flash pan and thus the charge within the barrel. It was almost foolproof and far easier to operate. All one had to do was load it, prime the pan, and when ready thumb back the hammer from the safety notch position and pull the trigger.

The design proved quite versatile and there were many variations, including side-by-side

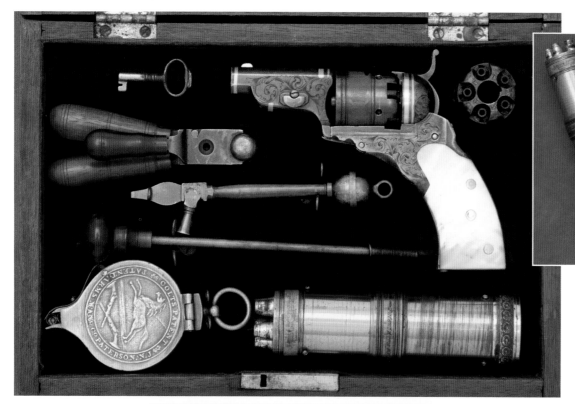

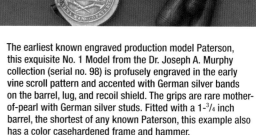

The earliest known engraved production model Paterson, this exquisite No. 1 Model from the Dr. Joseph A. Murphy collection (serial no. 98) is profusely engraved in the early vine scroll pattern and accented with German silver bands on the barrel, lug, and recoil shield. The grips are rare mother-of-pearl with German silver studs. Fitted with a 1-³/₄ inch barrel, the shortest of any known Paterson, this example also has a color casehardened frame and hammer.

First, Second, and Third Model Patersons each exhibit distinctive styling traits. At top the smallest of the Paterson models, a No.1, center a No. 2 with flat bottom grips, and a No. 3 with flared grips. A Paterson powder and ball flask is separated into its two halves to reveal the patented loading device which charged all five chambers with powder, and then dropped five round balls into place ready to be seated with the loading tool (bottom). The top of the loading tool unscrewed and was fitted with a steel pick to clean out clogged chambers in the cylinder. (Dr. Joseph A. Murphy collection)

double-barreled pistols, and innovative swivel barrel examples, providing a quick follow up shot by rotating a second barrel and lock into battery. The firing mechanism could also be scaled down, allowing a diversity of pistol sizes from long barreled, large caliber examples to small pocket pistols easily concealed in a waistcoat. For nearly two centuries the flintlock was unsurpassed until the Right Reverend Alexander Forsyth missed his dinner...quite literally.

An avid hunter and sportsman, inventor, and clergyman, Forsyth had grown frustrated with flintlocks, which though efficient had a momentary delay from the ignition of the primer to the actual discharge of the firearm, often giving his prey sufficient warning to avoid becoming the evening's repast. Thus, the good Reverend began development of a more efficient means of igniting the powder charge, and in 1807 patented both the percussion lock and the fulminating mercury process used to ignite the powder charge. His idea would take more than a decade to perfect.

Historian Keith R. Dill, writing in the August 2000 issue of *Man at Arms* noted, "There is hard evidence to support the claim of only one gunmaker [as the inventor of the percussion cap] Joseph Egg. There are examples that may be dated to 1819, and documentary evidence indicating that he was probably producing the system a year before that. On the case labels that he used in the 1820s, the [London gunmaker] rightfully made claim of being '*the inventor of the copper cap.*'"

By the late 1820s the percussion era was ushered into the fullness of its development. In the end it was all so simple, a copper cap containing the mercury fulminate (a gray, crystalline solid), was placed over a hollow tube and detonated by the impact of the hammer, producing a small flame that was sent directly into the powder charge causing almost instantaneous detonation. Taking the idea one step further was Samuel Colt's patents for the revolver in 1835-1836. The pistol had finally come of age.

Even with the introduction of the Colt revolver, many people still preferred a single or double barreled percussion pistol, and others still clung to their old flintlocks. Samuel Colt had more than a century of established arms making standing in the path of progress. In 1836, when Colt built his assembly plant in Paterson, New Jersey, then one of this nation's fastest-growing manufacturing centers, he was beginning an uphill battle against tradition and, above all, public and military skepticism, the latter of which would, in time, force Colt's first enterprise into receivership.

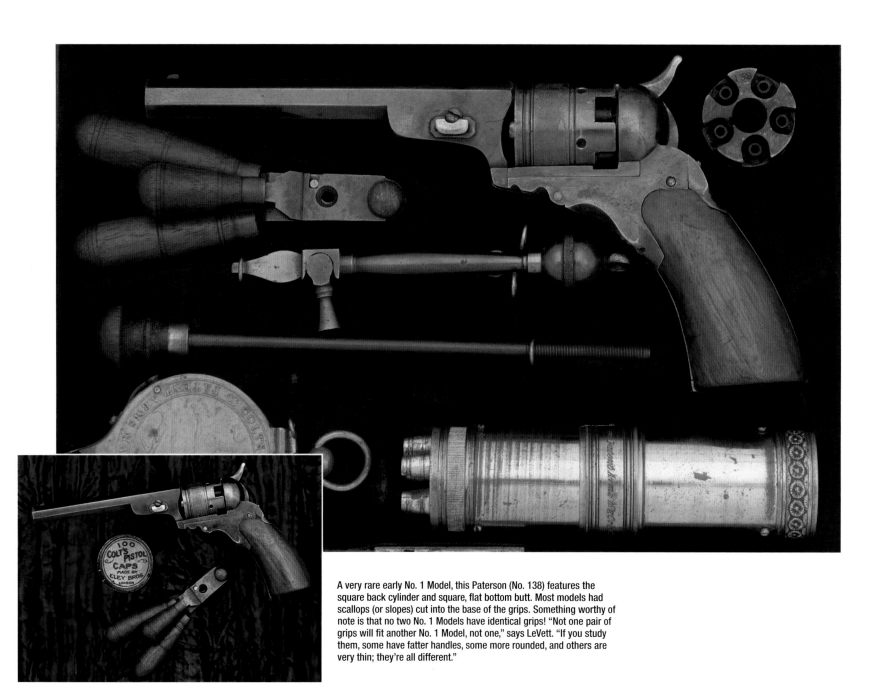

A very rare early No. 1 Model, this Paterson (No. 138) features the square back cylinder and square, flat bottom butt. Most models had scallops (or slopes) cut into the base of the grips. Something worthy of note is that no two No. 1 Models have identical grips! "Not one pair of grips will fit another No. 1 Model, not one," says LeVett. "If you study them, some have fatter handles, some more rounded, and others are very thin; they're all different."

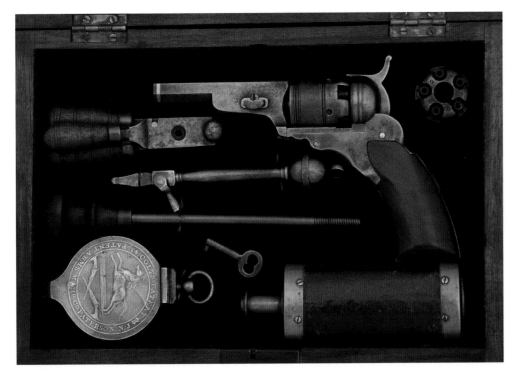

A No. 1 Model that was likely sold after 1840; this example has the round shoulder cylinders. Although not engraved, the gun has the German silver band embellishments. It is cased with a charger-type single nozzle powder flask of the period, but not of Colt manufacture.

Left: A typical cased No. 1 Model. Once again, this gun has been fitted with the later round shoulder cylinders c.1840.

By the end of 1837 Sam had developed three different revolvers: the pocket, belt, and holster models; and two types of long rifles, the first cocked by a finger lever, the second by a conventional hammer. Despite the generally favorable performance of Paterson revolvers and rifles in the hands of early buyers, sales remained below expectations. The U.S. government purchased small quantities of the Colt ring-lever rifle and Colt 1839 carbine, but those quantities appear to have totaled no more than 100 of both types.

The exact number of arms produced between 1836 and the date of Colt's petition for bankruptcy in 1841, as well as those produced by John Ehlers from late 1841 until the permanent closure of The Patent Arms Manufacturing Company in 1842, is an educated guess. Estimates have ranged from a low of under 2,000, which is unlikely as it would indicate a production rate of only about six guns per week, to a high of 6,000. The actual number of revolving rifles and pistols is now believed to be around 4,700 over a six-year period, taking into consideration the slow startup in 1836, and the equally slow sell-off of the so-called Ehlers Paterson models from 1841 to 1846.

According to research conducted by historian and author Herbert G. Houze for his book *Samuel Colt – Arms, Art, and Inventions* (2006 Yale University Press and Wadsworth Atheneum Museum of Art), Colt may have produced 1,992 assorted models by July 1, 1839, but also notes, that of the total only 890 arms had actually been sold. Additionally, there was dissention within the company regarding Colt's "sales techniques" which were founded on the principle of "one hand washes the other" and wherein Colt made gifts of guns to military and government officials in order to secure their favor and endorsements. His promotional ploys, often fortified by the free flow of spirits during sales demonstrations, and afterward at lavish dinner parties, brought Sam Colt the support of top military officers and Washington politicians, as well as the open contempt of his Board of Directors, principally its treasurer, Dudley Selden. Not only was he a board member, Selden was Samuel Colt's cousin and one of his largest investors, having provided a portion of the money used to build the Paterson, New Jersey factory. Growing impatient with Sam's lavish dinner parties, gifts of guns, and mounting expense account Selden chastised Colt first for his liquor bill: "I have no belief in undertaking to raise the character of your gun by old Madeira,"

Close-up of the early Paterson combination powder and ball flask, what Sam Colt called "ammunition flasks," shows the intricate detail in its design, and the small decorative rosettes. This was seen on No.1 and No. 2 Model flasks. The accompanying patent drawing shows how the flask came apart into two sections. The upper half was used to charge all five cylinder chambers at once, and the bottom of the flask to drop five round balls into place with a twist of the base ring. This was a complicated design and by far the most advanced means of loading a revolver in 1836-37. The cylinder was then placed back on the arbor and the combination tool (see the 1839 Paterson patent illustration on page 45) used to seat the balls in the chambers. (Dennis LeVett collection)

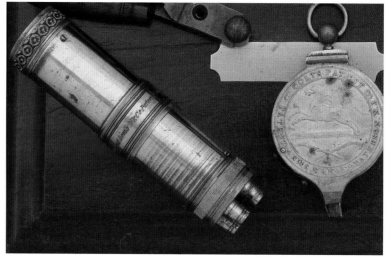

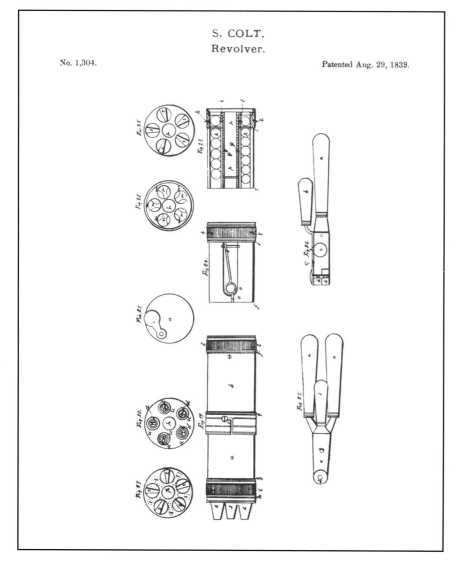

S. COLT.
Revolver.

No. 1,304.

Patented Aug. 29, 1839.

and then for his presentations of guns to government representatives: "I will not become a party to a negotiations with a public officer to allow him compensation for aid in securing a contract with the government...."[1] (Obviously, this was long before the advent of Lobbyists!) The admonishment from Cousin Dudley, however, did little to deter Colt's marketing techniques. It is noted in *Fine Colts* (1999 Republic Publishing Co.) that recipients of Paterson pistols included Commodore John Nicholson, Col. William S. Harney (who later wrote a letter of endorsement praising Colt's Revolving Rifles), D.E. Twiggs (Commissioner of the U.S. Patent Office), the Governor General of Cuba, Czar Nicholas I of Russia, and (reputedly) the President of the United States, Andrew Jackson.

Colt's efforts often paid off. In January 1838, General Thomas Jessup (to whom Colt had presented a cased pair of No. 1 Models), ordered 25 Paterson No. 3 Models and 50 No. 1 Rifles for his troops. There were also substantial orders from the Republic of Texas, all of which contributed to civilian sales of Colt's pistols and rifles. Sam Colt's behavior nevertheless put him on the outs with his financiers and Selden forced a "restructuring" of the relationship between the Patent Arms Manufacturing Co., and its founder, who, in reality was little more than an employee. After Selden finished with his young cousin, he wasn't even that. Beginning in 1838 Colt was reduced to the role of company agent, a salaried position. From a business standpoint it put Colt in his place but it also marked the

[1] *Samuel Colt – Arms, Art, and Invention* by Herbert G. Houze.

Here the square bottom No. 1 is seen in its case with accessories, including the patented Paterson two-piece powder and ball flask, bullet mold, combination (loading) tool, cleaning rod, patented Paterson capper, and spare cylinder. The facing No. 1 Model is an even earlier example, number 88, with a shorter barrel and yet another variation in the Paterson grip designs, this one showing only a slight scallop at the bottom. (Dennis LeVett collection)

The serial No. 138 Paterson is shown on top of its case with the primary accessories. Note the elegant beveled lid design. The close-up shows detail of the cylinder scene and Colt name. (Dennis LeVett collection)

beginning of the end. Colt had put his heart and soul into designing the Paterson rifles and pistols and more so into marketing them, regardless of his techniques. And while he had spent considerable funds playing host to Washington dignitaries he had also made sales and established the company's reputation as an arms maker. To Selden, however, the ledger sheets showed that Colt had spent almost as much as he made. Sam knew he had lost the support of his investors and, to some extent, his family. By 1839 sales were declining, hoped for contracts from the government failed to materialize, as did purchases that had been anticipated from the states of New York, Michigan, and Maine. Only Texas had come through with orders for both revolvers and rifles: 180 Holster pistols, and 180 Model 1839 Carbines. The Republic of Texas had also taken delivery of 100 Paterson Ring Lever Revolving Rifles for use in the ongoing border disputes with Mexico, and against attacks by Comanche Indians

Shown with powder and ball flasks and cappers to illustrate the diminutive size of the No. 1 Models, what becomes evident is the inconsistency of assembly from one gun to the next, regardless of barrel length. The grips on the bottom example are skinny, narrow, on the other short and wide. (Dennis LeVett collection)

A pair of No. 2 Models built c.1837-1838. The example at right is a rare model with a silver plated frame. It is also fitted with ebony grips with silver studs. A most unusual No. 2 Model. Barrel length is 5-inches. According to Dennis LeVett, no more than 10 No.2 Models were built with silver plated frames. The example at left, also with 5-inch barrel and chambered in .31 caliber, is an excellent presentation of the No. 2 Paterson. Both cased guns have the full accompaniment of factory accessories. (Dennis LeVett collection)

in the Texas-Mexico border regions. The arms of Samuel Colt had acquitted themselves in the hands of Texas Rangers and in use by the Texas Navy. Alas, the same could not be said of those Paterson arms being tested by the U.S. government.

By April 1840 a frustrated Selden had stepped down as treasurer only to be replaced by an even more mindful accountant, wealthy New Jersey arms and hardware merchant John Ehlers, who had an even more substantial investment in the Patent Firearms Manufacturing Company. Loyalties in Paterson were shifting away from Colt and he became further distant, though at first he thought he had found an ally in Ehlers. But this was not to be the case. Later on Colt revealed his innermost thoughts in a letter to a family member:

"To be a clerk or an office holder under the pay and patronage of Government, is to stagnate ambition & I hope by hevins I would rather be captain of a canal bote than have the biggest office in the gift of the Government...however inferior in wealth I may be to the many who surround

One of the best known examples of the No. 2 Model is Dennis Levett's large vine scroll engraved revolver with 5-inch barrel. Chambered in .31 caliber, this gun exhibits the excellent engraving seldom seen on early guns. This example also has the rare silver plated frame.

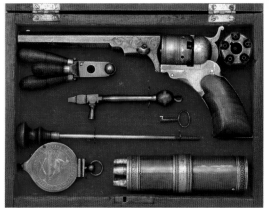

me I would not exchange for there treasures the satisfaction I have in knowing I have done what has never before been accomplished by man... Life is a thing to be enjoyed...it is the only certainty." One of those certainties, unfortunately, was Sam Colt's declining prestige among his investors.

In April 1840 factory superintendent Pliny Lawton had implemented several of Colt's improvements, including rounding of the shoulders on the Paterson cylinders. Previously they had been squared off and prone to cause jamming of the action if a split percussion cap became wedged. The rounded shoulders allowed easy removal of split caps. (This, unfortunately, did not prevent the other most common jam, a spent percussion cap falling into the space between the hammer and the back of the cylinder.) Additionally, by August 1840 an attached loading lever had become standard on the No.5 Holster Models. But it was all too little too late. Sam Colt was about to lose everything and the one person who could help him, John Ehlers, wanted nothing more than for Colt to fail, and might actually have contributed to ensuring that outcome.

Another engraved No. 2 Model showing the large vine scroll style. This cased model is fitted with the 3-inch barrel. Most No. 2 models had flat shouldered cylinders. As can be seen from the right side view, there was no cut out in the recoil shield for capping (capping was done with the cylinder removed), and thus a cap that may have split apart after firing could easily jam the action. Spent caps also had a tendency to fall into the recess in front of the hammer as the gun was cocked, once again possibly causing the action to jam.

R.L. Wilson outlined the demise of the Patent Arms Manufacturing Company in *The Book of Colt Firearms*. Control of the company was gradually being assumed by Ehlers who was now withdrawing his assets through inventory. Noted Wilson, "An injunction was soon filed by Colt, supported by a band of the stockholders, for a full accounting and to prevent Ehlers from selling arms to recoup his investments in the company. However, Ehlers continued the sales of arms he had himself confiscated (approximately 210 rifles, 260 carbines, 350 pistols) and in December 1841, he sold 100 carbines and 100 Holster pistols to Commodore Thomas Catesby Jones (for the Navy's Pacific Squadron).

"Finally the injunction was granted, but concurrently a severe blow to the Model 1839 carbines was dealt in a letter of February 8, 1842, addressed to Colt from Captain McLaughlan of the U.S. Marines. His note read in part: '*I am sorry to say that your arms have proved an entire failure when put to the test of actual service. Lieut Sloan Comdg the Marines on the 13th Jany addressed me as follows: 'I would respectfully suggest that Colts firearms be no longer used in my command.'*

*…I am perfectly satisfied that the principle of these arms is a good one and that they can be made the invaluable weapon they now pretend to be – but to effect this they must be made with a degree of attention and care which was sadly deficient in these.'"

This was the final blow. Colt, to his dying day, believed that Ehlers had sent deficient guns for the test so that they would fail and bring down the house around Colt's head. It was the outcome Ehlers had sought and in 1842 the company was forced into receivership. Ehlers acquired the remaining inventory, after which he continued to sell Paterson revolvers as "Colt's Repeating Pistols, With the Latest Improvement" from 1842 until the remaining inventory was exhausted in 1846.

Sam Colt had been outwitted and outgunned by Ehlers. Of course, in 1842 Colt was only 28 years old. His fight had not yet begun. Five years later he would be back, and not even the likes of a Dudley Selden or John Ehlers could stand in his way.

The Paterson Colts

Between 1837 and 1842 there were four different Paterson model revolvers, the No.1 or Pocket Model, also known as the Baby Paterson; the No. 2 Pocket Model; No.3 Belt Model; and the famous No.5 Holster Model, more popularly known as the Texas Paterson. Each was progressively larger in caliber and size, but shared a similarity that was distinctive to Colt's original design.

Only a handful of changes were implemented throughout the Paterson's brief production history, the most obvious being the addition of loading levers, the round shoulder cylinders, and late in No.3 production a change to larger flared grips.

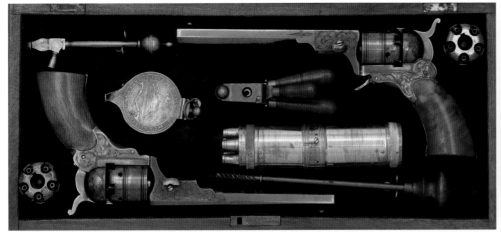

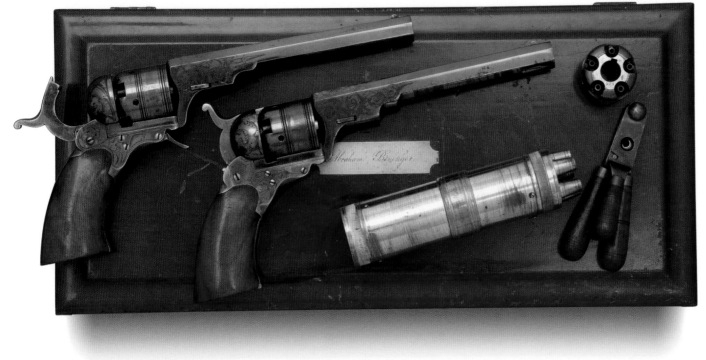

One of the most significant casings of No. 2 Models known is this set of engraved guns originally owned by Abraham Bininger. Research of the Bininger family suggests the purchaser of this exquisite pair of Colts may have been A.M. Bininger, a wealthy New York distiller and grocer whose family company produced an exceptional line of liquor bottles (and their contents) for over 100 years. Old A.M. Bininger liquor bottles are almost as collectible today as Colt pistols. The Bininger Patersons (whether or not they belonged to A.M. Bininger) are the only known cased pair of engraved No. 2 Models, serial numbers 626 and 878. Extremely rare even as single engraved guns, the pair is embellished in the large vine scroll style and features a seldom-observed dagger motif on the sides of the barrels. The guns also have rare squared off flat bottom grips. The cylinders are of the c.1840 round shoulder type. The close-up reveals the Centaur cylinder scene used on all No.1 through No.3 Patersons. (Dr. Joseph A. Murphy collection)

A superb group of No. 3 Models from the Dennis LeVett collection exhibit the late flared grip design, both versions of shell motif ivory grips, German silver bands, and typical factory engraving. Also note that both square and round shoulder cylinders are evident on models without loading levers.

Cased with 5-1/2 inch and 12-inch barrels, this No. 3 Model Paterson is embellished with German silver bands on both barrels, and on the recoil shield. This example also has shell motif ivory grips. This pattern varied on Patersons from a single carving (as shown) to grips with shell carvings at each corner. LeVett believes that anywhere from seven to twelve similar two barrel sets were made. One of the most unusual features of this set is the single nozzle brass powder flask, the only known flask of this type to be embossed with a Paterson pistol. (Dennis LeVett collection)

This is an unusual "upside down" casing with the barrel facing to the right. The reason for this is that it is a British casing. The gun and accessories were shipped to its original owner in England and the case was made there. The pistol has the early squared shoulder cylinders indicating that it was probably shipped before 1840. (Dennis LeVett collection)

Below, left & right: This flared grip No. 3 Model with 5-1/2 inch barrel is typical of the third model Paterson revolvers. A superb casing with original accessories, this example is chambered in .31 caliber. Take a close look at the patented Paterson capper and the two crossed revolvers in the cover decoration. They look remarkably similar to the Paterson Carbine Pistol conversions! Also note Colt's patented combination tool used to seat bullets into the chambers. It could be used as a mallet to knock the wedge loose and the top unscrewed to reveal a pick for cleaning nipples clogged with powder residue. (Dennis Levett collection)

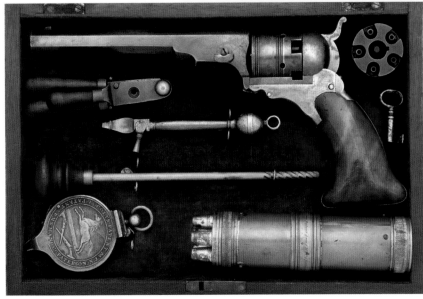

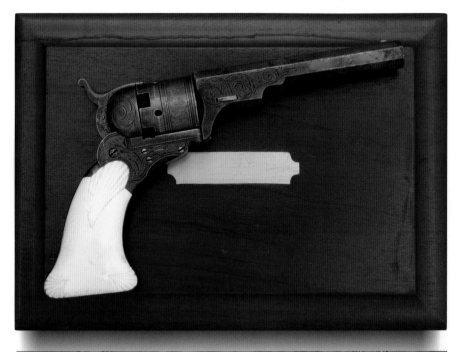

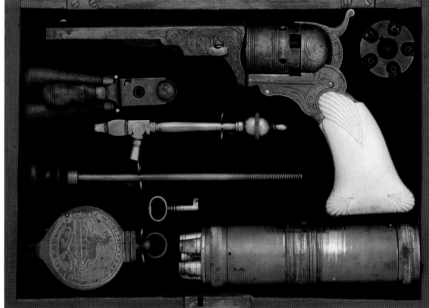

An exceptional No. 3 Model with large vine scroll engraving and shell motif ivory grips. This example shows the full shell design which carried to the corners of the grips. The engraving detail includes the hammer and backstrap. Colt presentation cases were varnished mahogany and most had elegant beveled lids with inset German silver or brass plaques. Only very early Paterson cases and a handful of rare later exceptions had flat topped lids. (Dennis LeVett collection)

A very unusual early No. 3 Model (no. 137) with a dovetailed rear sight on the barrel. This example also has the inlaid German silver bands frequently seen on No. 3 Models. (Dennis LeVett collection)

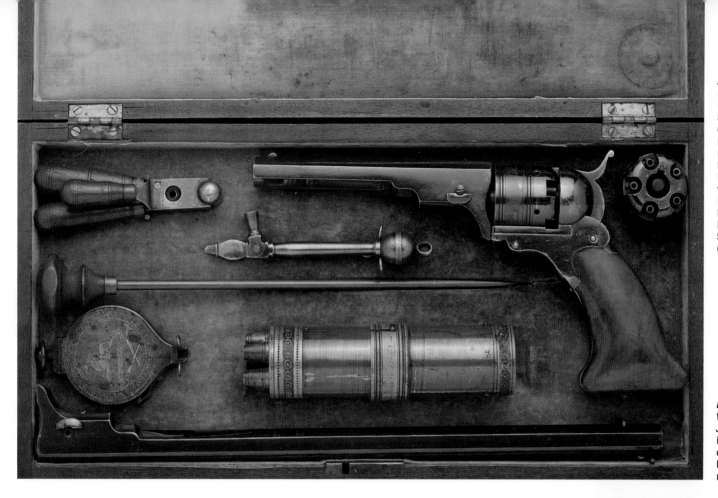

Another of the rare two barrel No. 3 Models, this example has a 4-11/16 inch barrel and extra 12 inch barrel (actually measuring 12-3/32 inch). Fitted with the later round shoulder cylinders, No. 770 was estimated to be worth $350,000 in 2002, which certainly points out the high value placed upon early Paterson models. This cased No. 3 was originally owned by Samuel Colt. (photo courtesy Greg Martin Auctions)

Below: A typical No. 3 Model, this example from the Dr. Joseph A. Murphy collection is an excellent representation of the third Paterson variation. Note that it is fitted with the round shoulder cylinder.

Grips are the one area where design appears to have been regarded either as individual to the assembler or gun. A study of No. 1 and No. 2 Models reveals that no two sets of grips are the same. There is absolutely no interchangeability between guns and size and shape vary dramatically among the earliest examples, particularly among No. 1 Models, indicating their almost handmade nature.

Though production numbers were only in the hundreds, with the exception of the Texas Patersons, the surviving examples remain testament to the quality and durability of Colt's firearms. And given the resounding success of Paterson arms sold to and proven in battle by the Republic of Texas, one

is given to believe Sam Colt's suspicions about John Ehlers might well have been correct.

The No. 1

Sam Colt called it the No.1, or Pocket Model revolver. It has since become more popularly known as the "Baby Paterson." No matter what you call it, this demure 5-shot revolver was the beginning of an era, the first production percussion revolver with a cylinder mechanically advanced to the next chamber by cocking the hammer.

The No. 1 was available in .28 and .31 caliber versions, both comparatively small but more than adequate for a pistol one could hide in a vest pocket or

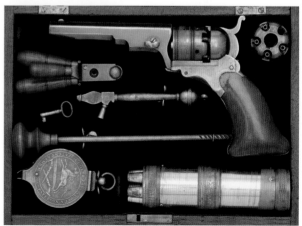

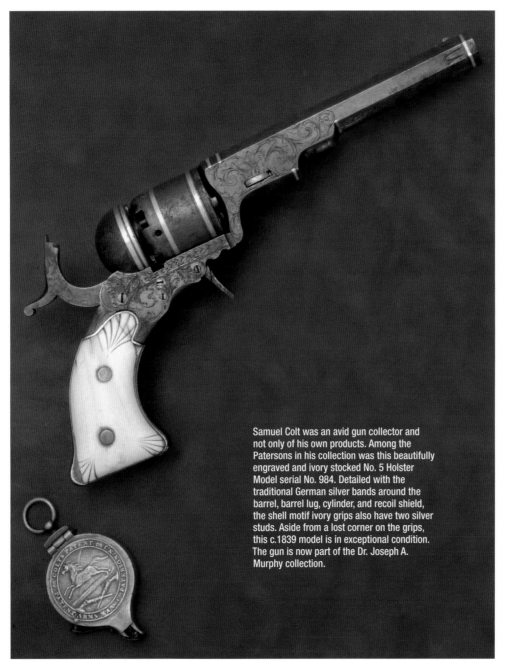

Samuel Colt was an avid gun collector and not only of his own products. Among the Patersons in his collection was this beautifully engraved and ivory stocked No. 5 Holster Model serial No. 984. Detailed with the traditional German silver bands around the barrel, barrel lug, cylinder, and recoil shield, the shell motif ivory grips also have two silver studs. Aside from a lost corner on the grips, this c.1839 model is in exceptional condition. The gun is now part of the Dr. Joseph A. Murphy collection.

palm from seemingly out of nowhere. Fitted with a 2-$\frac{1}{2}$ inch barrel, the gun was barely the size of a man's hand and weighed less than 12 ounces.[2] Even with the long 4-$\frac{3}{4}$ inch barrel, the No. 1 was easily concealed. And at close range, five shots were four better than a Henry Deringer.

Production began in 1837 and concluded roughly a year later in 1838. Perhaps because of its small size the appeal of the No. 1 was limited. Although 490 had been produced by July 1, 1839, all but 128 remained in Colt's inventory. The No.1, being the first model, was thus subject to later alterations, and many are seen today with loading levers and the round shoulder cylinders not available until 1840. Such factory upgrades were not uncommon to make older products appear newer or more marketable. These remaining examples were sold between 1841 and 1846, most by John Ehlers after the failure of the Patent Arms Manufacturing Company. The need to "update old inventory" would once again become paramount in the years following the Civil War when Colt's began offering cartridge conversion revolvers (c.1871-72) most of which were built upon left over Civil War percussion revolver frames refitted with altered cylinders and barrels.

The No. 2

Beginning in 1837 Colt introduced his second Paterson revolver, the No. 2. This version picked up where the No. 1 left off. Available in two calibers, .31 (the largest offered for the No.1) and .34 (at last on the way to something with a little punch), barrel lengths varied from the short 2-$\frac{1}{2}$ inch version to the long 4-$\frac{3}{4}$ inch model. Still a 5-shot pocket pistol, the No. 2 had a bit more heft, weighing 20 ounces in .34 caliber with the long barrel. Sales were far better with production reaching around 800 examples by 1840, the year No.2 Models were first offered with an attached loading lever and new round shoulder cylinder. Those with loading levers also had a contoured (dished) right recoil shield to make capping possible without removing the cylinder.

[2] Weight estimated for .28 caliber No.1 Model with 4-$\frac{3}{4}$ inch barrel.

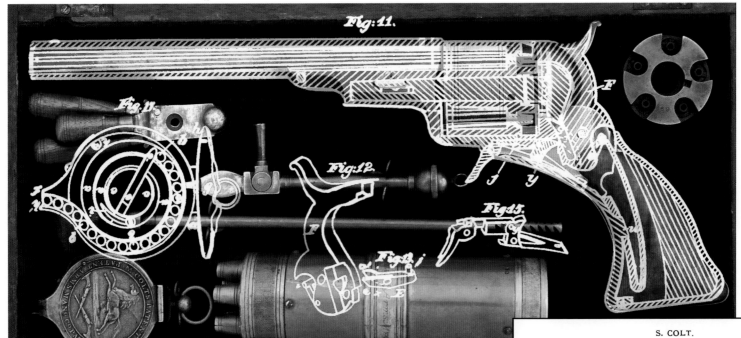

The No. 3

A year after the No.2 was added to the revolver line the Patent Arms Manufacturing Company introduced its first "large" revolver, the No. 3 or "Belt Model" as it is more commonly known. This was also the first transitional design which varies in configuration based upon year of manufacture. A larger gun with a medium sized frame, the No. 3 was offered in barrel lengths varying from 4 to 6 inches, and in increments of 4-$\frac{1}{2}$ inches, 4-$\frac{7}{16}$ inches, 5 inches, and 5-$\frac{1}{2}$ inches, as well as some with extra 12-inch barrels. One of the more distinctive visual differences (other than size) was a double step bevel in the lower portion of the frame (earlier models had a single bevel). Later versions of the No. 3 also came with flared grips, which would become standard on the large frame No. 5 Holster Model, also introduced in 1838.

No.3 Models were often sold as cased sets with extra cylinders. Other casings also came with an extra 12-inch barrel. The No.3 Models are rarely seen with loading levers. Those built prior to 1840 have square shoulder cylinders, those after 1840 the rounded style, although once again, early examples could have been refitted with the later style cylinders. Production of the No.3 is estimated at approximately 900 examples built between 1838 and 1840-41.[3]

[3] Production estimates for the No.3 vary from 800 to 900. The latter figure from R.L. Wilson's The Book of Colt Firearms.

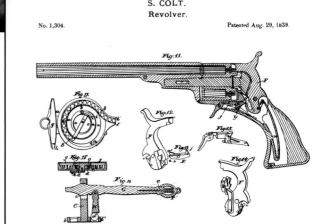

Samuel Colt's patent drawing for the No. 5 Holster Model is shown superimposed over an early No. 5 Model. The patent date shown is August 29, 1839. However, this is one of two pages detailing changes to accessories for the No. 5 Models, which had been in production since 1838. This patent drawing details the Paterson capper and combination tool. The gun illustration shows 10 moving parts in the Paterson Colt revolver. Colt simplified this to only six by the time the Walker Colt was built in 1847. (Dennis LeVett collection)

This very rare cased pair of No. 5 Holster Models with 9-inch barrels is one of only two cased sets known to exist. One set is in the Hartford Museum, and the other in the Dennis LeVett collection. LeVett's (pictured) is a very early set with square backed cylinders. No. 5 Models such as these were the guns used by Capt. Jack "Coffee" Hayes and the Texas Rangers in the famous Comanche Indian battle of 1844.

An early Texas Paterson, this example from the Dennis LeVett collection features scroll and border engraving, silver inlaid bands on the barrel, cylinder and frame, and replaced shell motif ivory grips that have aged to a remarkable finish. The flask and combination tool are accurate copies of rare originals; relined case with blue velvet.

The No. 5 Holster Model

This is the gun most people picture when they talk about Patersons. It is indisputably the most famous and best selling of the Paterson line built from 1836 to 1841. It was produced in two versions, those with and those without loading levers. Chambered in .36 caliber, it was the largest and most powerful of the Paterson revolvers. With a full size frame and weight of 2 pounds, 8 ounces (with the standard 7-1/2 inch barrel) this was the gun that gained fame in the hands of Capt. Jack Hayes, Samuel Walker, and the Texas Rangers during their legendary1844 Comanche Indian battle. The guns were known thereafter as Texas Patersons. The models used by Hayes and his Texas Rangers were fitted with 9-inch barrels, and were part of an order of 180 guns shipped in April 1839.

Approximately 1,000 Holster Models were manufactured with barrel lengths measuring anywhere from 4-inches to 12-inches. Samuel Colt's personal Texas Paterson with 6-inch barrel was heavily engraved (roughly 80 percent coverage), embellished with silver bands on the barrel and frame, and shell motif ivory grips accented with two silver studs. The same engraving pattern and grip design was used on a number of Texas Patersons, both with and without loading levers.

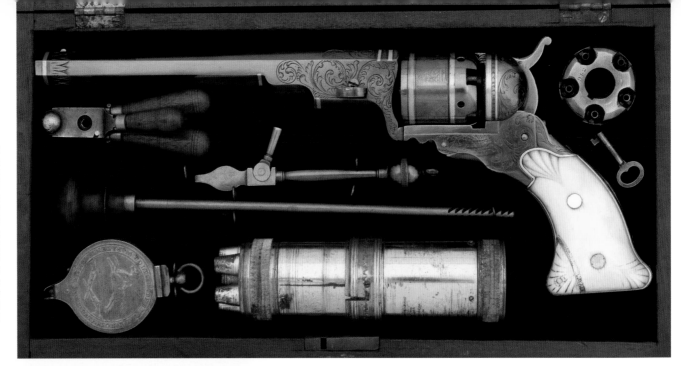

An exceptional No. 5 example that was possibly refinished by the factory. One corner of the shell motif ivory grips was broken and repaired in a unique fashion. The factory engraving and German silver bands are typical of deluxe No. 5 Models sold by the Patent Firearms Manufacturing Company in its last few years of operation. More No. 5 Models were engraved than any other. The close-up image shows the new stagecoach holdup cylinder scene introduced with the No. 5 Models. (Dennis LeVett collection)

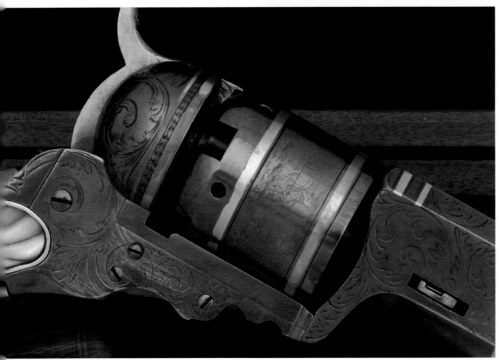

Among all Paterson variations there were more engraved No. 5 Holster Models than any other. Rarely were No. 1 Models engraved except for a handful of presentation guns, and even fewer among the No. 2 and No. 3 Models.

All No. 5 Patersons were fitted with large, flared grips. The standard barrel lengths were 7-¹/₂ or 9-inches. The 7-¹/₂ is the most customary. Nine inch models are regarded as rare. Most were shipped to Texas. The majority of No. 5 examples extant fitted with loading levers were built in 1840-41, but again earlier guns might have been refitted at the factory. As with everything else concerning the Colt Patersons, there are exceptions to the rules. Case in point, there is a No. 5 Holster Model in the Dennis Levett collection fitted with a 12-inch barrel. The author has also seen No. 5 Models with 4- and 5-inch barrels and one example on display at the Woolaroc Museum in Bartlesville, Oklahoma that was converted to fire metallic cartridges.

With the end of No. 5 production in 1841 the history of the Patent Arms Manufacturing Company essentially came to a close, but not entirely. Although Samuel Colt was no longer involved with the company and the doors in Paterson, New Jersey had been shuttered, Paterson revolvers were still being marketed and sold by John Ehlers.

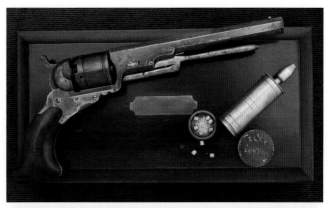

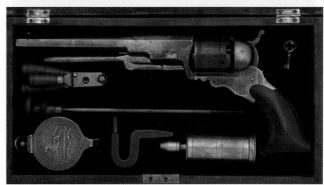

One of the most familiar Paterson models was the No. 5 with loading lever, more popularly known as a Texas Paterson. This example has the later single nozzle powder flask. Although this is the most recognized of all Patersons, the No. 5 with loading lever is the rarest. Note the round shoulder cylinder and dished right hand recoil shield, which was only done on guns with loading levers. (Dennis LeVett collection)

This view shows the two variations of No. 5 Holster Models, with and without loading levers. The levers became standard in August 1840. (Dennis LeVett collection)

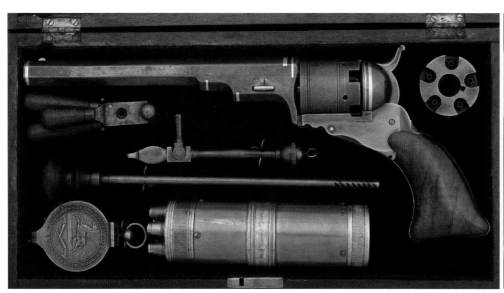

Left & right: Another Texas Paterson with 7-1/2 inch barrel and inlaid German silver bands. This was a typical presentation for the No. 5 Model. (Dennis Levett collection)

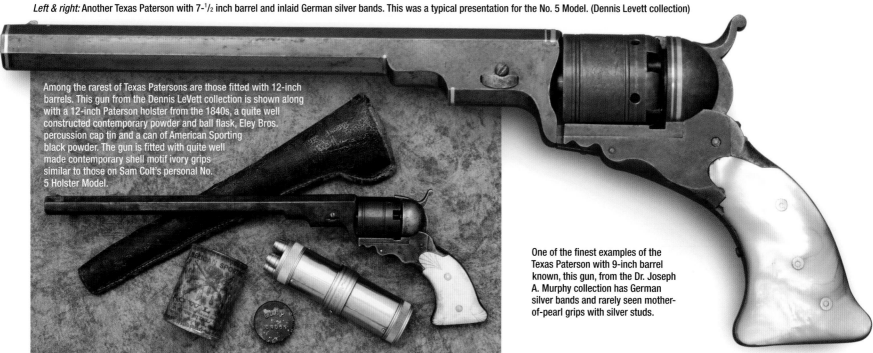

Among the rarest of Texas Patersons are those fitted with 12-inch barrels. This gun from the Dennis LeVett collection is shown along with a 12-inch Paterson holster from the 1840s, a quite well constructed contemporary powder and ball flask, Eley Bros. percussion cap tin and a can of American Sporting black powder. The gun is fitted with quite well made contemporary shell motif ivory grips similar to those on Sam Colt's personal No. 5 Holster Model.

One of the finest examples of the Texas Paterson with 9-inch barrel known, this gun, from the Dr. Joseph A. Murphy collection has German silver bands and rarely seen mother-of-pearl grips with silver studs.

The Ehlers Patersons

In 1842, following the failure of the Patent Arms Manufacturing Company in December, John Ehlers walked away with the remaining assets of Samuel Colt's first business venture, assets which included 536 uncompleted Paterson revolvers and anywhere from 150 to 160 rifles and carbines. He paid just a little over $6,000 for the above noted guns at a court ordered public auction of company inventory held in New York on December 9, 1842, but moreover, as the company's former treasurer, largest stockholder, and chief creditor, he had paid himself!

The remaining Paterson revolvers were completed at Ehlers' expense and updated with the features introduced in 1840, such as loading levers and round shoulder cylinders. The majority of the guns were a redesign Pocket known to collectors as the Fourth Model Ehlers Pocket or Improved No. 1 Pocket Model,

and a redesigned Belt Model known as the Fifth Model Ehlers Belt or Improved No. 2 Belt Model (with medium size frame). Both have distinct features which are at variance to the earlier No. 1 and No. 2 revolvers, as detailed in R.L. Wilson's *The Paterson Colt Book.* It took Ehlers until 1846 to completely dispose of his inventory. And here too he succeeded where Colt had failed, selling 100 Paterson Carbines and all of the remaining No. 5 Holster Pistols, approximately 50, to the Ordnance Department for use by the U.S. Navy.

Although the majority of guns disposed of by Ehlers were indistinguishable from those marketed by the Patent Fire Arms Manufacturing Company, many of the unfinished Pocket Models were different in fit and finish. This is sometimes evident in grip contours but more conspicuously in the shape and fitting of loading levers to guns not originally designed for them.

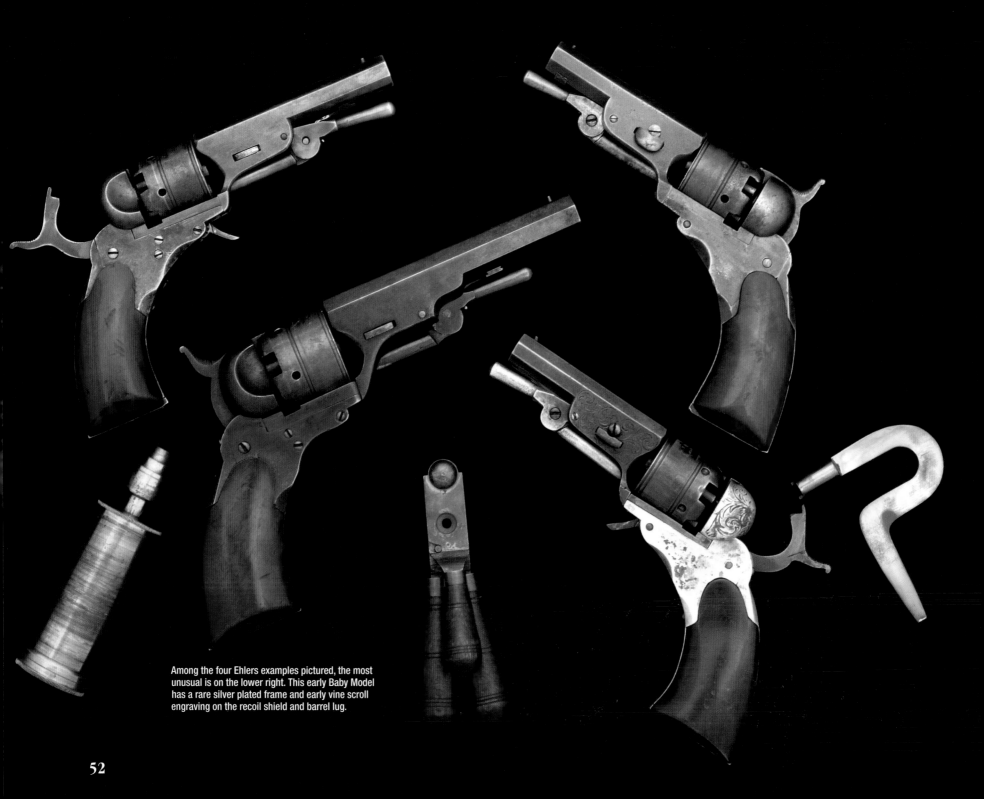

Among the four Ehlers examples pictured, the most unusual is on the lower right. This early Baby Model has a rare silver plated frame and early vine scroll engraving on the recoil shield and barrel lug.

Here & right: Throughout Colt's early history there were various copies of Colt revolvers, some built under license from Colt, others simply built by European gunmakers in disregard for Colt's British and French patents. The elegantly styled Paterson Brevete from the Dennis LeVett collection is of the later, handcrafted in Suhl, Germany by the firm of J.P. Sauer and Sohn. Different from the Paterson in more ways then it is similar, the Sauer revolver has very flowing, articulate lines more accustomed to single shot European percussion pistols, particularly in the hammer design. The barrel also flares slightly toward the muzzle. The front sight is dovetailed into the barrel and the engraving is accented with gold inlay. Even the maker's name is engraved in gold. The accessories were held in drawers in the presentation case, which held the gun upright in the top compartment.

Looking very much (perhaps too much) like a New Jersey built Paterson, this Brevete model of the No. 2 was made in Belgium and sold in England. (Dennis LeVett collection)

A categorical knockoff of the No. 3 Paterson, this Brevete even has the squared back cylinder and later flared grips of the No. 3 Models. The addition of silver inlays, at the outer edges of the grips, adds a very distinctive touch. One wonders why this example wasn't also engraved. The gun is shown in a manufactured case with Colt accessories. Dennis LeVett is "almost convinced" this is a European Brevete, but suspects it might also be a rare 20th Century American copy made in Winterset, Iowa, the birthplace of John Wayne, home to the Bridges of Madison County, and possibly one of the many gunmakers who copied Samuel Colt's designs in the 1800s.

53

Four remarkable copies of the Colt Paterson are among the guns in Dennis LeVett's collection. At far left is a limited edition Paterson model produced in 2005 by American Remembers. The gun was designed by the author and built for America Remembers by R.L. Millington of ArmSport LLC in Brighton, Colorado, engraved by Conrad Anderson in Kingston, Idaho, and fitted with authentic shell motif ivory grips by Dan Chesiak and Dennis Holland in Naugatuck, Connecticut. The presentation boxes were handcrafted by Pennsylvania furniture maker Duncan Everhart. Less than 100 were built. To the right is another limited edition model produced by Colt (through license to Colt Blackpowder Arms in Brooklyn, New York) c.1998-2002. Fewer than 100 were made. Back in 1989 the U.S. Historical Society produced a series of No. 5 Holster Models cased with authentic accessories (included the Colt capper) along with a signed and numbered copy of Philip R. Phillips and R.L. Wilson's book Paterson Colt Variations. The last example is the first model offered in the America Remembers Paterson Heritage Series. Like the engraved version sold in 2005, this edition of 100 guns built in 2004 was based on the Paterson Belt Model revolver.

The rarest of all Paterson reproductions are the examples built by the author and R.L. Millington for America Remembers in 2005. Fewer than 100 were manufactured. The gun's design was based on the late model Ehlers Improved Belt Model No. 2. This particular variation of the Paterson had never been reproduced. (Author's collection)

With Ehlers' final disposition of Paterson inventory in 1846 it seemed as if the book on Samuel Colt as an armsmaker had been closed. A year later, in 1847, he would open it again.

Paterson Statistics

No. 1 Pocket Model
Caliber: .28 or .31
Capacity: 5 shots
Frame: Small Frame
Barrel length: 2-^{1}/$_2$ to 4-^{3}/$_4$ inches
Average Weight: 11 ounces

No. 1 through No.3 Models featured a roll engraved cylinder scene with the horse head COLT emblem, three men, a horse and rider, a centaur, and a dismounted rider and horse. The background pattern was comprised of erratic vertical lines with the overall scene grounded on a solid field. The centaur theme was evolved from those used on the Paterson Ring Lever Rifles, but was completely different for the pistols.

Markings: Top of the barrel marked
— *Patent Arms M'g Co. Paterson, N.J. – Colt's Pt.*—

Production: Approximately 500 beginning with serial number 1. Produced 1837-1838.

No. 2 Pocket Model
Caliber: .31 or .34
Capacity: 5 shots
Frame: Small Frame
Barrel length: 2-^{1}/$_2$ to 4-^{3}/$_4$ inches
Average Weight: 20 ounces

Roll engraved cylinder scene was enlarged on this and No. 3 Models to include a second Centaur (holding a Paterson Revolving Rifle) between the COLT emblem and the original cylinder scene.

Markings: Top of the barrel marked
— *Patent Arms M'g Co. Paterson, N.J. – Colt's Pt.*—

Production: Approximately 800 beginning with serial number 1. Produced 1837-1840. Late models manufactured in 1840 were fitted with loading levers, round shoulder cylinders and capping channel cut into the right recoil shield. Some earlier models left in inventory were also converted to the later design.

No. 3 Belt Model
Caliber: .31 or .34
Capacity: 5 shots
Frame: Medium Size Frame
Barrel length: 4-inches to 6-inches. Also some cased with extra 12-inch barrel.
Average Weight: 20 ounces
Markings: Top of the barrel marked
— *Patent Arms M'g Co. Paterson, N.J. – Colt's Pt.—*

Extra 12-inch barrels marked
~~~~* *Patent Arms M'g Co. Paterson, N.J. –Colt's Pt.* *~~~~

Production: Approximately 900 beginning with serial number 1. Produced 1838-1840. Late models manufactured in 1840-41 were fitted with loading levers, round shoulder cylinders and capping channel cut into the right recoil shield. Some earlier models left in inventory were also converted to the later design. Grip design changed during production to the flared grips used on the No. 5 Holster Model.

No. 5 Holster Model (Texas Paterson)
Caliber: .36
Capacity: 5 shots
Frame: Large Frame
Barrel length: 4-inches to 12-inches with various increments in between. Standard lengths were either 7-1/2 or 9-inches.
Average Weight: 40 ounces (2 lbs. 8 oz.)
Roll engraved cylinder changed to new stagecoach holdup scene and new COLT block letter emblem.
Markings: Top of barrel marked
~~~~* *Patent Arms M'g Co. Paterson, N.J. –Colt's Pt.* *~~~~

Production: Approximately 1,000 beginning with serial number 1. Produced 1838-1841. Late models manufactured in 1840-41 were fitted with loading levers, round shoulder cylinders and capping channel cut into the right recoil shield.

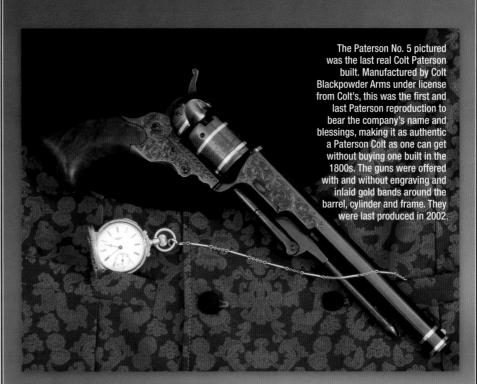

The Paterson No. 5 pictured was the last real Colt Paterson built. Manufactured by Colt Blackpowder Arms under license from Colt's, this was the first and last Paterson reproduction to bear the company's name and blessings, making it as authentic a Paterson Colt as one can get without buying one built in the 1800s. The guns were offered with and without engraving and inlaid gold bands around the barrel, cylinder and frame. They were last produced in 2002.

Reproductions of the Colt Paterson No. 5 Holster Model, both with and without loading lever, have been produced in Italy since the 1990s. A. Uberti in Serezzo produced both versions through 2005. They have since been discontinued. The example shown was built in the late 1990s and finished at the factory as shown. The Paterson capper is another fine reproduction that is no longer made. Fratelli Pietta in Brescia remains the only manufacturer of Paterson reproductions today. The photograph is from the 1860s and shows the original Paterson factory as it stood on the banks of the Passaic River at Van Houten and Mill Streets. It is referred to in Paterson as "The Old Gun Mill." The stone is a piece from one of the original buildings. (Author's collection)

Chapter Three
Samuel H. Walker
Colt's Resurrection

"If I can't be first, I won't be second in anything..."

—Samuel Colt

Samuel Colt was about to go bankrupt. It was 1840 and his young enterprise founded in 1836, The Patent Arms Manufacturing Company of Paterson, New Jersey, was on its last legs. With increasing debts and the failure of the Paterson Model 1839 Carbine to pass military tests in February 1842, the company was finally forced by court order to dispose of all properties, most of which were purchased by his treasurer and largest stockholder, John Ehlers.

Colt regarded Ehlers as a treacherous schemer, but rather he was a hard-nosed businessman. After the foreclosure, Ehlers modified the remaining No1. through No. 3 Paterson revolvers in inventory, fitting them with loading levers and round shoulder cylinders, and marketing them as the Ehlers Models. By 1846 he had earned back a good deal of his lost investment. Moreover, he had helped, in a somewhat backhanded way, to keep the Colt name alive until 1846, the year Sam Colt met Captain Samuel Hamilton Walker. A year later, Colt would experience a reversal of misfortune.

During the years between 1840 and 1846 he had endeavored to establish himself in the munitions field, developing several defensive weapons systems with the intent of selling them to the government. Among Colt's inventions was the submarine torpedo (mine), a device detonated by electric wire conduction. The Navy granted him $6,000 for a series of tests, one of which blew up and sank a 60-ton schooner on the Potomac, as a gallery of congressmen and government officials watched in horror. It was a little too overwhelming a sight for the 1840s and neither the military nor Congress liked what they

Far left: What some might consider the Holy Grail of post-Paterson Colts, the Walker Walkers are the guns presented by Colt to Capt. Samuel H. Walker in 1847. These are the very guns that he was carrying at the time of his death on October 9, 1847 while leading a charge into Huamantla, Tlaxcala, Mexico. (Dr. Joseph A. Murphy collection)

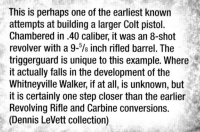

This is perhaps one of the earliest known attempts at building a larger Colt pistol. Chambered in .40 caliber, it was an 8-shot revolver with a 9-5/8 inch rifled barrel. The triggerguard is unique to this example. Where it actually falls in the development of the Whitneyville Walker, if at all, is unknown, but it is certainly one step closer than the earlier Revolving Rifle and Carbine conversions. (Dennis LeVett collection)

This is the first "Walker" prototype c.1846, built for Samuel Colt by Blunt & Syms in New York and presented for review to the Secretary of War, William L. Marcy, and Captain Samuel Walker, prior to signing the January 1847 contract. Elements of the final rendition are evident as are ties to the Paterson in the grip, barrel, and frame design. This gun was chambered in .47 caliber (closer to the original specifications set forth in the contract, "of a bore suited to carrying round balls, fifty to the pound..." Walker's suggestions were for a different grip design, the addition of a loading lever, and better sights. Colt's final interpretation exceeded everyone's expectations. What is interesting in this design, even though the gun does not have a loading lever, the right recoil shield is dished to allow capping the cylinder. This gun can be seen on display at the Wadsworth Atheneum Museum of Art in Hartford, Connecticut. (photo courtesy Herbert G. Houze and Wadsworth Atheneum Museum of Art)

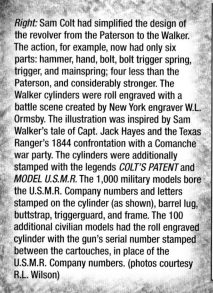

Right: Sam Colt had simplified the design of the revolver from the Paterson to the Walker. The action, for example, now had only six parts: hammer, hand, bolt, bolt trigger spring, trigger, and mainspring; four less than the Paterson, and considerably stronger. The Walker cylinders were roll engraved with a battle scene created by New York engraver W.L. Ormsby. The illustration was inspired by Sam Walker's tale of Capt. Jack Hayes and the Texas Ranger's 1844 confrontation with a Comanche war party. The cylinders were additionally stamped with the legends *COLT'S PATENT* and *MODEL U.S.M.R.* The 1,000 military models bore the U.S.M.R. Company numbers and letters stamped on the cylinder (as shown), barrel lug, buttstrap, triggerguard, and frame. The 100 additional civilian models had the roll engraved cylinder with the gun's serial number stamped between the cartouches, in place of the U.S.M.R. Company numbers. (photos courtesy R.L. Wilson)

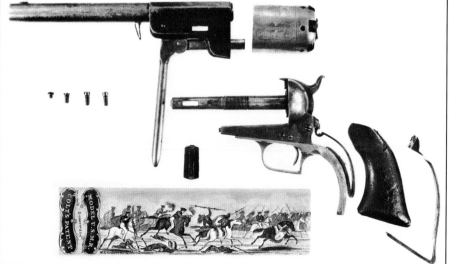

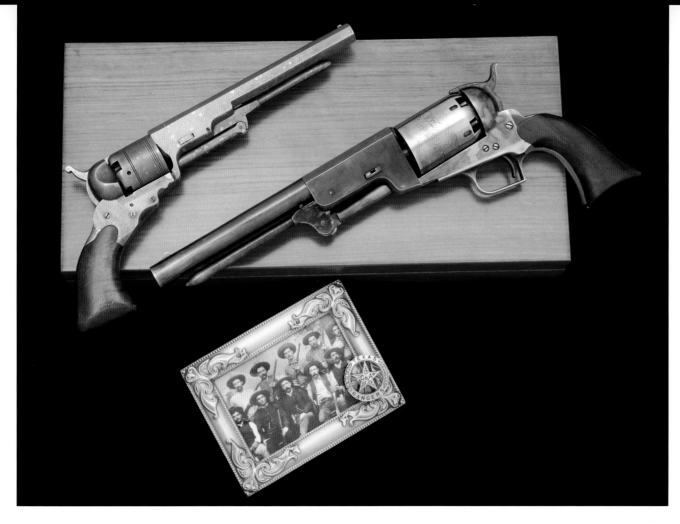

The difference between the last Paterson Models, also known as Texas Patersons, and the 1847 Holster Model (later renamed the Whitneyville Walker or Walker Colt) was a substantially larger and heftier sidearm for the Texas Rangers and United States Mounted Rifles. The best feature, as far as the Rangers were concerned, was having six .44 caliber rounds, verses only five .36 caliber charges in the Paterson. As *Texas Ranger Dispatch Magazine* editor and author Robert Nieman once noted, "The [Walker] was as effective as a common rifle at one hundred yards, and superior to a musket even at two hundred." With a maximum load of 60 grains of black powder the Walker delivered its charge at 1,200 feet per second and a force of 450 foot pounds.

saw. John Quincy Adams branded Colt's invention an "un-Christian contraption." They were more impressed with his design for waterproof cartridges which had already been endorsed by Winfield Scott, General in Chief of the Army. In 1845 Congress spent one quarter of its $200,000 state militia appropriation on Colt's ammunition.

Although his submarine torpedo had been a political failure, the electronic wire conduction method used for detonation ended up having a more civilized use. The cable Colt designed to trigger an explosive charge carried an electrical impulse under water. Soon after the torpedo test Colt befriended Samuel Morse who developed underwater cable communications based in part on Colt's electronic wire conduction method, an

achievement for which his name is barely remembered. It was his patents for the revolving pistol that would ultimately lead to success in 1847. The year before, he had made the acquaintance of Samuel H. Walker, a young Texas Ranger who had attained national celebrity status from his daring exploits in the border wars between the Republic of Texas and Mexico, and in battles with Comanche Indians.

A newly appointed Captain of the United States Mounted Rifles, Walker had favored Colt's new Paterson revolvers in battle. Before the Paterson the Rangers had carried single shot percussion pistols, which left them at a decided disadvantage when fighting Indians. In the time it took to reload a pistol, a Comanche warrior could accurately fire five or six arrows!

One interesting detail of the Walker revolvers was the U.S. 1847 stamping above the wedge slot on the right side of the barrel. The "8" was stamped upside down, with the smaller loop at the bottom.

At the time of his death, Walker's fame was nationwide. His passing was news in every major newspaper in America. In 1846, there was even a Broadway play, *The Campaign on the Rio Grande, or, Triumphs in Mexico*, whose main character was Sam Walker.

Although reports from the field stated that Captain Walker was shot to death in the Battle of Huamantla on October 9, 1847, this famous painting shows him being run through by a Mexican soldier's lance. (Painting reproduced courtesy of Dennis LeVett collection and Greg Martin Auctions)

guns. A purchase order for 1,000 Colt Holster Models was passed on to Ordnance Chief, Lieutenant Colonel George Talcott.[2] This was the news Sam Colt had only dreamed of receiving. It was a second chance. All he needed now was a factory and the means to build 1,000 revolvers!

Money had never been one of Sam Colt's personal concerns, not that he was wealthy, quite the opposite in fact, he just didn't care about money. "*Money is a trash I have always looked down upon that I never had any to know how to appreciate it, it is true. Neither would I long were my income that of John Jacob Astor,*" he had written to his brother William in 1844. Two

years later, he wrote to a friend in Washington D.C. remarking that he, Colt, was as "*poor as a church mouse.*" Now, with the possibility of starting anew he not only needed a factory, but one that was well funded in order to fulfill the Ordnance Department commission. Colt turned to Eli Whitney, Jr., son of the inventor of the cotton gin, who was then producing rifles for the government in Whitneyville, Connecticut. Whitney, though somewhat reluctant, agreed to produce the tooling and manufacture the guns for Colt at his Whitneyville armory.

To ensure that the new gun would meet government standards, and more importantly those of Sam Walker

[2] Ibid.

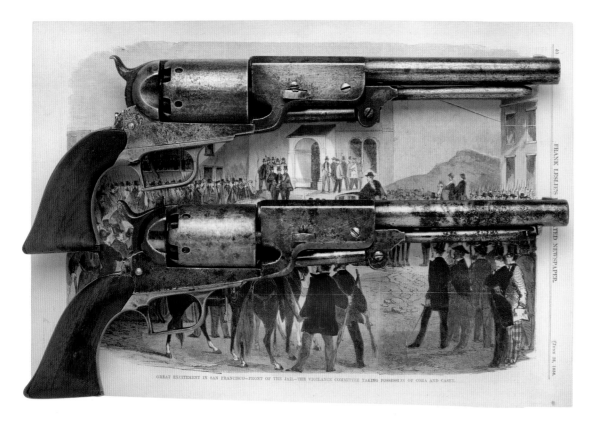

Pictured is a rare matched pair of Colt Walker revolvers, serial numbers B Co. No. 25 and B Co. No. 26. Although the blued finish is worn from the barrels, they have aged to match the cylinder which was originally left un-blued by Colt's. The brass triggerguards and oil stained walnut grips still show remarkable finish for a pair of revolvers built 160 years ago. One unique feature is seen on gun B Co. No. 26, which has been fitted with a loading lever latch, which was not standard until the Whitneyville Hartford Dragoons (successor to the Walker) manufactured at Colt's new Hartford, Connecticut factory in the latter part of 1847. (photo courtesy of Greg Martin Auctions)

This is the only known Walker with period engraving. The early foliate or vine scroll style pattern is seen on the frame, recoil shield, backstrap, triggerguard and barrel lug. This example is also a U.S.M.R. model and is stamped E Co. No. 22. In the early 1980s, American master engraver Alvin A. White engraved a 2nd Generation Walker in a similar pattern. (photo courtesy of Greg Martin Auctions)

and his Texas Rangers, Colt asked him to take an active role in the revolver's design. To Colt's good fortune the Ordnance Department had already appointed Walker to act as its representative. On the fourth of January 1847, the government contract was signed by Samuel Colt and Samuel Walker for 1,000 Holster Model pistols. At the time, neither man realized that they were about to change the history of the American firearms industry.

The requirements for the new Colt revolver were set forth in the contract, which stated in part that the gun be, "of a bore suited to carrying round balls, fifty to the pound…" thus the new revolver would be chambered in .44 caliber. The requirements also stipu-

lated "…a barrel length of nine inches…and cylinders to be made of hammered cast steel with chambers for six charges each." Colt was to be compensated for the guns at a rate of, "[not less than] $25 each on delivery."

It was apparent from the onset that this was going to be a much larger revolver than the Paterson. Walker had envisioned a side-arm of substantial size and power that could be carried on horseback, either single or in pairs within a pummel holster. Thus the guidelines were established, and Colt set about building a gun that was to surpass even Walker's vision.

The first 100 examples were to be ready within three months of the contract signing,

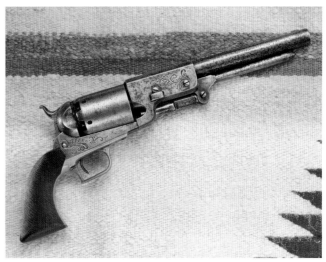

A big gun with a lot of clout, until the Colt New Service chambered in .45 ACP was developed, the .44 caliber Walker Colt reigned as the most powerful revolver in the world.

Another interesting detail of the Walker revolvers was the U.S. 1847 stamping above the wedge slot and screw on the right side of the barrel. The "8" was stamped upside down, with the smaller loop at the bottom. (This is one of the essential clues in determining a fake Walker revolver. Aside from known reproductions built by Colt and several Italian gunmakers[3], there were examples fabricated by hand in the early to mid 20th century intended by their makers to be passed off as originals, right down to the serial numbers. But even these counterfeiters missed the inverted "8".)

As soon as production was under way, Colt dispatched a pair to Texas Ranger Captain (now Colonel) John Coffee "Jack" Hayes. And as Walker had requested, paired sets were also shipped to top military officials, including Brigadier General David E. Twiggs, Col. W. S. Harvey, and Generals Persifer Smith, Winfield Scott, and W. J. Worth. A matched set of Holster Models, serial numbers 1009 and 1010, was shipped from Colt to Walker, in addition to a pair of military issued revolvers. All of the guns presented by Colt were in a special serial number range beginning with 1001 and concluding with 1020. Tragically, Sam Walker never lived long enough to take receipt of his issued guns. The latest war with Mexico, which had begun in 1846, claimed his life on October 9, 1847 during the battle of Huamantla, Tlaxcala, Mexico.

Walker had gained national fame doing what Texas Ranger commanders had done in battle since their beginning – he led from the front. He had ordered his men to draw sabers and charge, hitting the Mexican Army a full 45 minutes ahead of the main U.S. Army contingent and crippling Santa Ana's defenses. His bravery this time came at a high price. At age 32, Samuel Hamilton Walker lay dead after being been shot off his horse. There are conflicting reports as to how he was killed. In one historic painting of the battle, Walker is shown atop his horse impaled on the lance of a Mexican soldier, but he was most definitely shot according to military reports. One states that it was a bullet to the head, another that he was shot in the back, with the bullet passing through the left shoulder and above the heart. At the time of his mortal wound Walker was carrying the pair of guns sent to him by Sam Colt.

The first 220 guns that had been delivered were specially marked as Walker had requested, "C-Company" (his Company) and then the serial number beginning from 1 to 220. Additional deliveries bore the individual Company letters and numbering until the commission was fulfilled. After the first contract order had been completed, U.S. Secretary of War, William L. Marcy, placed an order

an almost impossible task considering that on January 4 neither the gun's final design nor the tooling to build it at Whitneyville was ready. Colt pressed to have Walker present as often as possible to observe the progress. Since he was in Washington recruiting troops for the U.S.M.R. Walker was able to lend his expertise from the field. With his suggestions implemented the design was finalized and Colt delivered the first 220 revolvers for government inspection on June 7, 1847.

The weight of the new revolver (Colt initially referred to the gun in his letters as a "holster model" and did not call it a Walker pistol until after Walker's death), was a massive 4 pounds, 9 ounces, with six .44 caliber chambers packing 50 grains of black powder behind a 220 grain lead ball. (The loading lever was designed as specified to load both round ball and conical bullets).

Colt hired Waterman Lilly Ormsby, a renowned New York engraver, to design a cylinder scene suggested by Captain Walker: the famous "Hayes fight." Because Ormsby had never seen a Texas Ranger, he mistakenly placed them in the uniforms of the United States Dragoons. The roll engraved cylinders were additionally stamped with the legends *COLT'S PATENT* and *MODEL U.S.M.R.* The flat top of the breech was marked *ADDRESS. SAM^L COLT NEW-YORK CITY.* All Walker cylinders were left in the white.

[3] Colt's sold two "2nd Generation" versions of the Walker between 1980 and 1982. Walkers were also sold by the Colt Blackpowder Arms Co., and manufactured under license from Colt's as 3rd Generation models from 1992-2002. Italian gunmaker A. Uberti has built an excellent copy of the Walker since the 1980s. Other examples were also produced by Armi San Marco and Palmetto, the latter almost exclusively for Dixie Guns Works, which sells both the Palmetto and Uberti versions. Armi San Marco ceased production in 2000. All of the Italian reproductions are readily distinguishable from original 19th century models. Fourth Edition Blue Book of Modern Black Powder Arms, by John B. Allen and Dennis Adler.

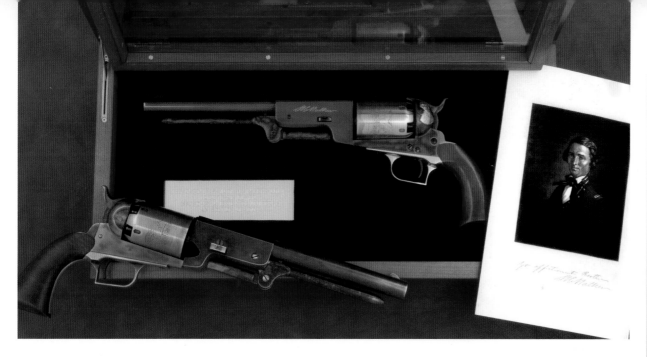

for another 1,000 of Colt's "Walker" revolvers.[4] Within the year Samuel Colt had moved into a new factory in Hartford, Connecticut, designed and put into production a second model, the transitional Whitneyville-Hartford Dragoon (first successor to the Walker), a small pocket pistol known as the Baby Dragoon introduced in 1848, and by the end of the decade established the foundation for an entire line of revolvers that would make the Colt's Firearms Manufacturing Company the most important American arms maker of the 19th century.

The Guns of Samuel Walker

Although Walker and his men were officially Mounted Riflemen of the United States Army, they continued to operate as Texas Rangers during the war with Mexico and in the late summer of 1847 had turned their attention toward Mexican guerrillas who were working to keep the American Army's supply line severed. In October General Joseph Lane was moving his troops toward Puebla, where it was estimated Santa Anna had 4,000 men garrisoned. Lane stopped in Perote and conferred with Walker, after which

both men decided to attack the Mexican forces with Walker and his Texas Rangers leading the assault. Even though instructed by Lane to stay within support distance of his force, about three miles from Puebla, Walker decided to surprise the Mexican troops in the hopes of weakening their defenses. Though he lost his life in the attack, his plan succeeded, and Lane's army defeated Santa Anna's troops.

Although born in Maryland, Walker's body was returned to San Antonio for burial. Twenty years later, on April 21, 1856, San Jacinto Day, his body was exhumed and re-interred in the Odd Fellow Cemetery beside another great Texas Ranger, Richard Gillespie.[5]

Although Sam Walker did not survive the battle of Huamantla his presentation guns did, and today they are part of the Dr. Joseph A. Murphy collection in Pennsylvania. The pair, serial numbers 1009 and 1010, have been cased together in a custom presentation box with a portrait of Walker mounted inside the lid. The guns were on display from July through December 1999 at the National Firearms Museum in Fairfax, Virginia, and have since been shown at major gun shows and at NRA annual meetings around the country.

In 2006, to commemorate the first meeting of Samuel Colt and Samuel H. Walker, America Remembers released a limited edition of 100 authentic Colt Walker revolvers (from the remaining inventory of Colt Blackpowder Arms Co.) with cylinders in the white, Samuel Walkers signature reproduced on the left barrel lug and high relief solid gold bust of Walker on the left recoil shield. The guns were done with the cooperation of Dr. Joseph A. Murphy, whose Walker case was copied for this limited edition. The engraving, gold bust, and finish work was done by Andrew Bourbon, the late Alvin A. White's protégé. (Author's collection)

[4] This order was subsequently filled by Colt's new, lighter weight Dragoon models.
[5] Texas Ranger Dispatch Magazine, Texas Ranger Hall of Fame and Museum.

Among the legendary guns of the Texas Rangers were Samuel Colt's Dragoons. Pictured atop a painting of the Texas Rangers by Jack Terry, are an engraved Third Model, top, a First Model, center, and a

Chapter Four

Colt Single Action Models of the 1840s and 1850s
Dragoons, Pocket Pistols and the Legendary 1851 Navy

With his profits from the sale of 1,100 Walker revolvers and an order for 1,000 additional guns from the Ordnance Department in hand, Samuel Colt was no longer "poor as a church mouse."

After paying off Eli Whitney, Jr., Colt still had a sizable stake remaining from his $25,000 in government sales, plus earnings from the approximately 81 civilian models sold[1] and profits from powder flasks and accessories purchased by the Ordnance Department. Thus with cash in hand he set up shop in Hartford in the summer of 1847. What was to become the greatest arms manufacturing company in American history began humbly that year within a leased building located on Pearl Street. As the works began to shape up Sam wrote to a friend in Illinois: "*I am working on my own hook and have sole control and management of my business and intend to keep it as long as I live without being subject to the whims of a pack of dam fools and knaves styling themselves a board of directors... my arms sustain a high reputation among men of brains in Mexico and...now is the time to make money out of them.*"

To acquire everything necessary to begin manufacturing in Hartford, Sam told his cousin Elisha Colt, he required another $5,000, which Elisha (who conveniently happened to be a banker) provided. The money was used, along with other funds, to purchase the Walker tooling from Whitney and set up additional machinery in Hartford. The first product of his new endeavor appeared in the fall of 1847; a gun built on the Whitneyville tooling but modified to make the new model a bit lighter and more reliable than the Walker. A century later the first revolvers built in Hartford would come to be known by historians and collectors as the Whitneyville-Hartford Dragoons.

The Walker had nearly been "*...the most perfect weapon in the World for light mounted troops...*" except for a few minor refinements which Sam Colt began to make by the summer of 1847. In battle, the Walkers had "occasionally" been prone

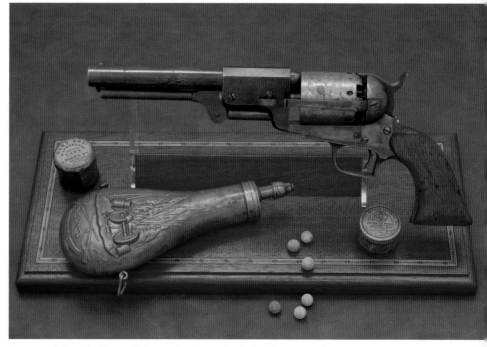

Often regarded as "the Dragoon between the Dragoons" following the success of the 1847 Whitneyville-built Walkers, Sam Colt established his own armory in Hartford and began producing an improved model known as the Whitneyville-Hartford Dragoon.

[1] Colt had used 19 guns from the civilian 100 civilian models as presentation pistols in 1847, serial numbers 1001 to 1020.

inch, 5-inch, and 6-inch lengths and, like the first Paterson Pocket Models, without loading lever. Chambered in .31 caliber, the new pocket model harkened back to its New Jersey heritage by being a 5-shot revolver.

The Dragoon miniature bore the same cylinder scene as the First Model (although cropped tightly to fit the smaller circumference of the .31 caliber cylinder), a square back triggerguard, round cylinder stop slots (later changed to oval and toward the end of production rectangular, thus keeping pace with changes to the full size Dragoon models) and a cupped cylinder arbor intended to serve as a loading rammer. To say that the 1848 was a success would be an understatement. Between late 1847 and 1850 Colt's produced more than 15,000 examples (serial numbers 1 to approximately 15,500).

Beginning in 1849 Sam Colt took a page from John Ehlers' book and added a loading lever to his popular Pocket Revolver, creating the Model 1849. This however, was an entirely new gun, and not the updating of an old model, as Ehlers had done in 1842.

The 1849 Pocket Revolver had a new cylinder design with rectangular cylinder stop slots, a round back triggerguard (the first Colt to offer this feature) and a new "Stagecoach Holdup" roll engraved cylinder scene designed by W.L. Ormsby. (This same scene was used on later models of the Baby Dragoon c.1849-1850, and would reappear on later Colt Pocket Models, as well as some Roots Pistols, and 1870s era cartridge conversions of Police and Pocket Models of Navy Caliber.)

When Sam Colt introduced the Model 1849 he had no idea that this would be the most successful gun of his career. With sales beginning in 1850, this diminutive revolver remained in production through 1873 with sales in America exceeding of 325,000 over 23

A civilian First Model Dragoon cased with accessories; 500 count Eley Bros. cap tin, "Walker" style powder flask, large nipple wrench, and brass and iron bullet mold. Serial number 6116, this is one of the finest examples known of the First Model Dragoon. (Dr. Joseph A. Murphy collection)

years, plus an additional 11,000 sold in England. No other American revolver, not even Colt's 1851 Navy and 1860 Army, would ever outsell the 1849 Pocket Model.

Aside from retailers flocking to Colt's door to order the guns in quantity was a new client that had more to do with what came *after* the sale of goods; the banking and express firm of Wells Fargo & Co.[2]. In the early 1850s the home office in San Francisco requested a short barreled 1849 Pocket Model, specially built without a loading lever, which would be issued to Wells Fargo & Co. stagecoach and railway agents. Approximately 6,000 were produced, although it is highly doubtful that Wells Fargo & Co. purchased very many. Therefore, thousands of 1849 Pocket Models without loading levers would have been sold to the public, making the gun briefly available in two versions.

Easily concealed in a small belt holster or simply in a coat pocket or waist sash, the lightweight 24 ounce, 5-shot (and 6-shot beginning in 1861) pistol became the concealed carry gun of choice in the 1850s, during the Civil War, and well into the 1880s. Throughout its production life, and even afterward, there were more variations of the 1849 Pocket Model than any other Colt revolver. We say "afterward" because the 1849 continued on as a .38 caliber cartridge conversion revolver manufactured by Colt's until 1880, giving this gun a total production history spanning three decades.

[2] Wells Fargo & Company was organized on March 18, 1852.

Close-up of First Model Dragoon No. 6116 shows the defining characteristic of oval (also referred to as round) cylinder bolt stops. This design was changed to rectangular in 1850 when the Second Model Dragoon was introduced.

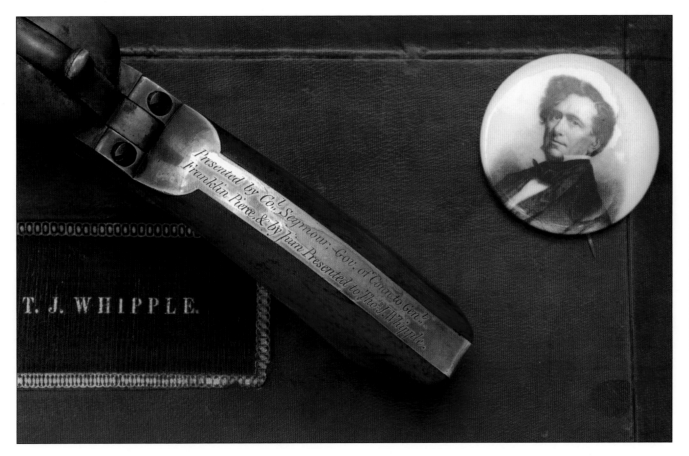

This historically significant First Model Dragoon, serial number 3969, was originally a gift from Connecticut Governor Thomas H. Seymour to Franklin Pierce (later to become 14th President of the United States 1853-1857). At the outbreak of the Mexican War in 1846, the former New Hampshire Senator and U.S District Attorney enlisted in the Army as a private. Serving under General Winfield Scott in the campaign against Mexico City, he was commissioned a Brigadier General. Pierce later presented the cased Colt Dragoon to Colonel Thomas J. Whipple (a fellow veteran of the Mexican campaigns, and later commander of the 4th New Hampshire during the Civil War). All of this is handsomely documented by the revolver's inscription on the silver-plated brass backstrap. (Dr. Joseph A. Murphy collection)

Serial numbers for the 1849 Pocket Model overlapped with the 1848 Baby Dragoon, beginning at around 12000[3] and concluding in 1873 at 331000. This takes into account 1849 Pocket Model frames used to build factory cartridge pistols from 1876 to 1880, which were in the serial number range beginning at approximately 274000 through 328000; an estimated 6,700 cartridge models.

The 1849 Pocket Models were stamped with a two line barrel address:

ADDRESS SAM^L COLT
NEW-YORK CITY

The style used changed three times during manufacture and in the serial number range from 187000 became a one line address:

ADDRESS COL. SAM^L COLT NEW-YORK U.S. AMERICA.

In addition, London Models (built for sale in England) were marked:

ADDRESS. COL: COLT.
LONDON.

Design changes to the 1849 (and over 30 years there were many) include different front sights varying from a simple

[3] Given the known overlap with 1848 Pocket Models, the beginning serial numbers for the 1849 Model could be in the 14400 range rather than 12000.

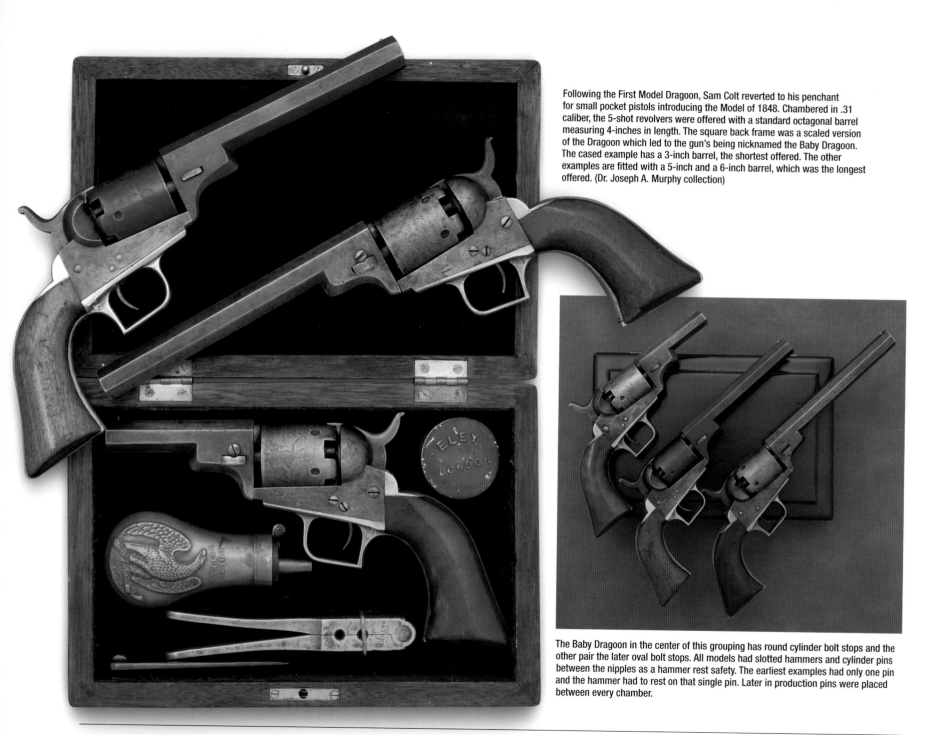

Following the First Model Dragoon, Sam Colt reverted to his penchant for small pocket pistols introducing the Model of 1848. Chambered in .31 caliber, the 5-shot revolvers were offered with a standard octagonal barrel measuring 4-inches in length. The square back frame was a scaled version of the Dragoon which led to the gun's being nicknamed the Baby Dragoon. The cased example has a 3-inch barrel, the shortest offered. The other examples are fitted with a 5-inch and a 6-inch barrel, which was the longest offered. (Dr. Joseph A. Murphy collection)

The Baby Dragoon in the center of this grouping has round cylinder bolt stops and the other pair the later oval bolt stops. All models had slotted hammers and cylinder pins between the nipples as a hammer rest safety. The earliest examples had only one pin and the hammer had to rest on that single pin. Later in production pins were placed between every chamber.

Left: This rare 3-inch Baby Dragoon is cased with powder flask, Colt's patent brass bullet mold, the Eley Bros. percussion cap tin, and the combination tool. Loading of cylinders was accomplished with the cylinder arbor which was cupped on the end to serve as a rammer. (Dennis LeVett collection)

A rare engraved Baby Dragoon in the popular early large vine scroll or foliate pattern of the period. Although there is not a great deal of embellishment the detail is exceptional. Even the barrel wedge is finely engraved. This is an early gun and is cased similarly to late model Paterson revolvers with the bullet mold held in place by staple, the gun, flask and early Eley Bros. cap tin set into formed recesses but not of the later French Fit style. (Dr. Joseph A. Murphy Collection)

brass pin to German silver or iron blade sights dovetailed onto the barrel, and German silver blade sights mounted into the barrel. The capping cutout on the recoil shield varied from none to two different versions, the latter being dished a bit deeper. Additionally, there were minor changes in the barrel lug, loading levers, latches, and triggerguard contours. None of this is unexpected from a production run that outlasted every other percussion model ever built at Hartford. There were also more engraved 1849 Models than any other percussion Colt.

In 1850, as the popularity of the Pocket Models soared, Sam Colt also made improvements to the large .44 caliber Dragoon, introducing the Second Model at approximately serial number 8000, a continuation of First Model serial numbers. Changes and improvements included rectangular cylinder stops and stop slots (guide grooves), a slotted hammer face and pin safeties between each chamber and, after serial number 10000, a change from the earlier "V" shaped mainspring to a flat mainspring. A roller bearing was also added at the base of the hammer where it engaged the mainspring. There were minor changes in the triggerguard contours and loading lever latches as well.

There were enough improvements over the First Model Dragoon that Colt secured new patents on September 10, 1850 to protect the rectangular cylinder stops and guide grooves,

Anther pair of early Baby Dragoons with round cylinder bolt stops. The top example has a 5-inch barrel and the engraved gun the standard 4-inch. Also shown are the Colt's patent brass bullet mold, an early package of paper cartridges, Colt's patent powder flask and the rarely seen loading tool. (Dr. Joseph A. Murphy collection)

slotted hammer face, and pin safeties. The latter were intended to secure the hammer at rest between chambers. Cocking the hammer from this position completed the rotation of the cylinder into battery. This was a significant improvement but hardly a safety by today's standards. On Walkers, Whitneyville-Hartfords and First Model Dragoons, placing the hammer at rest between chambers was not even recommended, as the cylinder could easily rotate and allow the hammer to rest on a loaded chamber. In theory this was not a problem unless one dropped the gun and it fell on the hammer, or the hammer was struck inadvertently; in either instance the gun would more than likely discharge. The slotted hammer face and pin safeties added an extra margin of confidence when carrying a fully loaded six gun.

The Second Model was essentially an interim design replaced in 1851 by the further improved Third Model Dragoon. Only around 2,700 Second Models were built, with a portion of those examples used to fill a government order for 1,000 Army pistols received in February 1850. The serial number range for the Second Model runs from approximately 8000 to 10700 produced between 1850 and 1851, a very significant year in Colt history.

Wild Bill and the 1851 Navy

In 1851 Sam Colt introduced one of the most important single action revolvers in the company's history, the medium frame, six shot, .36 caliber Model 1851 Navy. Despite the greater sales success and longevity of the 1849 Pocket, the 1851 Navy is the most famous percussion gun in Western firearms lore. This was the preferred sidearm of one James Butler Hickok, better known as lawman and gunfighter Wild Bill Hickok. For most of his career as a lawman, gambler, and gunfighter, he carried a brace of engraved Colt 1851 Navy revolvers. He had other guns, including S&W pocket pistols, but the Colts were his favorite. Many a gunman, outlaw, and errant gambler lost his life to that pair of Navy revolvers.

Hickok's most publicized gunfight took place in the public square in Springfield, Missouri on July 21, 1865. Hickok and a gambler named David Tutt had agreed to disagree

Reverse view of the previous pair of Baby Dragoons shows the fine engraving on the 4-inch model and COLT'S PATENT frame stamping surrounded by scrollwork.

This is an excellent cased example of a Baby Dragoon with 4-inch barrel. This gun has the single pin safety at the breech but later oval cylinder bolt stops. This also presents an excellent study of the Colt's patent brass-mounted copper powder flask embossed with American eagle clutching a Colt square back revolver. (Photo courtesy Greg Martin Auctions)

Colt followed the 1848 Baby Dragoon with the most successful percussion revolver ever built, the Model 1849. This extraordinary cased example with a 6-inch barrel shows the finest engraving of the period on a pocket model Colt. The 1849 was also a 5-shot pocket pistol like the 1848, but with the addition of a loading lever. Later models (after 1850) could also be purchased with a 6-shot cylinder. The Model 1849 remained in production as a cap-and-ball revolver until 1873. Note the new Colt's patent powder flask now with crossed Dragoons beneath the American eagle, which is now grasping arrows, an olive branch and a shield. The legend E. Pluribus Unum appears below within a banner. (Dr. Joseph A. Murphy collection)

One of the changes made to the pocket pistol design beginning with the Model 1849 was a rounded triggerguard. A change summarily made on the Third Model Dragoon. This superbly engraved example, possibly done at Gustave Young's Hartford shop in 1854, was a gift from Sam Colt (The Inventor) to Marshfield Fair.

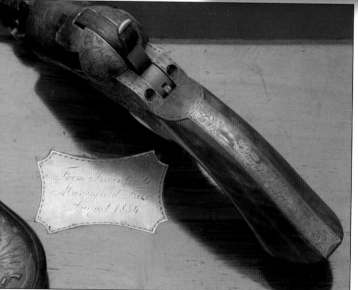

over a card game, and Tutt wanted to settle the dispute with a gunfight. At 6:00 in the evening the two men began walking toward each other from opposite ends of the square. When they were almost 150 feet apart, Tutt drew and fired. He missed. Hickok returned fire striking Tutt in the heart at 50 yards. This was the first recorded example of two men taking part in a quick-draw duel. Hickok was charged with murder but acquitted the following month after pleading self-defense, since Tutt had fired first.

Hickok's adventurous life took a tragic turn while he was Marshal of Abilene, Kansas. Local salon owner Phil Coe and Hickok were on the outs, in part because of Coe's business partner, outlaw Ben Thompson. On October 5, 1871, while Hickok was standing off a crowd during a street brawl, Coe took advanatge of the opportunity and fired two shots at Hickok but missed. He turned and shot Coe dead. In all of the confusion that followed Hickok caught a glimpse of someone coming up behind him and instinctivly wheeled around and fired. The man advancing on the Marshal was his own deputy, Mike Williams, now fatally shot by Hockok. It was a turning point in his career. Combined with advancing glacoma, which no doubt contributed to his accidental shooting of Williams, the events of October 1871 ushered the end of his days as a lawman. Five years later, on August 2, 1875, Wild Bill Hickok was assassinated in Deadwood Dakota Territory by Jack McCall, who walked into Nuttal & Mann's Saloon No. 10 and shot Hickok in the back of the head. It was the only time Wild Bill had sat at a card table with his back to the door.

One could say that Sam Colt wrote the book on self defense with a handgun, or at least he put the gun in the book. Among the famous casings of Colt's revolvers were those designed to appear as bound books. The 1849 was an ideal candidate for this style of casing, as were the later Pocket Police and Pocket Model of Navy Caliber. The spine reads" "**Colt's Pioneer. To Civilization & Christianity.**" There were numerous titles used including "**Colt Bible**", **Law For Selfdefence**", [sic] and "**Colt On The Constitution – Higher Law And Irrepressible Conflict**". The casings were designed to hold the revolver and all accessories. (Dr. Joseph A. Murphy collection)

The engraving on this book cased, 6-shot, Model 1849 fitted with 5-inch barrel, is of presentation grade in the late vine scroll style. From the serial number, 292256/HE and larger style triggerguard this example is from antebellum period, c.1867. (Dr. Joseph A. Murphy collection)

In his defense McCall claimed that the Marshal had killed his brother. Despite the obvious facts, he was aquitted in his first trial, such as it was in Deadwood. But after bragging about killing Wild Bill Hickok he was rearrested and tried a second time. Since Deadwood was not regarded as a "legal city" nor the trial a legal decision, the statutes regarding double jeopardy did not apply. McCall's second trial was held in Yankton, South Dakota and this time he was found guilty and hanged. After his execution it was discovered that Jack McCall never had a brother. Perhaps he killed Wild Bill for whatever fame it would bring him. Possibly, some speculate, he was a paid assassin. Either way, Jack McCall was a coward.

On August 3, 1876 James Butler Hickok was laid to rest in a simply marked grave in Deadwood. He was only 40 years old. Three years later, at the urging of Calamity Jane, his body was re-interred in a ten foot square plot at the Mount Moriah Cemetery.

The site was surrounded by a cast-iron fence with an American flag flying nearby. Twenty-four years later, in August 1903, Martha Jane Cannary was buried next to Wild Bill Hickok. She was 51 years old.

When Colt introduced the .36 caliber Navy Model in 1851, he had finally produced the perfect gun, small enough to be carried in comfort, powerful enough to get the job done. Both the U.S. military and civilian market was once again standing at Samuel Colt's doorstep saying "more please." There were two basic versions of the elegant octagonal barreled repeater, one with a square back triggerguard and another with a round triggerguard. The gun's name was not derived from its use by the Navy (although it was used by both the U.S. Navy and Army), but rather from its Ormsby engraved cylinder scene depicting the famous May 16, 1843 battle between the Texas and Mexican Navy.

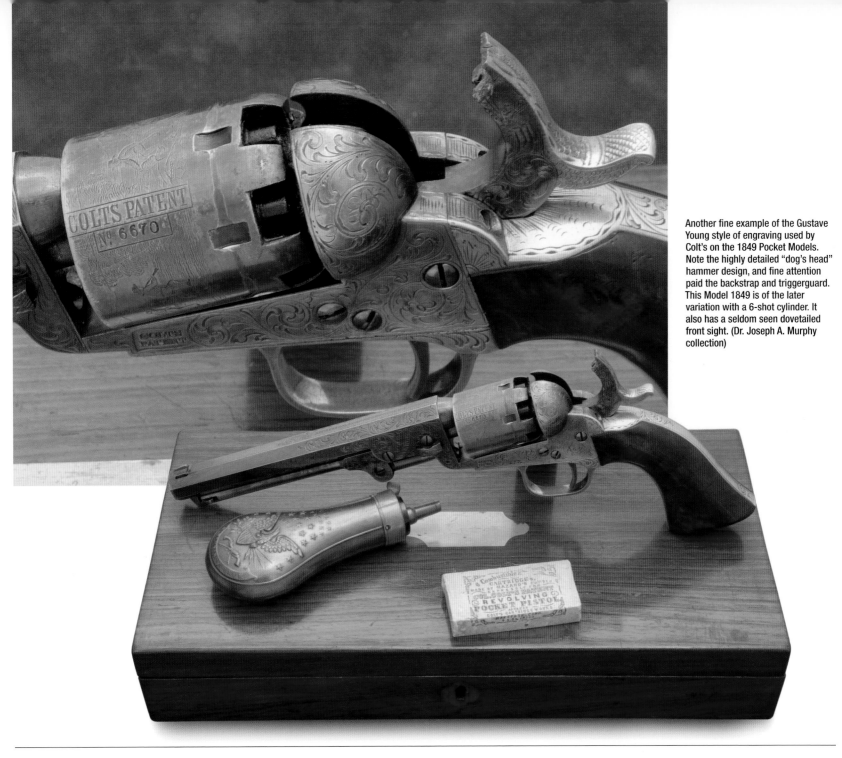

Another fine example of the Gustave Young style of engraving used by Colt's on the 1849 Pocket Models. Note the highly detailed "dog's head" hammer design, and fine attention paid the backstrap and triggerguard. This Model 1849 is of the later variation with a 6-shot cylinder. It also has a seldom seen dovetailed front sight. (Dr. Joseph A. Murphy collection)

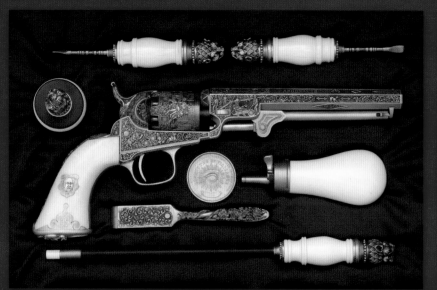

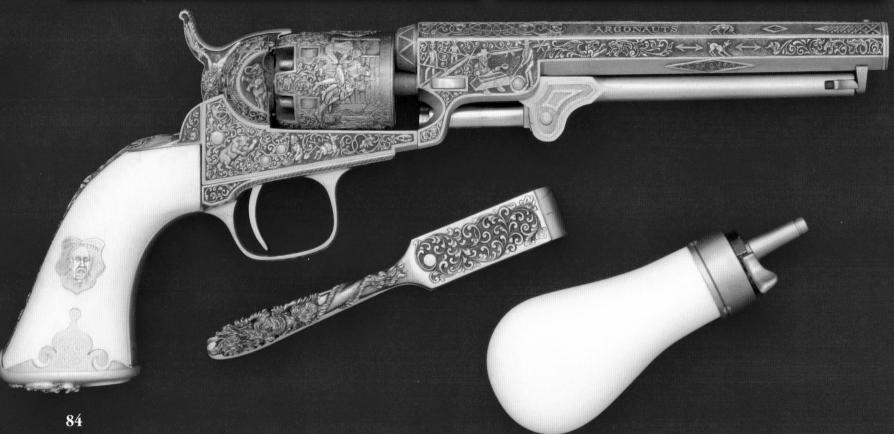

"THE FORTY NINERS"

This is the most intricately engraved Colt ever made. More than an embellished Model 1849 Pocket Revolver, the contemporary engraving on this original gun by sculptor and master engraver Bryson Gwinnell tells the story of the 1849 Gold Rush in 15 individual gold inlaid scenes. The work took two-and-a-half years to complete, and encompasses within its gist all that transpired during the California Gold Rush.

The scenes, which cover nearly 90 percent of the surface area, depict everything from miners panning for gold, the Wickenburg Massacre, the Panama Passage to the Pacific Ocean, gambling, fist fights, and vigilantes, to the simpler things of life in 1849, men washing their clothes, racing horses, and attending a bible reading alongside a cabin. Some of the inspiration for the designs says Gwinnell came from a painting by

Charles Nahl after his arrival in California in 1850, a later piece by Nahl titled "Fandango, and "The Prospector" by E. Hall Martin c.1850.

Among the important figures and images of the period are portraits of John Sutter and James Marshall on the ivory grips, a Masonic motif of The All Seeing Eye, and the Great Seal of the State of California.

Gwinnell also created the unique case and accessories for the gun. The magnificent ivory sculpture atop the lid depicts a bull and grizzly bear locked in combat, a symbolism for Wall Street and the battle for wealth at the heart of the Gold Rush.

"You can look at this gun a hundred times," says Dr. Murphy, "and always find something you've never seen before." It is truly the gun as art.

– Dennis Adler

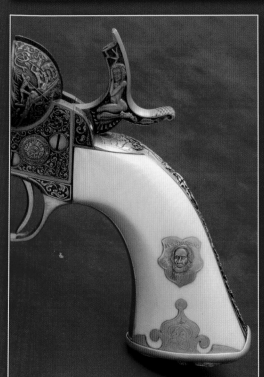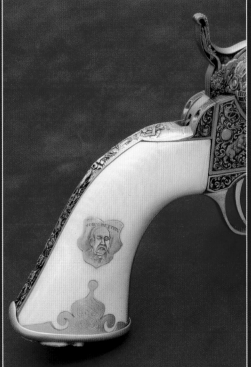

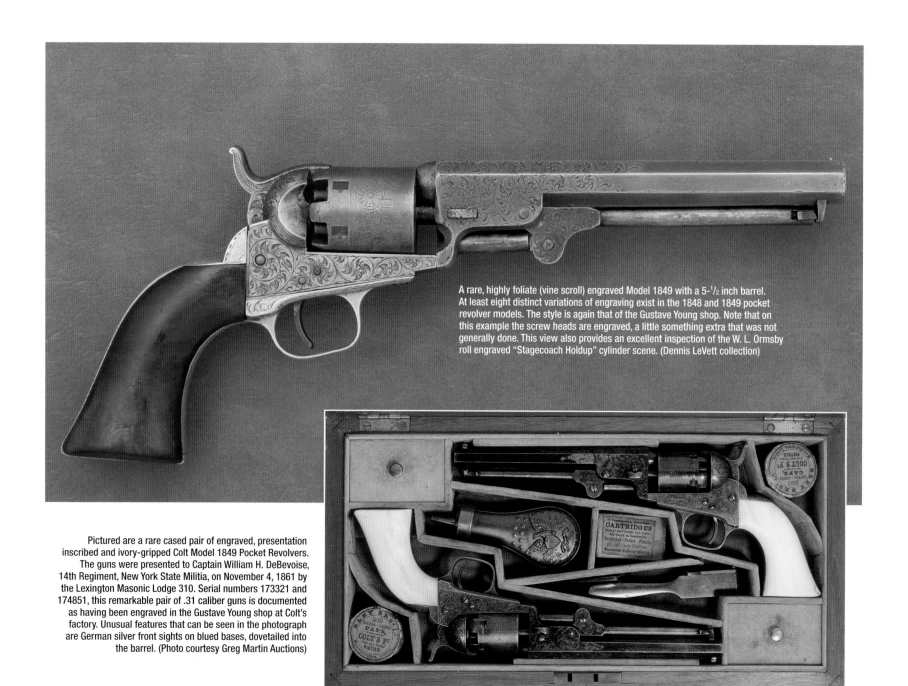

A rare, highly foliate (vine scroll) engraved Model 1849 with a 5-1/2 inch barrel. At least eight distinct variations of engraving exist in the 1848 and 1849 pocket revolver models. The style is again that of the Gustave Young shop. Note that on this example the screw heads are engraved, a little something extra that was not generally done. This view also provides an excellent inspection of the W. L. Ormsby roll engraved "Stagecoach Holdup" cylinder scene. (Dennis LeVett collection)

Pictured are a rare cased pair of engraved, presentation inscribed and ivory-gripped Colt Model 1849 Pocket Revolvers. The guns were presented to Captain William H. DeBevoise, 14th Regiment, New York State Militia, on November 4, 1861 by the Lexington Masonic Lodge 310. Serial numbers 173321 and 174851, this remarkable pair of .31 caliber guns is documented as having been engraved in the Gustave Young shop at Colt's factory. Unusual features that can be seen in the photograph are German silver front sights on blued bases, dovetailed into the barrel. (Photo courtesy Greg Martin Auctions)

Aside from moderate wear and bluing that has faded to a light brown and gray patina, this cased presentation is a perfect example of the standard Model 1849 Pocket Pistol with 4-inch barrel. Most cased examples came in a regular partitioned walnut box with velvet lining, powder flask, bullet mold, Eley cap tin and nipple wrench. Most of the silver plating on the backstrap and triggerguard remain and the grips are in very good condition. (Photo courtesy Greg Martin Auctions)

Below: This is a beautiful but well worn example of a cased 4-inch Model 1849 with factory engraving from the Gustave Young shop. The silver plating has worn away from the engraved backstrap and triggerguard and the ivory grips show a mellow patina. While this gun obviously saw some use in its lifetime, as evidenced by the wear to the cylinder bolt stops, it is nevertheless an excellent example of a factory engraved model. (Photo courtesy Greg Martin Auctions)

Patented in September 1850, the first examples of the 1851 Navy or Belt Model were being produced by early fall. As R.L. Wilson notes in *The Book of Colt Firearms*, "the Navy was the '38' caliber of its day, and quickly outshone the Dragoon arms in commercial sales." By 1855 the Navy Model had also been adopted by the U.S. government, which ultimately purchased 35,000 guns. Total production, which continued through 1873, amounted to more than 255,000 guns, including another 40,000 manufactured in London.[4]

In 1853 Samuel Colt became the first American manufacturer to open a plant in England, thereby solidifying the company's reputation in Great Britain where he had filed his original patent in 1836. The Colt property was on

[4] There were a total of four variations of the 1851 Navy, two with square back triggerguards differentiated primarily by the location of the wedge screw, below the wedge and then above it, respectively, the latter with the wedge passing through the cylinder arbor. The first example rested atop a notch in the arbor. The third variation has a small oval triggerguard, the fourth a large oval triggerguard. In addition, the placement of screws changed within the four versions, as did minor alterations in the barrel lugs, loading lever latches, front sights, and recoil shield capping contours.

Another example of the "donut scroll" this time on an 1849 Pocket Model, serial number 19016. This is an unusual two barrel, 4-inch and 6-inch, cased set that was made for H.B. Beach of Hartford, Connecticut. H.B. was Hetty Beach, Mrs. Elizabeth Colt's younger sister. The engraving, though somewhat whimsical in places, is beautifully done and perfect for a Lady. The gun is believed to have been presented sometime in the early 1850s. (Dr. Joseph A. Murphy collection)

the Thames and Sam had envisioned building as many guns in England as he did in America. But there was difficulty from the very start. He found England's mechanical competence wanting, and was forced to send over both journeymen and machines from Hartford. Colt was ultimately unable to convince the English of the superiority of machine labor, and the London factory was sold in 1857.

In Hartford, he had begun purchasing parcels of property in 1853, in what was then called the South Meadows, an area that fronted on the banks of the Connecticut River. As lowland, it was swampy, prone to spring flooding, and considered of little value, thus Colt was able to acquire the land, 250 acres total, at a remarkably low price of $60,000. He then spent another $125,000 to build a dike nearly two miles long between the river and the ground upon which his new factory was to be built. By August 1855 the Colt assembly plant fronting the Connecticut River shoreline was open for business. The new facilities were equipped with the most up-to-date metalworking machinery available, the installation of which had been overseen by Colt's childhood friend, Elisha King Root, one of the most talented mechanical engineers of the era.

The two had met when Sam was 15 years old. While attending private school at Amherst he became interested in chemistry and electricity, and it was here that Colt first conceived of the idea for underwater explosives. He fashioned a rudimentary mine filled with gunpowder that could be detonated from shore by an electric current passing through a wire wrapped inside a tarred rope. On July 4, 1829, he distributed a handbill boasting that, "Sam'l Colt will blow a raft skyhigh on Ware Pond." His proclamation brought out a crowed of curious locals dressed in their holiday best to witness this improbable feat. Young Sam's experiment worked as declared, in fact, better. The raft exploded with such force that everyone along the shoreline was doused with water. Soaked to the skin the crowd ran after Colt, probably with the intension off tossing him headfirst into Ware Pond. Their pursuit ended when a tough looking young man who had watched the events unfold placed himself between Colt and the mob. His name was Elisha King Root. A quarter of a century later he was setting up the tooling in Hartford.

Regarded as one of, if not the finest example of Gustave Young's work on the Model 1849, this gun was used by Samuel Colt as a "Sample of The Artistry and Quality of Colt Firearms." The 5-shot, 5-inch model has full coverage with gold bands (and borders) around the muzzle, barrel lug, frame cylinder, recoil shield, loading lever lug, and hammer. The roll engraved cylinder scene was hand-accentuated by Young, who also added engraving on the cylinder shoulders. The backstrap and triggerguard are gold plated. The case colored frame, hammer, and loading lever remain excellent. This is the earliest known example of only five gold inlaid and engraved 1849 Pocket Pistols. The gun is valued today at nearly $1 million. (Photos courtesy Greg Martin Auctions)

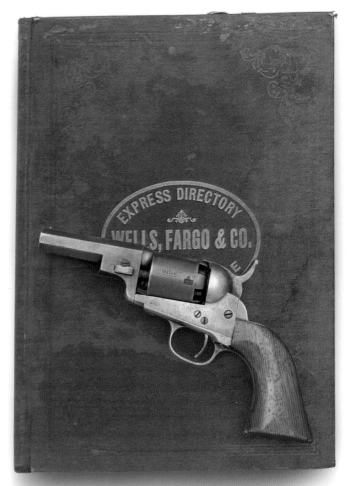

This pair of well preserved 1849 Well Fargo models, shown with accessories, illustrates how compact and easily concealed the pistols could be. It is not known how many Wells Fargo & Co. agents actually carried these guns. (Dennis LeVett collection)

The banking and express firm of Wells Fargo & Co. requested that Colt's make a short barreled 1849 Pocket Model without a loading lever which could be carried discretely by Wells Fargo & Co. stagecoach and railway agents. Colt's produced approximately 6,000 similar guns in varying barrel lengths, however, There is no record of Wells Fargo ordering a quanitiy of such arms, though an example is in the Wells Fargo Bank Museum collection, with backstrap inscription.

Along with the new assembly plant, the Colt's Patent Fire Arms Manufacturing Company was officially incorporated in Connecticut in 1855, with an initial issuance of 10,000 shares of stock, of which Sam Colt retained ownership of 9,996 shares, giving one share to each of his business associates, including Root, now his factory superintendent. Within a year Colt's was manufacturing 150 weapons a day and "Colonel" Samuel Colt had become one of the ten wealthiest businessmen in America. As a loyal Democrat he had finally won his long-sought military commission, becoming a colonel and aide-de-camp to his good friend, Connecticut Governor Thomas Seymour. Even though it was an honorary commission, like everything else, Colt used it to his best advantage for sales and marketing. Decades later Sam Colt would be recognized by industry as one of the earliest Americans to take full advantage of marketing and sales promotion programs through publicity, product sampling, advertising, and public relations. Colt's cousin Dudley Selden must surely have been spinning in his grave!

By 1855 Colt's Third Model Dragoon (put into production back in 1851) was the best selling large caliber revolver in America. The 1851 Dragoon was a continuation of the Second Model but easily distinguished by its oval triggerguard. All of the improvements from the Second Model were carried over, including the flat mainspring, notched roller bearing hammer, and cylinder locking pins.

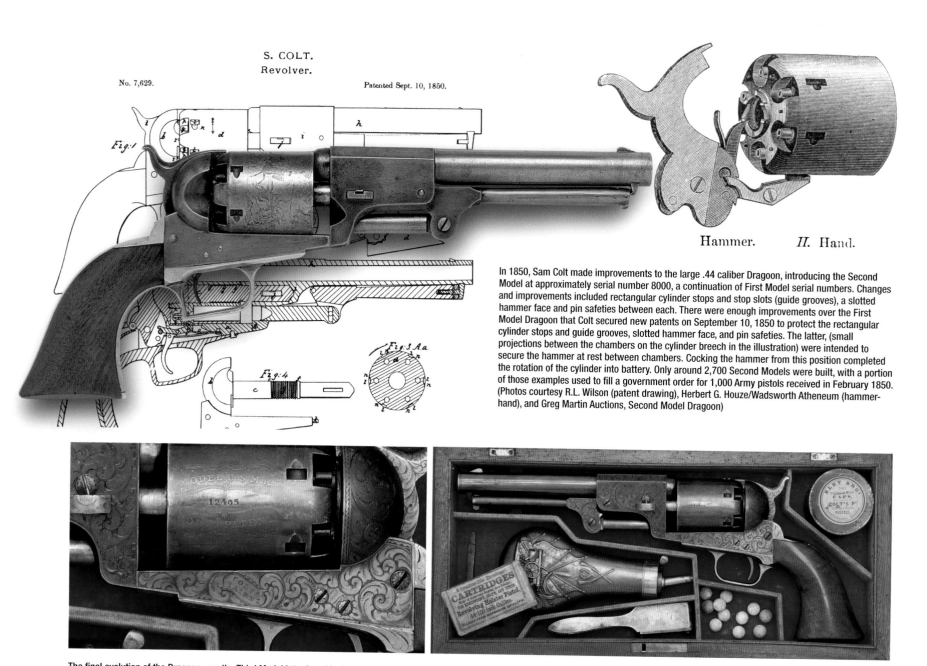

S. COLT.
Revolver.

No. 7,629.

Patented Sept. 10, 1850.

Fig. 1

Fig. 3 A a

Fig. 4

Hammer.   H. Hand.

In 1850, Sam Colt made improvements to the large .44 caliber Dragoon, introducing the Second Model at approximately serial number 8000, a continuation of First Model serial numbers. Changes and improvements included rectangular cylinder stops and stop slots (guide grooves), a slotted hammer face and pin safeties between each. There were enough improvements over the First Model Dragoon that Colt secured new patents on September 10, 1850 to protect the rectangular cylinder stops and guide grooves, slotted hammer face, and pin safeties. The latter, (small projections between the chambers on the cylinder breech in the illustration) were intended to secure the hammer at rest between chambers. Cocking the hammer from this position completed the rotation of the cylinder into battery. Only around 2,700 Second Models were built, with a portion of those examples used to fill a government order for 1,000 Army pistols received in February 1850. (Photos courtesy R.L. Wilson (patent drawing), Herbert G. Houze/Wadsworth Atheneum (hammer-hand), and Greg Martin Auctions, Second Model Dragoon)

The final evolution of the Dragoon was the Third Model introduced in 1851 and manufactured through 1861. The most successful of the Dragoons, approximately 10,500 were built. This particular example with fine "donut scroll" engraving, serial number 12405, was a presentation from Samuel Colt to Eli Whitney, Jr. This style of engraving was only seen briefly at Colt's, roughly from 1851 to 1852 and was a departure from the popular vine scroll and similar foliate styles from Gustave Young shop beginning in 1852. (Dr. Joseph A. Murphy collection)

The Third Model Dragoon was also manufactured with a removable shoulder stock. The "Carbine Pistol" was specially designed with cutouts in the base of the recoil shield and large "4th" screws at the back of the frame to engage the yoke of the shoulder stock. A channel cut into the base of buttstrap, corresponding to a latch at the bottom of the yoke, was used to lock the stock to the frame. The example shown, serial number 17462 is one of the finest examples extant. (Dr. Joseph A. Murphy Collection)

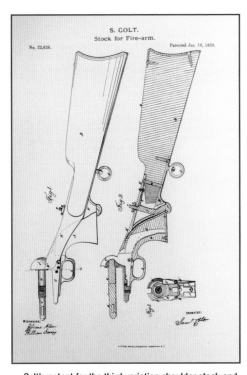

Colt's patent for the third variation shoulder stock and modifications to the Colt frame is dated January 18, 1859. The various components, bottom latch and knurled screw for tightening, yoke contour and recoil shield cutouts are illustrated. (Photo from author's collection)

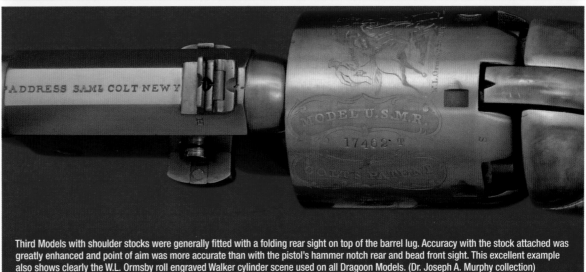

Third Models with shoulder stocks were generally fitted with a folding rear sight on top of the barrel lug. Accuracy with the stock attached was greatly enhanced and point of aim was more accurate than with the pistol's hammer notch rear and bead front sight. This excellent example also shows clearly the W.L. Ormsby roll engraved Walker cylinder scene used on all Dragoon Models. (Dr. Joseph A. Murphy collection)

93

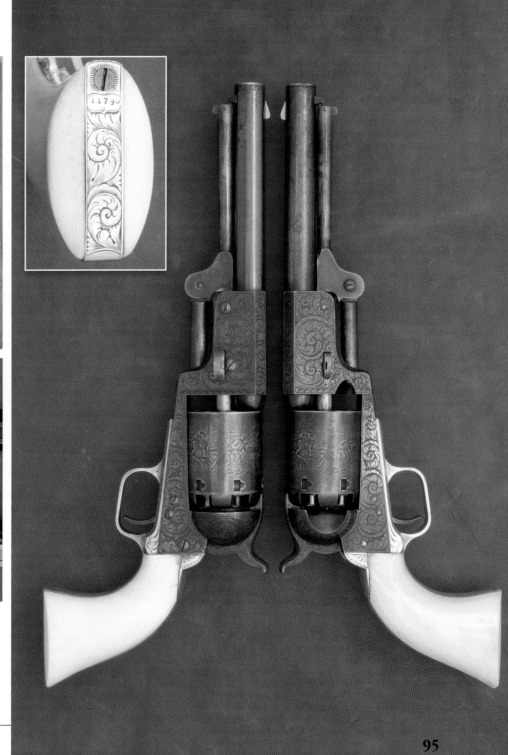

Sam Colt made presentations of cased engraved models to military and government officials as a common practice. He also made presentations to foreign leaders in hopes of gaining foreign contracts for guns. Often this ploy was quite successful. Pictured is an exquisite pair of engraved Third Model Dragoons, serial numbers 11790 and 11850, presented by Col. Colt to King Victor Emmanuele II, of Italy in 1851 (or 1852). Both guns are profusely engraved and have blued frames (rather than case colored), silver plated backstraps and triggerguards, and ivory grips. The undersides of the triggerguards are engraved with the Coat of Arms of The House of Savoy and the United States, respectively. (Dr. Joseph A. Murphy collection)

Some guns have histories of their own. This Third Model Dragoon was owned by W. W. McCrackin of the Iowa 4th Cavalry. When sold by Greg Martin Auctions in November 2004, the gun was offered as shown along with McCrackin's personally inscribed cane, his diary, Civil War Veteran Medal, plus holster and accessories. What sets this example apart is the barrel; it is the rare 8-inch variety, $1/2$ inch longer than most Third Models produced. The gun was also drilled through the backstrap and buttstrap to mount the early style shoulder stock. (Photo courtesy Greg Martin Auctions)

The Third Models were also produced as a "Pistol Carbine" with a detachable shoulder stock. The majority of shoulder stocked Dragoons have cutouts in either side of the recoil shield and a large, protruding screw at the back of the frame to engage the tapered brass yoke of the shoulder stock. The stock was secured at the bottom of the grips by an adjustable catch that slipped into a groove in the buttstrap. The whole affair was then locked down by tightening a large knurled knob at the top of yoke.[5] Some shoulder stocked Third Model Dragoons were also fitted with a folding rear sight mounted on top of the barrel lug. This same basic shoulder stock design was used for the 1851 Navy, and later 1860 Army and 1861 Navy models.

Production of the Third Model continued through 1861 with total production over a 10 year period reaching 10,500 of which approximately 4,330 were Ordnance issue. Of that number 946 were supplied with detachable shoulder stocks. As noted by R.L. Wilson in *The Book of Colt Firearms*, "Government issued Pistol Carbines were in pairs, with only an issue of a single matching detachable shoulder stock." These have become the rarest and most desirable sets of Third Model Dragoons.

Still weighing 4 pounds, 2 ounces, the Third Model Dragoon marked the end of Colt's large frame, 1847 Walker derived revolvers. The .44 caliber mantle would be passed to a new generation of smaller, lighter Colt revolvers in 1860.

[5] There were three types of shoulder stocks, each with a specific mounting system. The earliest attached using two prongs that locked into a cutout in the backstrap and were secured by tightening a knurled nut at he bottom of the yoke. The second design used a single prong inserted into the backstrap and a cutout in the base of the buttstrap to receive the latch hook from the stock. The works was tightened by a knurled knob on top of the yoke. This design evolved into the final version which used the recoil shield cutouts and frame screw combined with the cutout in the buttstrap.

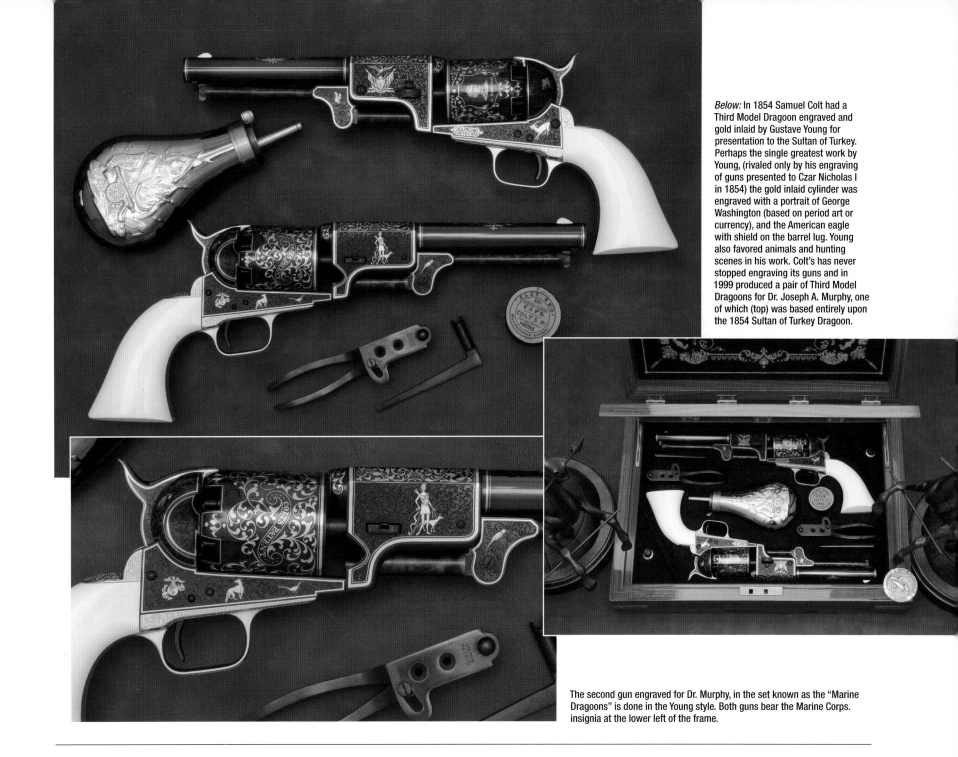

Below: In 1854 Samuel Colt had a Third Model Dragoon engraved and gold inlaid by Gustave Young for presentation to the Sultan of Turkey. Perhaps the single greatest work by Young, (rivaled only by his engraving of guns presented to Czar Nicholas I in 1854) the gold inlaid cylinder was engraved with a portrait of George Washington (based on period art or currency), and the American eagle with shield on the barrel lug. Young also favored animals and hunting scenes in his work. Colt's has never stopped engraving its guns and in 1999 produced a pair of Third Model Dragoons for Dr. Joseph A. Murphy, one of which (top) was based entirely upon the 1854 Sultan of Turkey Dragoon.

The second gun engraved for Dr. Murphy, in the set known as the "Marine Dragoons" is done in the Young style. Both guns bear the Marine Corps. insignia at the lower left of the frame.

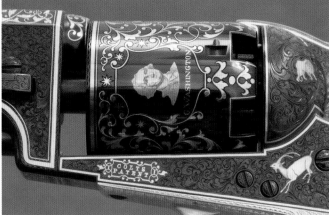

Regarded as the finest contemporary engraving in Colt's history, the detail in which the Custom Shop duplicated the Sultan of Turkey Dragoon, "…set a standard for excellence," according to R.L. Wilson, "which proves that today's gunmakers are capable of equaling, or surpassing, any who preceded them." One gun duplicates the cylinder with George Washington, and for the second gun Abraham Lincoln's bust was used. The work was done by Colt Master Engravers George Spring and Steve Kamyk. (Dr. Joseph A. Murphy collection)

Pictured is another Colt 2nd. Generation (c.1974-78) Third Model Dragoon engraved at the factory in a contemporary presentation grade design. The workmanship again exhibits the same characteristics of presentation guns produced by Colt's in the 1850s. The overall design depicts military battle and hunting scenes, but also shows extensive engraving and shadow detail around the backstrap and triggerguard, and a beautifully engraved rosette treatment on the screw heads. (Dr. Joseph A. Murphy collection)

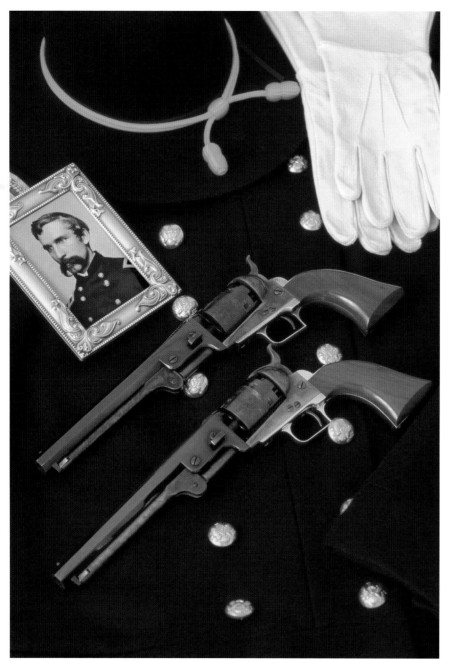

The Guns of Elisha King Root

In many ways Sam Colt was to the handgun what Henry Ford and Henry Martyn Leland would be to the automobile. In 1902 Leland established the Cadillac Automobile Company. Six years later his cars won the coveted Dewar Trophy in England, successfully completing a standardization test involving parts interchangeability. Three Cadillacs were disassembled, their 2,163 components completely intermixed and then another 89 random parts removed and replaced with spares. The three cars were then reassembled from the commingled parts, started up and driven for 500 miles! Cadillac became the first American automaker ever to win the Dewar Trophy. What does this have to do with Colt? Henry Leland began his engineering career in Hartford, Connecticut working for Samuel Colt. Other famous Colt alumnus included Christopher M. Spencer (inventor of the Spencer rifle used in the Civil War; the first hammerless slide action shotgun; and the first screw-making machine), Francis A. Pratt, and Amos Whitney.

Although two other Connecticut gunmakers, Simeon North and Whitney, had attempted to standardize parts, by the late 1850s Colt had perfected the technique to the point where eighty percent of his gun making was done by machine alone. Hartford was where the standards for mass production and parts interchangeability were established in the 1850s; the very underpinning of American auto making in the early 20th century. Leland had learned the value of precision engineering at Colt and put it to use in the auto industry. Henry Ford was similarly inspired by Colt's in his establishment of the moving assembly line.

The man who had been behind much of this, and behind Sam Colt from 1849 on, was Elisha King Root. As noted by historian Herbert G. Houze in *Samuel Colt, Arms, Art and Invention*, "…had it not been for Root's inventive genius, Colt's dream of mass production would never have been realized."

The quintessential Colt of the 1850s and 1860s, the Model 1851 Navy was used by both the U.S. Army and Navy, and on both sides throughout the Civil War. Pictured with a Union officer's tunic, hat, and gauntlets is Col. Joshua Lawrence Chamberlain, Commander of the 20th Maine, the unit credited with turning the course of the Battle of Gettysburg on July 2, 1863 in its defense of Little Round Top. Chamberlain led a bayonet charge against a superior Confederate force, surprising and overwhelming them. They surrendered to fewer men, most who had empty guns! Chamberlain was given a field promotion to Brigadier General by Ulysses S. Grant in 1864, and later promoted to Brevet Major General by President Lincoln. Chamberlain survived the war, was elected Governor of Maine four times and later awarded the Congressional Medal of Honor (August 11, 1893) for his heroics in the battle of Little Round Top. (Author's collection)

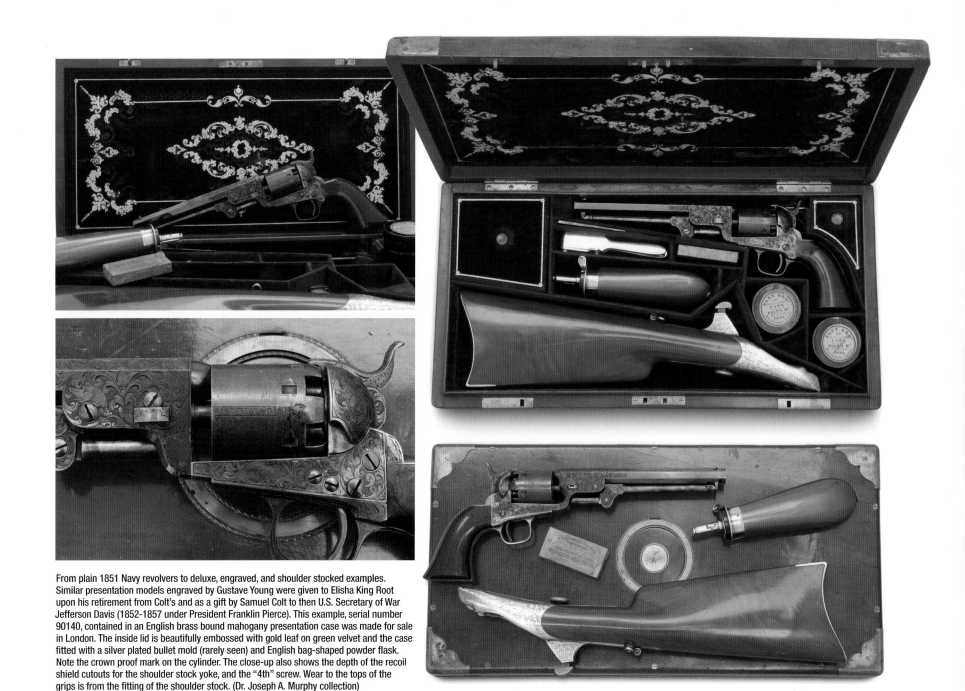

From plain 1851 Navy revolvers to deluxe, engraved, and shoulder stocked examples. Similar presentation models engraved by Gustave Young were given to Elisha King Root upon his retirement from Colt's and as a gift by Samuel Colt to then U.S. Secretary of War Jefferson Davis (1852-1857 under President Franklin Pierce). This example, serial number 90140, contained in an English brass bound mahogany presentation case was made for sale in London. The inside lid is beautifully embossed with gold leaf on green velvet and the case fitted with a silver plated bullet mold (rarely seen) and English bag-shaped powder flask. Note the crown proof mark on the cylinder. The close-up also shows the depth of the recoil shield cutouts for the shoulder stock yoke, and the "4th" screw. Wear to the tops of the grips is from the fitting of the shoulder stock. (Dr. Joseph A. Murphy collection)

They called him the deadliest pistolero of the West, and James Butler "Wild Bill" Hickok lived up to that reputation. His gun of choice for most of his career as a Union Scout during the Civil War, a lawman, and gambler, was the Colt's 1851 Navy. He carried a pair either in reverse draw holsters or simply within a waist sash. His relationship with Martha Jane Cannary, better known as Calamity Jane, has been written as everything from intimate to mutual admiration. It was certainly more than that on Jane's part. Her deathbed request was to be buried next to Hickok in Mount Moriah Cemetary, where she had his body reinterred three years after his murder in Deadwood on August 2, 1876. In August 1903, she was buried next to Wild Bill Hickok. (The copy of Hickok's engraved and ivory gripped 1851 Navy revolver was done by former Colt engraver John J. Adams, Sr. The serial number from one of Hickok's guns, 138813, was duplicated by Colt for this presentation, with the exception of an "A" prefix.)

In addition to setting up the assembly lines in Hartford, Root the machinist was also Root the teacher, instructing his personnel (including Leland and Spencer) in manufacturing techniques. And as Colt's factory superintendent, he was also Root the inventor.

Colt has often been accused of "staying too long at the fair," building open top revolvers for decades when it had long been established that a revolver with a solid frame and topstrap was a stronger design. E. Remington & Sons knew this is 1858 when they introduced their first revolvers. Horace Smith and Daniel B. Wesson knew this too when they began selling their first cartridge revolvers in 1857, the same year Sam Colt's patent extension expired. Why then did Colt's continue to manufacture open top revolvers until 1873? There are two answers. First, they didn't, and secondly, sales of established models, such as the 1849 Pocket Revolver, Third Model Dragoon, and 1851 Navy were so lucrative only a fool would dare tamper with such success.

There were a handful of experimental revolvers built by Sam Colt and E. K. Root that employed a topstrap (these experimental models are on display at the Wadsworth Atheneum), as well as various means of fixed barrels and break open designs. None were as good as the original save for E. K. Root's 1855 patent model revolver, the fountainhead for a separate line of Colt's pistols and rifles featuring a solid frame and unique side mounted hammer. The prototype design had been finalized by Root and Colt in 1854 and a patent issued in E. K. Root's name on Christmas day 1855. Subsequent patents for the Root pistols (May 4, 1858) bore Samuel Colt's name with Root signing as witness. The first patent issued (December 25, 1855) had been for the prototype, which was never put into production. It employed a unique self cocking method activated by sliding the trigger ring forward and pulling it back, the rearward motion also discharging the weapon. A zig-zag channel in the cylinder (see patent illustration), acted upon by sliding the trigger rotated the cylinder.[6]

[6] Although this version of the Root revolver was never manufactured, a similar concept utilizing a zig-zag channel on the cylinder to actuate chamber rotation appeared in 1902 on the British Webley-Fosbery automatic revolver.

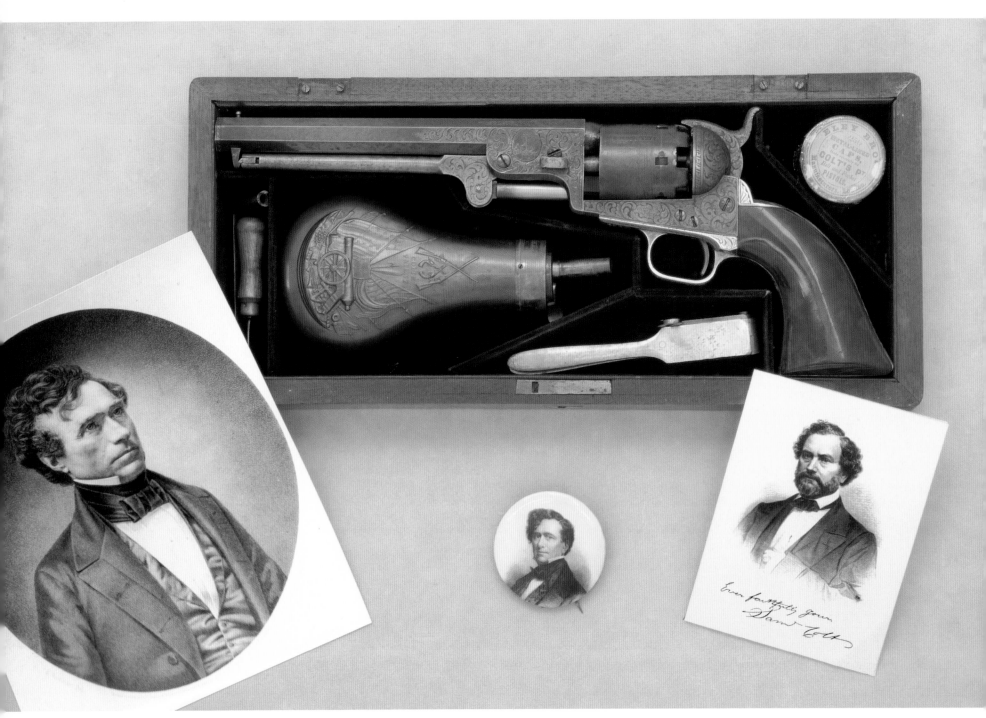

In 1852 Samuel Colt presented this donut scroll engraved 1851 Navy to then General Franklin Pierce. Shortly thereafter he became the 14th President. A former veteran of the Mexican War, Pierce was familiar with the value of Colt's revolvers and was among many military officers who wrote glowing endorsements. "…I do not hesitate to give [the Colt revolver] a decided preference in cavalry service in Mexico, over all other species of fire-arms, and recommend its general use in that service." The barrel lug patterns are unique and feature a nautical theme, an anchor on the left side and man-of-war on the right. (Dr. Joseph A. Murphy collection)

This example shows typical early factory engraving for the 1851. (Dr. Joseph A. Murphy collection)

The Root pistols and rifles had mixed popularity during the War Between the States, due to the Longarms' occasional multi-discharges, the firing of the charge so close to the shooter's face, and the risk of shots hitting the hand extended to secure the forend.[7]

The Root pistols were built from 1855 through 1873 in seven different series variations chambered in either .28 or .31 caliber. Seven versions for a gun that saw no more than 40,000 examples built might sound strange but Colt and Root were continually changing the design, and to such extent that there are distinctive physical and mechanical differences from one version to another.

The most obvious visual changes are from the octagon barrels used in the First through Fourth series to the round barrels used on Fifth through Seventh. Cylinders changed from round

[7] The Root rifles were chambered in a variety of calibers including: .36, .44, and .56. The first two chamberings were 6-shot, the latter 5-shot. The military rifles and rifled muskets were chambered in .44, .50, and .56 caliber, the latter being a 5-shot. A full stock Root sporting rifle was offered in chamberings from .36 through .56 caliber, the latter once again limited to 5-shots. The popular revolving carbine favored during the Civil War was offered in the same chamberings as the sporting rifle. Shotguns were all 5-shot in either 10 gauge (.70 caliber) or 20 gauge (60 caliber). Frame sizes on all Root revolving rifles and shotguns varied according to caliber or gauge.

Built c.1856, this early Third Model 1851 Navy, serial no. 5605 is the only example known with a gold plated triggerguard and backstrap. Likely made for presentation or display, it is in the donut scroll motif with a wolf head in the circle on the frame and hammer. The work is definitely that of the Gustave Young shop. This gun was also featured in R.L. Wilson's *Colt Engraving Vol. 1*. The gun is cased in a traditional American walnut presentation box with deluxe one-sided powder flask, Colt's Patent brass two-cavity bullet mold, combination tool (nipple wrench and screw driver) Eley Bros. cap tin and two packages of Colt Cartridge Works .36 caliber paper cartridges. (Dr. Joseph A. Murphy collection)

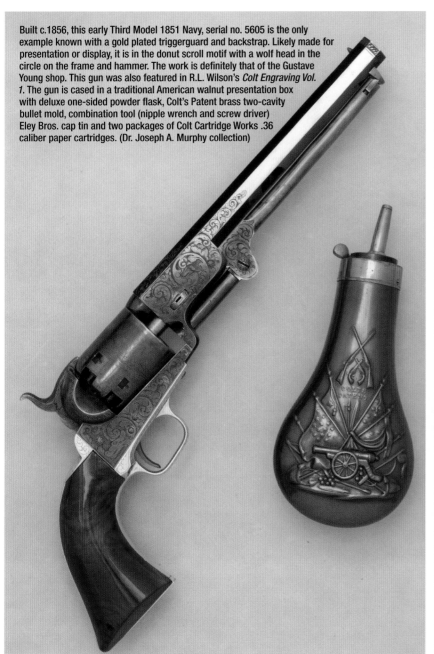

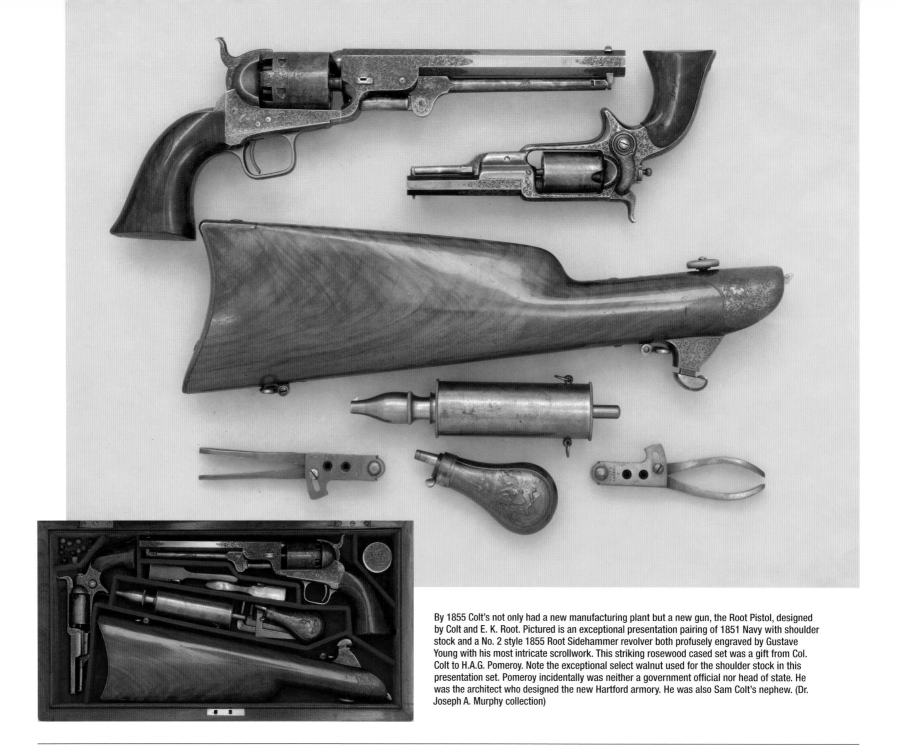

By 1855 Colt's not only had a new manufacturing plant but a new gun, the Root Pistol, designed by Colt and E. K. Root. Pictured is an exceptional presentation pairing of 1851 Navy with shoulder stock and a No. 2 style 1855 Root Sidehammer revolver both profusely engraved by Gustave Young with his most intricate scrollwork. This striking rosewood cased set was a gift from Col. Colt to H.A.G. Pomeroy. Note the exceptional select walnut used for the shoulder stock in this presentation set. Pomeroy incidentally was neither a government official nor head of state. He was the architect who designed the new Hartford armory. He was also Sam Colt's nephew. (Dr. Joseph A. Murphy collection)

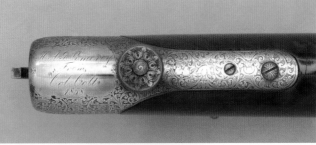

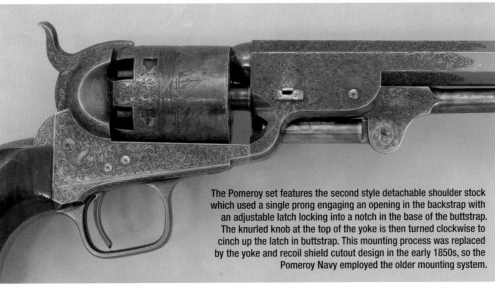

The Pomeroy set features the second style detachable shoulder stock which used a single prong engaging an opening in the backstrap with an adjustable latch locking into a notch in the base of the buttstrap. The knurled knob at the top of the yoke is then turned clockwise to cinch up the latch in buttstrap. This mounting process was replaced by the yoke and recoil shield cutout design in the early 1850s, so the Pomeroy Navy employed the older mounting system.

in the First and Second Models, to fluted cylinders on the Third and Fourth Models, and then back to round cylinders. Cylinder scenes changed from the first round cylinder series to the second. The original engraving by W. L. Ormsby was a settler armed with a pair of pistols fighting Indians in front of his cabin. The second cylinder scene used was Ormsby's Stagecoach Holdup adopted from 1849 Pocket Pistol. Changes too were made in loading lever designs and shapes, and factory patent stampings.

As a small caliber pocket pistol, both the .28 and .31 caliber Root Models were only modestly successful despite being the highly touted solid frame design. The traditional small caliber open top Colt revolvers of the late 1840s continued to outsell and outlast the Root Pistols.

One of the most famous cased sets of 1851 Navy and 1849 Pocket Models (serial Nos. 2847 and 84624) built at Colt's was a Gustave Young engraved and gold inlaid pair presented to Captain James West on January 4, 1854 by the 30 passengers who had crossed the Atlantic aboard the U.S.M. Steamer Atlantic. The set was in appreciation for Capt. West's heroics in saving the ship during its 1853 trans-Atlantic voyage. The plaque on the lid is gold, and inscribed to Capt. West. The pair of Colts was uniquely engraved by Young at the request of the passengers, and both have flush gold inlaid 24 karat gold bands around the cylinders and select ivory grips. Both the guns and grips have aged beautifully over time and still retain nearly all of their original beauty. (Dr. Joseph A. Murphy collection)

The right side barrel lug engraving on this pair of Colts is unique both in its design and its intricacy, as evidenced by the macro close-up of the U.S.M. Steamer Atlantic on the 1851 Navy, in which can be seen the entire rigging of the masts and even the forms of passengers and crew on deck. A dog's head and serpent adorn the 1849 barrel lug.

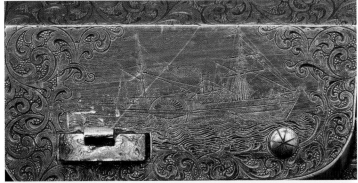

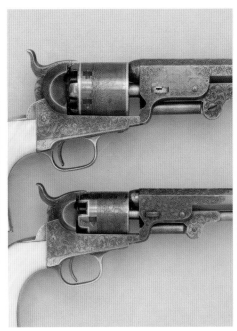

As can be seen in the close-ups, the roll engraving on the cylinders was hand chased by Young to provide more depth to the cylinder scenes. The gold bands and extensive engraving make this one of the finest pairs Young engraved guns not presented by Colt to a foreign dignitary. The left barrel lug of the 1851 Navy is engraved with an American Eagle.

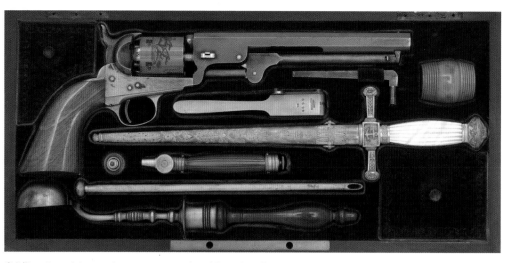

Colt/Brevete models are not uncommon as copies of the various Colt models produced from the Paterson to the 1860 Army and Pocket Models were manufactured (some even under license) in Belgium, Germany, and Austria, among others. Pictured is a fine Colt/Brevete Model 1851 (serial No. 4625) cased set manufactured in Liege, Belgium under license from Colt's. The revolver looks essentially the same as an 1851 Navy (many copies did not) with an etched cylinder battle scene of Mounted Dragoons and Indians. The European style accessories, and a handsomely engraved naval dirk (a dagger to us landlubbers) are all French fitted into an elegant presentation case. (Dr. Joseph A. Murphy collection)

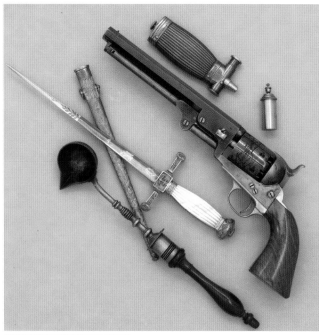

There were seven variations of the 1855 Root Sidehammer pistol incorporating numerous design changes and improvements. Pictured are three variations (left to right) a No.4 with 3-inch octagon barrel, fluted cylinder and ivory grips, a rare No.6A with round barrel and round cylinder, and two No. 5A Models with 4-inch round barrels and fluted cylinders. (Dennis LeVett collection)

This pair of beautifully engraved Sidehammer Pistols from the Dr. Joseph A. Murphy collection exhibits some of the finest engraving on this model. The ivory gripped No. 7 Model, serial No. 12076 I.E., was factory engraved and presented by Colt to James McClatchie, a longtime employee of the company, and Samuel Colt's timekeeper. He worked for Colt's from 1853 through 1864, two years after Sam Colt's death. One of the finest Root Sidehammer pistols known, the cost of this beautifully engraved gun was $28.88. The second example, shown from behind, is a No. 2 Root Pistol known as the "Charter Oak Model 1855 Sidehammer. No. 5886, it is from a series of guns presented to Colt's wholesalers or "jobbers" in 1856. The name comes from the wood used to make the grips, the famed Charter Oak, which had been toppled by a storm in that year. It had been used centuries before to conceal the charter from the British King to the Connecticut Colony, when the British government demanded it be revoked.

Two examples of the Root Sidehammer Pistol from the Dennis Levett collection exhibit the two primary types of cylinders, fluted and round. Not all round cylinders were roll engraved, however.

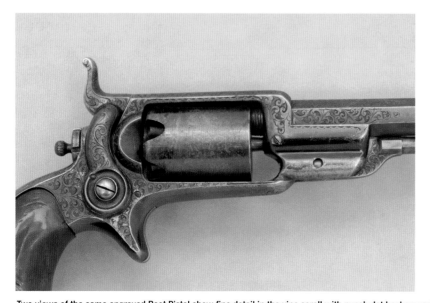 

Two views of the same engraved Root Pistol show fine detail in the vine scroll with punch dot background. (Dr. Joseph A. Murphy collection)

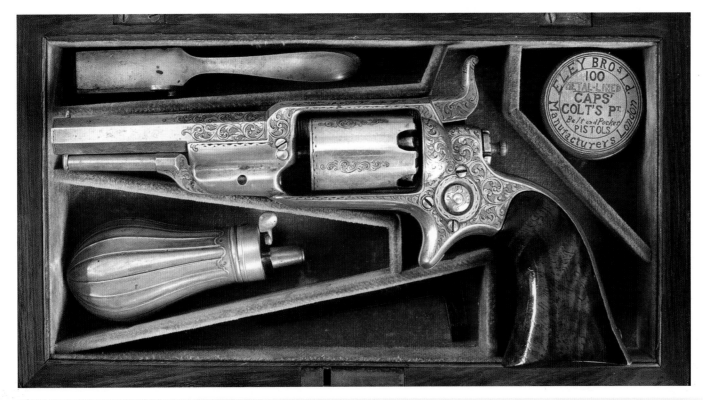

One of the rarest of all Root Sidehammer models, this No. 2 (or Model 2) bears elegant scrollwork by Gustave Young, and is silver plated with a matching silver plated powder flask.

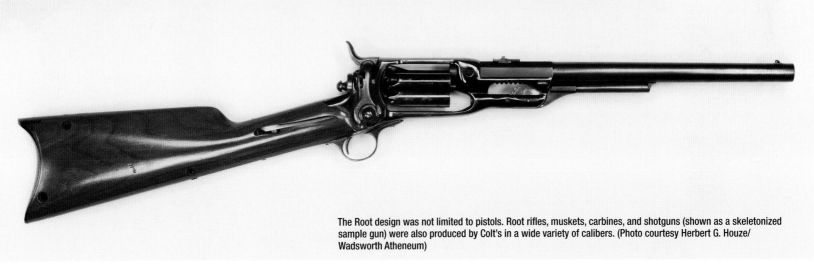

The Root design was not limited to pistols. Root rifles, muskets, carbines, and shotguns (shown as a skeletonized sample gun) were also produced by Colt's in a wide variety of calibers. (Photo courtesy Herbert G. Houze/ Wadsworth Atheneum)

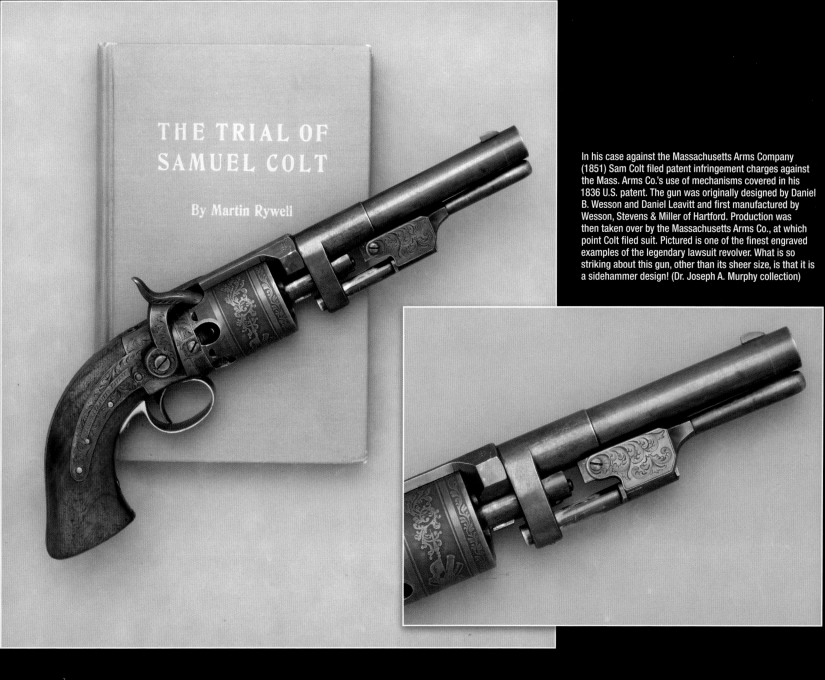

THE TRIAL OF SAMUEL COLT

By Martin Rywell

In his case against the Massachusetts Arms Company (1851) Sam Colt filed patent infringement charges against the Mass. Arms Co.'s use of mechanisms covered in his 1836 U.S. patent. The gun was originally designed by Daniel B. Wesson and Daniel Leavitt and first manufactured by Wesson, Stevens & Miller of Hartford. Production was then taken over by the Massachusetts Arms Co., at which point Colt filed suit. Pictured is one of the finest engraved examples of the legendary lawsuit revolver. What is so striking about this gun, other than its sheer size, is that it is a sidehammer design! (Dr. Joseph A. Murphy collection)

Chapter Five
Samuel Colt and the War Between the States
The Model 1860 Army, 1861 Navy, and Colt's Pocket Models

By 1860 Samuel Colt was the largest private purveyor of arms to the U.S. government. For nearly a decade he had been providing 1851 Navy models to both the Army and Navy, as well as fulfilling the last requisitions for Third Model Dragoons. In addition, Colt's Pocket Models were the best selling small caliber revolvers in America and among the most popular sold throughout Europe and Great Britain. However, while Colt's star continued to rise in the late 1850s, the stars on the American flag were growing further apart with each passing year. By 1860 it appeared that the Union was on the verge of a social division over the issues of slavery, and more importantly, the separation of industry between the Northern and Southern states, a political imbroglio that had been festering for nearly a decade.

As the nation raced toward cataclysm, Sam Colt was selling arms to Southern State militias, as well as the U.S. military. He sarcastically referred to his sale of arms to clientele whose political sentiments were from either side of the aisle, as "...his latest work on 'Moral Reform.'" He had even considered establishing a second armory in either Virginia or Georgia before the war. The threat of war was profitable; the reality of war, which began in 1861, increased the bottom line from annual earnings of around $237,000 to over $1 million. His last shipment of 500 guns to the South left for Richmond three days after Fort Sumter, packed in boxes marked "hardware."

Shown at left is a deluxe engraved and cased pair of 1862 Police models, consecutively serial numbered, 15859/I and 15860/I, the guns were engraved by the Gustave Young shop and presented to Major General James B. McPherson along with a cased pair of engraved 1861 Navy revolvers. (Dr. Joseph A. Murphy collection)

Right: The most popular sidearm of the Union Army throughout The War Between the States was Colt's new Model 1860 Army. The .44 caliber revolvers were lighter in weight and easier to handle than the heftier and less manageable Third Model Dragoons. Both examples are military models with the recoil shield notches and protruding fourth screw used to anchor the shoulder stock yoke. (Author's collection)

This beautifully engraved 1860 Army, shown with an original Mathew Brady portrait of General Ulysses S. Grant, exhibits the high level of embellishment and detail from the Colt's engraving shop. Note the eagle's head above the barrel wedge screw, elegant vine scrollwork on the cylinder shoulders, the word *Union* in a banner along the left side of the barrel, and the **COLTS PATENT** within a cartouche. The right side of the gun, (shown on top of the presentation box) shows the continuation of the banner with the words *And Liberty*. The hammer is profusely engraved with an eagle's head (rather than the traditional wolf's head) to match the barrel. This gun has the recoil shield notches but was never intended for a shoulder stock, as it does not have the fourth screw in the frame or the notch in the bottom of the buttstrap. The grips are another rarity, they are ebony. Serial number 151718/E, the cased 1860 Army was presented to General Grant but was never used by him. It remained in his family for generations. (Dr, Joseph A. Murphy collection)

A year before the onset of hostilities Colt had introduced the most advanced and powerful medium frame handgun of his career, the .44 caliber Model 1860 Army. The secret of the 1860 Army was in its construction, a new type of metal advertised as "Silver Spring Steel," a lighter yet stronger steel that allowed the 1860 Army to withstand the pressures of .44 caliber loads formerly limited to the heavier Dragoons, and do so in a revolver that weighed 2 pounds, 8-1/2 ounces, almost half that of a Third Model Dragoon, which tipped the scales at 4 pounds, 2 ounces. Not only was the 1860 Army lighter, but smaller, measuring 13-5/8 inches overall with an 8-inch barrel, compared to the Third Model Dragoon at just under 14-inches with a 7-1/2 inch barrel. The extra half inch in barrel length gave the 1860 Army a bit more weight up front and a longer sight radius. When fitted with a detachable shoulder stock, the military version of the 1860 Army made a reasonably decent six shot carbine.

The 1860 was more than a new handgun, it was a work of design art, as different in appearance from the 1851 Navy and Dragoons as the Walker had been from a Paterson. Here was a slim firearm with a tapered round barrel, compound curves, a trim, shallow frame, and a long, contoured grip[1]. It was an elegant looking gun.

Among the 1860 Army's distinguishing features was a roll engraved rebated cylinder, which was larger in circumference forward of the bolt stops, corresponding to a drop in the frame's contour. The reason for the step in the frame and the rebated cylinder was that the 1860 Army was actually a modification of the 1851 Navy frame, thus helping rationalize production and manufacturing costs and allowing use of the Navy's lockwork. The Army also featured a new type of loading lever derived from the 1855 Root Sidehammer pistol. The design, referred to as a "creeping" loading lever, was so named because a cog in the rear of the lever forced it to solidly pivot or "creep" when seating a ball into the chamber. The earlier lever designs used on the 1851 Navy and Colt Pocket Models pivoted freely under the barrel.

The Union gun of choice, the 1860 Army shown with rebated cylinder and fluted cylinders and in nickel finish. These examples were built by Colt's in the 1980s as part of a new line of historic Colt models known as the Second Generation. They have since become collectible (as the last percussion Colts that can be lettered by the factory) but have not achieved anywhere near the value of their 19th century predecessors. (Author's collection)

Top: Shown is a rare "experimental" 1860 Army, serial number 78, fitted with a 7-1/2 inch barrel and Navy style grips. The gun is cased with an Army powder flask, .44 cal. dual cavalry nipple wrench, bullet mold, an original, unopened packet of paper cartridges, and Eley Bros. cap tin. (Dr. Joseph A. Murphy collection)

[1] Additionally, a number of 1860 Army models were built with the smaller 1851 Navy size grips.

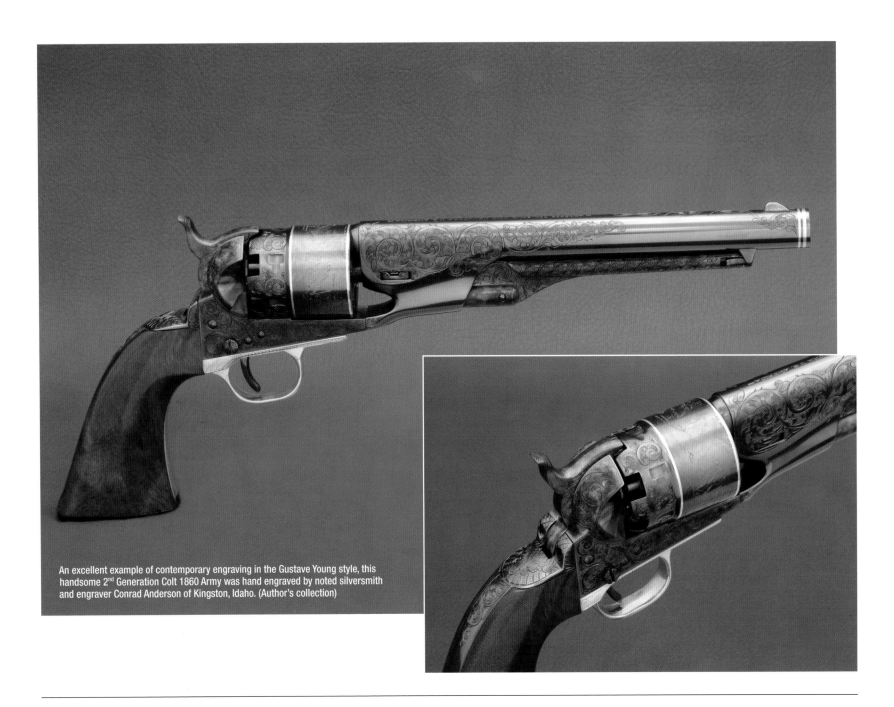

An excellent example of contemporary engraving in the Gustave Young style, this handsome 2nd Generation Colt 1860 Army was hand engraved by noted silversmith and engraver Conrad Anderson of Kingston, Idaho. (Author's collection)

The 1860 Army used the same roll engraved scene as the 1851 Navy. The barrel address was stamped either

– ADDRESS COL. SAM^L COLT NEW-YORK U.S. AMERICA –
– ADDRESS SAM^L COLT HARTFORD CT. –

or on London models:

– ADDRESS COL. COLT LONDON –

COLTS/PATENT was stamped on the left side of the frame, a feature often embellished, surrounded with a cartouche, or removed during engraving. The left shoulder of the triggerguard was stamped with 44 CAL. Other Colt's models were similarly stamped with their respective calibers.

Among variations of the 1860 Army were those fitted with fluted cylinders, and examples produced in special barrel lengths of 6 and 7-1/2 inches. Other 1860's are known to have had their barrels cut down to lengths as short as 2-1/2 inches and were often carried as hideaway guns during the Civil War. In later years these same guns, sometimes referred to as a Natchez Special, became a favorite among riverboat gamblers, outlaws, and after the assassination of President Lincoln, a discrete sidearm carried by Secret Service Agents assigned to protect the President.

Not surprisingly, with the start of the Civil War, the United States government became the single largest purchaser of the 1860 Army. Military models often had notched recoil shields and a fourth screw in the frame to mount a detachable shoulder stock, and this applied to both rebated and fluted cylinder variations. All civilian models had full recoil shields. Between rebated and fluted cylinders, the latter are the rarest. It is estimated that Colt's produced only around 4,000 fluted models (referred to in factory records as the "cavalry" model), out of a total production run exceeding 200,000 built between 1860 and 1873. Army frames, barrels, and cylinders were also used c.1873 to the early 1880s for Richards Type I, Type II, and Richards-Mason cartridge conversions of the 1860 Army. Later examples used Army frames remaining in inventory fitted with newly manufactured barrels and cartridge cylinders.

In 1861, just before the Civil War began, Sam Colt introduced another model, a slightly scaled down version of the 1860 Army chambered in .36 caliber. Since .36 caliber was regarded as a "Navy" caliber (.44 being the Army caliber), the new gun was named the Model 1861 Navy. Although a successor to the 1851 Navy, both guns remained in production through 1873.

Another rare and collectible example from Colt's c.1977-80 was the 1860 Army U.S. Cavalry Commemorative Cased Pair. A continuation of the shoulder stocked Colts issued to the U.S. Cavalry during the Civil War (two revolvers, one shoulder stock) only 17 engraved and gold inlaid pairs were built. No. 11 in the series, these are among the rarest of all Second Generation Colt's. Their value today is around $6,500. (Author's collection)

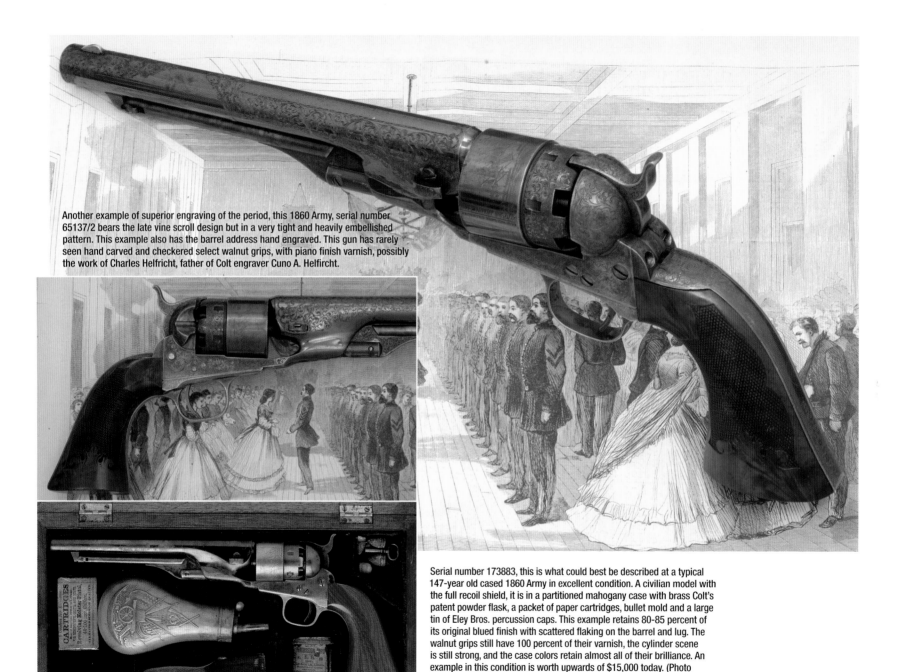

Another example of superior engraving of the period, this 1860 Army, serial number 65137/2 bears the late vine scroll design but in a very tight and heavily embellished pattern. This example also has the barrel address hand engraved. This gun has rarely seen hand carved and checkered select walnut grips, with piano finish varnish, possibly the work of Charles Helfricht, father of Colt engraver Cuno A. Helfircht.

Serial number 173883, this is what could best be described at a typical 147-year old cased 1860 Army in excellent condition. A civilian model with the full recoil shield, it is in a partitioned mahogany case with brass Colt's patent powder flask, a packet of paper cartridges, bullet mold and a large tin of Eley Bros. percussion caps. This example retains 80-85 percent of its original blued finish with scattered flaking on the barrel and lug. The walnut grips still have 100 percent of their varnish, the cylinder scene is still strong, and the case colors retain almost all of their brilliance. An example in this condition is worth upwards of $15,000 today. (Photo courtesy Greg Martin Auctions)

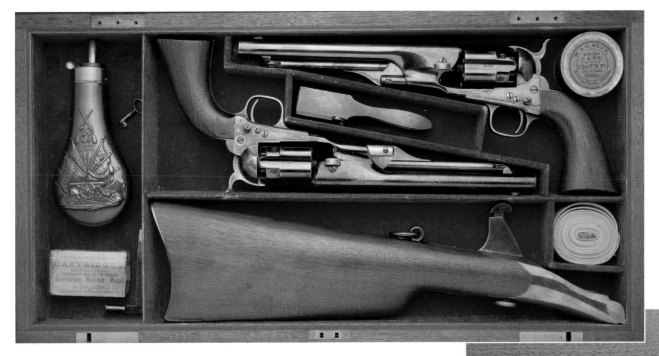

Fluted 1860 Army models are rare. A cased pair with shoulder stock is exceptionally rare! This consecutively numbered pair, 2259 and 2260, were a presentation from Samuel Colt to Colonel Charles Augustus May, a longtime friend and supporter. May was a distinguished Dragoon officer in the Mexican war and Colt had also presented him with a pair of shoulder stocked Third Model Dragoons. Col. May was among the pall bearers at Colt's funeral in January 1862. The fluted pair of 1860 Army revolvers remain in exceptional condition and were offered for sale through Greg Martin Auction in June 2002. The estimate for this cased pair was $150,000 to $250,000. (Photos courtesy Greg Martin Auctions)

In all of Colt's pre-cartridge era history, the 1861 Navy is arguably the most perfect revolver ever made in terms of design, appearance, balance, and caliber. It is also the basis for the most famous pair of military presentation pistols delivered from Samuel Colt to an officer of the U.S. Army. The gift was made to General Robert Anderson, the commander of Ft. Sumter.

General Anderson is remembered today as the heroic defender of Ft. Sumter in Charleston Harbor, South Carolina, but his distinguished military career dated back to the Seminole Indian Wars of the 1830s, and the Mexican American War, where he served with General Winfield Scott in the siege of Veracruz in March 1847, and Brevet Brigadier General John Garland in the battle of El Molino del Rey in September.

A U.S. Military Academy graduate, Anderson had returned to West Point after the Black Hawk War of 1832 as an artillry instructor. Highly regared as an authority, two years after leaving his teaching position, he literally wrote the book on artillery, *Instruction for Field Artillery, Horse and Foot* published in 1839.

By 1857 he had become Major of the 1st. Artillary. In November 1860, as the threat of a civil war loomed, Secretary of War John B. Floyd ordered Anderson to command a Federal garrison at Charleston Harbor, South Carolina.

A rarely seen combination: a gun with its original holster and belt. This example, originally owned by Corporal John Gilbert Ray, Jr., Company E, 43rd Regiment of Infantry, 1st Brigade, 1st Division of the Volunteer Militia of Massachusetts, remains intact with a Bowie Knife and scabbard and cartridge pouch. Ray, who later became a Union Pacific Railroad construction engineer, is pictured in the tintype photo c. 1867, wearing the belt, holster and his 1860 Army, serial number 155981. Traveling through the American West it was claimed that he smoked the pipe of peace with the chief of the Sioux tribe, and was present when they drove the golden spike that connected the east and the west by rail on May 10, 1869. Born in 1843, Ray lived long enough to see the turn of the century and even own a Stanley Steamer before he died on October 28, 1907. (Photo courtesy Greg Martin Auctions)

Below: Deluxe engraved presentation Colts were not uncommon in Sam Colt's day. This cased military Model 1860 Army, serial number 63091, was engraved in the shops of L.D. Nimschke with coverage on the barrel, frame, hammer (with wolf's head), backstrap and triggerguard. There is a waved line and dot border motif added to the cylinder, the barrel and frame are silver plated, with a gold washed cylinder, loading lever, and hammer. The grips are checkered one-piece ivory with hand checkering and a carved Mexican eagle and snake motif. Part of an order of standard 1860 Army models delivered to Schuyler, Hartley & Graham in June 1863 the New York retailer often made use of Nimschke's shop to produce spectacular and expensive guns for its wealthy clientele. (Photo courtesy Greg Martin Auctions)

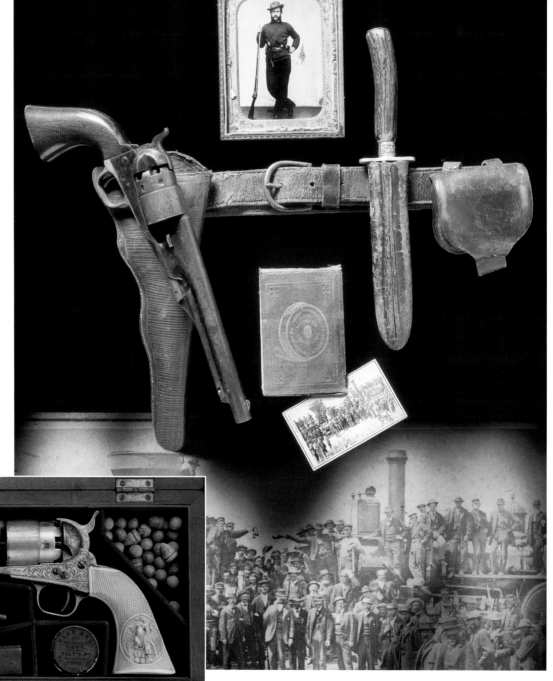

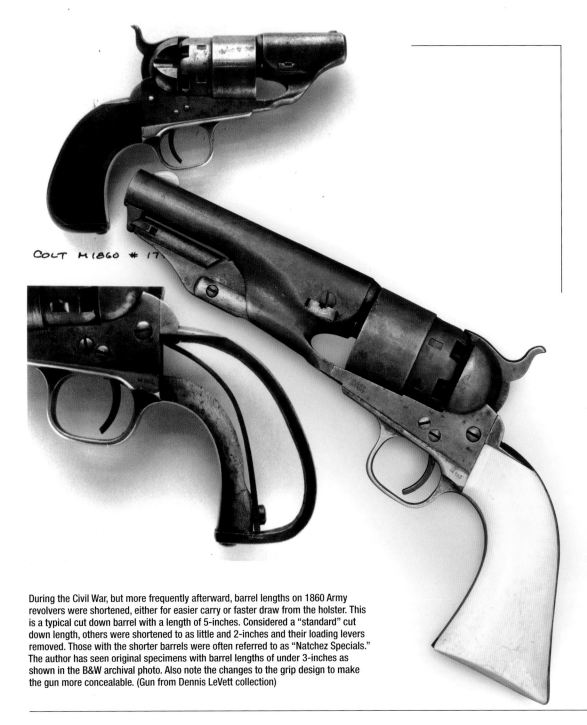

COLT M1860 # 17

During the Civil War, but more frequently afterward, barrel lengths on 1860 Army revolvers were shortened, either for easier carry or faster draw from the holster. This is a typical cut down barrel with a length of 5-inches. Considered a "standard" cut down length, others were shortened to as little and 2-inches and their loading levers removed. Those with the shorter barrels were often referred to as "Natchez Specials." The author has seen original specimens with barrel lengths of under 3-inches as shown in the B&W archival photo. Also note the changes to the grip design to make the gun more concealable. (Gun from Dennis LeVett collection)

Though Anderson was a southerner by birth (a Kentuckian), married to a woman from Georgia, sympathetic to slavery, and not honestly convinced that military efforts could stop the South from seceding, when it appeared secession was inevitable he remained loyal to the Union and his President, Abraham Lincoln, (who had served as a Captain under Anderson's command in the Illinois Volunteers during the Black Hawk War of 1832).

After a gallent three-day standoff in April 1861 against Confederate artillary, in which the fort had been heavily damaged by 34 hours of bombardment (its main gates destroyed, walls breached, and the magazine surrounded with fire), Brig. Gen. P.G.T. Beauregard (Anderson's former student at West Point), initiated a series of cordial letters couriered back and forth asking for Anderson's surrender. With food running out and what all parties agreed was a hopeless situation, Anderson finally ordered the evacuation (surrender) of Ft. Sumter on the April 14, 1861. Accomplished without a single shot fired on either side as the Union forces withdrew, this marked the "official" beginning of The War Between the States.

Anderson, who at the time of the battle bore the rank of Major, was promoted to Brigadier General by President Lincoln on May 15. Anderson received a hero's welcome in New York City, where he proudly carried Fort Sumter's 33-star American Flag to a Union Square patriotic rally regarded today by historians to have been the largest public gathering in North America up to that time. Gen. Anderson then went on a highly successful recruiting tour of the North before taking a leave of absence due to ill health. He retired from the Army on October 27, 1863.

His gallantry at Ft. Sumter was never forgotten by President Lincoln. Just days after Robert E. Lee's surrender at Appomattox on April 9, 1865 and the effective conclusion of the war, Robert Anderson was invited to return to Charleston in the uniform of a Brevet Major General and four years to the day

Although the fluted cylinder was intended for the 1860 Army, this gun, serial number 29, is an 1861 Navy, one of the few examples to be built with a fluted cylinder. One of the flutes is stamped **PAT. SEPT. 10TH 1850** the same as an 1851 Navy cylinder. (Dr. Joseph A. Murphy collection)

after lowering the 33-star flag in surrender, he raised it in triumph over the recaptured, but badly battered Fort Sumtner during ceremonies there. That same evening, April 14, 1865, President Abraham Lincoln was assassinated.

The pair of Gustave Young engraved 1861 Navy models presented to General Anderson bore the standard factory markings which included the barrel address:

– ADDRESS COL. SAMᴸ COLT   NEW-YORK U.S. AMERICA. –

and the **COLTS/PATENT** stamping on the left side of the frame. The cylinders used the roll engraved naval engagement scene from the 1851 Navy and 1860 Army.

The .36 caliber revolvers were fitted with 7-¹/₂ inch barrels and weighed 2 pounds, 10 ounces empty. The military demand for this model was modest and between April 1861 and the end of the Civil War only 2,363 were purchased. The civilian market, on the other hand, gladly embraced the new model with sales reaching over 25,000 by 1866. By the time Colt's discontinued the 1861 Navy in 1873, more than 38,000 had been sold.

The 1861 Navy has been called the most elegant Colt percussion pistol ever made. It is without question a superbly well balanced gun, the perfect combination of power, .36 caliber, six shots, with the grace of design established with the larger .44 caliber Model 1860 Army. The example shown is one of a limited number of guns built for a shoulder stock, and has the same recoil shield notches and fourth screw as an 1860 Army. (Author's collection)

This deluxe engraved and cased pair of 1861 Navy Models, engraved by the Gustave Young shop, was presented to Major General James B. McPherson along with a cased pair of engraved 1862 Police revolvers. The inscribed ivory grips read: *Maj. Gen. Jas. B. McPherson 17th Army Corps.* (Dr. Joseph A. Murphy collection)

The presentation to General McPherson (pictured to the left in a copy of *Harpers Weekly*), was inscribed on the backstraps: *FROM HIS FRIENDS/O.N. CUTLER; W.C. WAGLEY.* The sequentially serial numbered guns, 11756/I and 11757/I were done en suite with the matching 1862 Police models. McPherson was an 1853 West Point graduate, the same class as Sheridan, Schofield, and Hood, all of who were destined for glory in The War Between the States. McPherson, however, graduated head of the class. Promoted to Lt. Col. in 1861, by the autumn of 1862 he was in command of an infantry brigade at the battle of Corinth. His outstanding service led to a field promotion to Major General of volunteers and command of an entire division. After his success in the battle of Vicksburg in 1863, McPherson was promoted to the regular rank of Brigadier General on the recommendation of General Grant. Tragically, engaged in battle against one of his old West Point classmates, John Bell Hood, McPherson was mortally wounded on July 22, 1864. Ulysses S. Grant wept at the news, saying "The country has lost one of its best soldiers, and I have lost my best friend." (Dr. Joseph A Murphy collection)

Samuel Colt presented this pair of Gustave Young engraved 1861 Navy revolver to one of the Civil War's most renowned Union officers, General Robert Anderson, the commander of Ft. Sumter. The guns are pictured with a display of Anderson memorabilia including family portraits, his military belt, medals, and engraved ivory handled saber. (Dr. Joseph A. Murphy collection)

Below: The threat of Civil War was provoked in 1859 by John Brown's attack on the Harpers Ferry Arsenal, but the war didn't begin until the morning Confederate General P.G.T. Beauregard opened fire on Ft. Sumter in April 1861. Commander of Ft. Sumter, Major Robert Anderson, is pictured seated second from the left in this March 23, 1861 issue of *Harpers Weekly*. Less than three weeks later, on April 12, Ft. Sumter would come under fire, and on April 14, would fall to Confederate forces beginning The War Between the Sates.

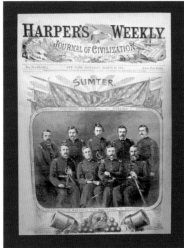

At the beginning of The War Between the States, Sam Colt had not been ambivalent about the issues. He regarded slavery not as much a moral issue but one of poor economics. After the October 16, 1859 attack on the Harpers Ferry arsenal, Colt had denounced John Brown as a traitor, and he had opposed the election of Abraham Lincoln for fear it would divide the Union. In this Colt had been correct.

As the Civil War carried into 1862, Colt added another revolver to his line, the Police Model, an even more compact version of the 1861 Navy, again chambered in .36 caliber but restricted to only five chambers in a new semi fluted, rebated cylinder. Another Pocket model of Navy size caliber followed in 1865, also chambered in .36 caliber, and resembling a compact 1851 Navy. This, however, was a model that Sam Colt would never know. On January 10, 1862, at the age of 47, Samuel Colt died after suffering a brief illness. Bothered by frequent attacks of inflammatory rheumatism and distressed by the death of an infant daughter, he drove himself as if he knew his days were numbered. Smoking Cuban cigars, Colt ruled his domain from a roll-top desk at the Hartford Armory.

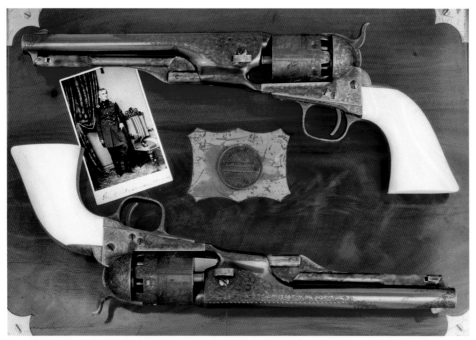

Representing some of the finest work done for Samuel Colt by master engraver Gustave Young, the presentation 1861 Navy Models of General Robert Anderson are regarded as two of the most beautiful engraved Colts in the world.

The fine engraved Colt 1861 Navy models presented to General Anderson are inscribed on the backstrap: To Gen. Robert Anderson U.S.A. with compliments of Colt's Pt. F.A. Mfg. Co.

Another remarkable 1861 Navy and an example of the exquisite engraving of L. D. Nimschke. Serial number 21838, the gun was almost totally engraved by Nimschke, silver plated, and accented with gold washed cylinder, loading lever, hammer and trigger, and blued screws. The grips are hand checkered ivory with an American eagle and shield. Another Nimschke job for Schuyler, Hartley & Graham, in New York, it is believed that the gun was presented to an aide to Emperor Maximilian. (Photo courtesy Greg Martin Auctions)

One of the more interesting casings for the 1862 Police Model was the "book-style". This particular design, there were several others, was titled on the spine, COLT/ON THE CONSTITUTION/HIGHER LAW & IRREPRESSIBLE CONFLICT...DEDICATED BY/THE AUTHOR/TO...with a blank space following the TO for the recipient's name. This beautifully engraved vine scroll pattern 1862 Police, accented with a rosette above the barrel wedge on both sides, was presented to a member of the Freemasons, and bears a Freemasons symbol, the key and scroll, on the grip strap. (Dr. Joseph A. Murphy collection)

Deluxe engraved and cased pair of 1862 Police models, consecutively serial numbered, 15859/l and 15860/l, were engraved by the Gustave Young shop and presented to Major General James B. McPherson. Pictured with the cased guns is an August issue of *Harper's Weekly* telling of the death of General McPherson. Also shown is a portrait of McPherson alongside his Medal of Honor for the Vicksburg Campaign, and Ellsworth's own Zouave Medal from the 17th Corps. at far right. (Dr. Joseph A. Murphy collection)

Though one of the wealthiest men in the country, Sam Colt was short on heirs; two of his brothers, John and William had died, and the third, James, had proven to be a hot tempered ne'er-do-well who could neither be trusted with money nor responsibility. At the time of his death Colt's estate was reportedly worth $15 million, a vast sum for the 1860s. He was survived by his wife Elizabeth and their son Caldwell. Elizabeth, whom he had only married in June of 1856, was the daughter of the Reverend William Jarvis. It would be in her brother Richard that Colt would find the assurance of talent and dedication necessary to carry on the family business. Shortly before he died, he handed the family reins to his brother-in-law, writing to Richard in 1862: "You and your family must do for me now as I have no one else to call upon. You are the pendulum that must keep the works in motion."

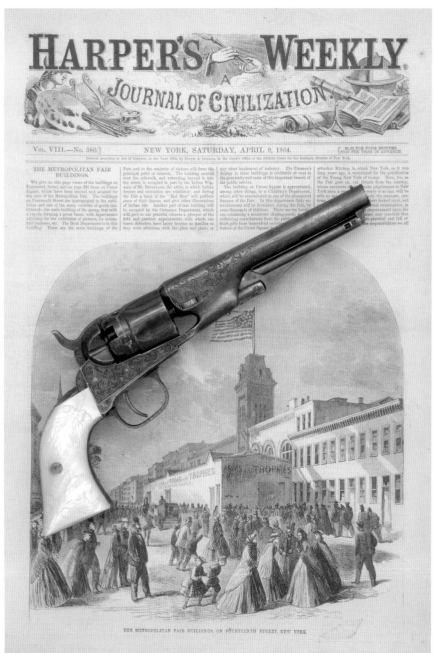

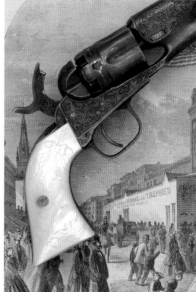
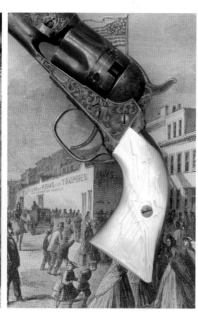

For the 1864 Metropolitan Fair in New York, a massive public trade show set up along Fourteenth Street and Union Square, Colt's created two special display guns, a handsomely engraved 1855 Sidehammer with ivory grips and this striking 1862 Police Model, both engraved by Gustave Young. The rare mother of pearl grips on the 1862 were carved in low relief with a patriotic stand of flags, liberty cap, musket and star devices on the left grip panel, and oak leaf motifs on the right. (Dr. Joseph A. Murphy collection)

Richard Jarvis saw the company through the end of the Civil War and into the postwar era. Control of Colt's remained in the hands of Elizabeth and her family until 1901, when the company was sold to a group of investors.

The last model of Sam Colt's design, the 1862 Police, and the Navy version that followed in 1865, were to be the final percussion guns built at the Hartford Armory.

The Police Model was available in four barrel lengths, 3-$\frac{1}{2}$, 4-$\frac{1}{2}$, 5-$\frac{1}{2}$ and 6-$\frac{1}{2}$ inches. As to production numbers, the serial number sequence for the Police begins at 1 and ends at 47,000 in 1873. However, the serial numbers for the Pocket Model of Navy Caliber, also erroneously known as a Pocket Navy, are in their own sequence, begining with 1. It is estimated that the ratio of Police to Navy Caliber revolvers is 60/40.

The rarest of 1862 Police Models are those with special 2-inch and 2-1/2 inch barrels. The first Colt snub nose revolvers, between 25 and 50 were manufactured with at least one having been sold to Wells Fargo & Co. Most of the guns are reputed to have been sold to the Mormon Church in Salt Lake City, for use by the Mormon Police, a de facto secret organization known as the Danites, headed by William A. "Wild Bill" Hickman (pictured), Hosea Stout, chief of the Mormon police, and Orrin Porter Rockwell, all of who were also Joseph Smith's and Brigham Young's bodyguards. The guns earned the rather disquieting sobriquet "Avenging Angel." This example has a dovetailed brass blade front sight. Others had simple brass bead sights and a few no sights at all, as they were generally used at very close range! (Author's collection)

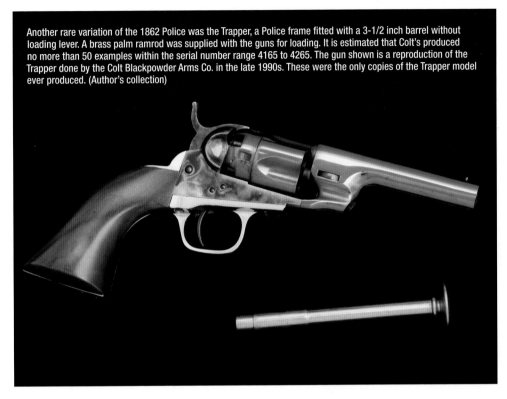

Another rare variation of the 1862 Police was the Trapper, a Police frame fitted with a 3-1/2 inch barrel without loading lever. A brass palm ramrod was supplied with the guns for loading. It is estimated that Colt's produced no more than 50 examples within the serial number range 4165 to 4265. The gun shown is a reproduction of the Trapper done by the Colt Blackpowder Arms Co. in the late 1990s. These were the only copies of the Trapper model ever produced. (Author's collection)

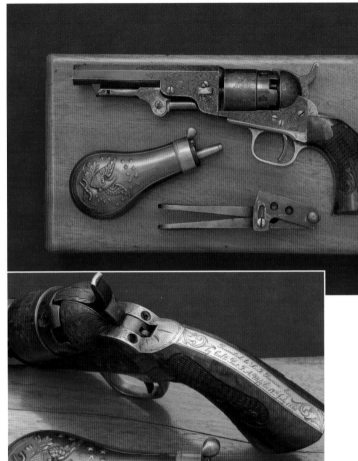

The Police Model was stamped with two different barrel addresses, as well as the London address on guns sold in Great Britain. The principal style seen is:

– ADDRESS COL. SAM^L COLT   NEW-YORK U.S. AMERICA –
Alternately the address was also stamped in two lines:

ADDRESS SAM^L COLT
HARTFORD CT.

The **COLTS/PATENT** stamping was also used on the left side of the frame. The half fluted rebated cylinders were stamped **PAT. SEPT. 10th 1850** on one of the flutes. The left shoulder of the triggerguard was marked **36 CAL.**

Not as concealable as Colt's earlier Pocket Models, there was one very limited exception, which has become the most intriguing pocket pistol of the percussion era, the so called "Avenging Angel" snub nose revolver.

Often called a Pocket Navy, the Pocket Model of Navy Caliber was introduced in 1865, a year after the fire that razed part of the Colt factory in 1864. A throwback to the extremely popular 1849 Pocket Model, the new model used the same frame as the 1849, and the same roll engraved cylinder scene. Chambered in .36 caliber, the 5-shot revolver became nearly as popular as the 1849, remaining in production through 1873. This particular example was a presentation gun from Colt's to L. T. Pearson, Esq. Serial number 16619/E it exhibits the late vine scroll style of engraving. The grips are hand checkered walnut in a volute (decorative spiral) motif. This same type of grip design was used on an 1860 Army and was also likely done by Charles J. Helfricht. (Dr. Joseph A. Murphy collection)

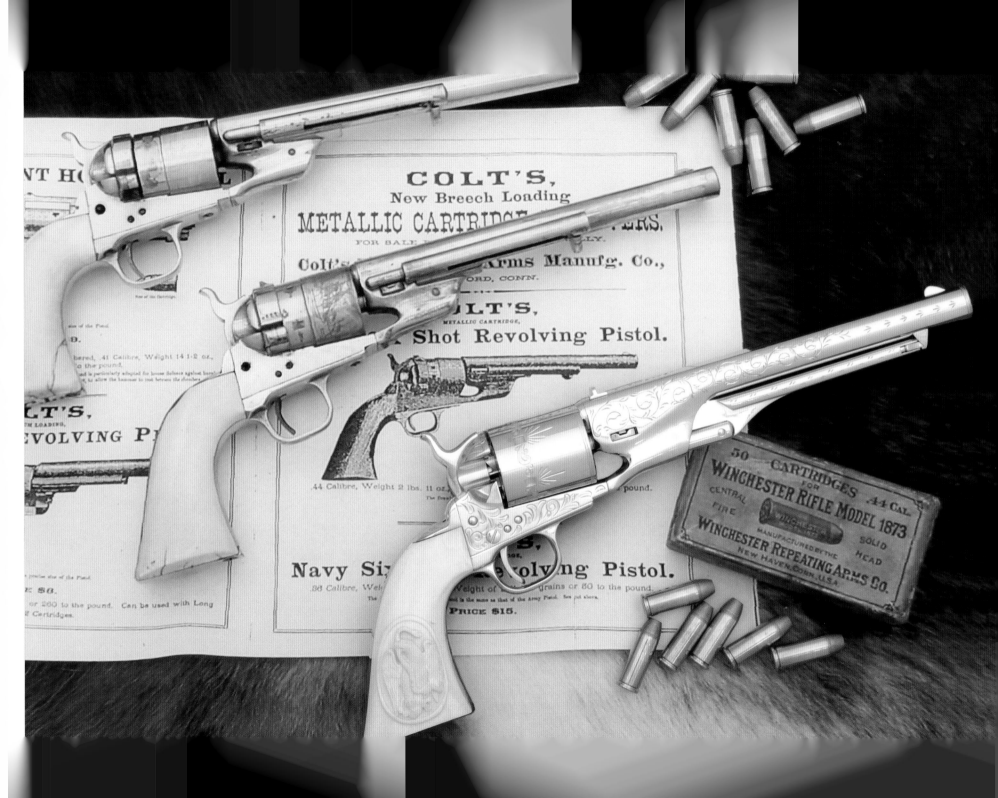

Chapter Six
Coming of Age in America
The Metallic Cartridge and Colt's Conversion from Cap and Ball

Although Colt and Remington cap-and-ball revolvers were regarded as contemporary firearms in this country, pistols designed to fire metallic cartridges had been in use throughout Europe since the 1840s. During The War Between the States tens of thousands of European cartridge revolvers would be imported by both Union and Confederate forces thereby changing the face of the American firearms industry.

As far back as the mid 1840s rimfire cartridges had been in common use throughout Europe, and by 1854 the first centerfire ammunition had been developed. However, in 1843 a third type of cartridge had been invented by French gunmaker Casimir Lefaucheux. It was known as the Lefaucheux pinfire, which literally meant that a firing pin was contained within each individual bullet. The operation was quite clever. The hammer fell on a cartridge pin extending above the rim of the cylinder through a notch, the pin in turn struck a percussion cap inside the chambered round, igniting the powder. While very effective, each Lefaucheux bullet was a very *live* round and it was in one's best interest never to fumble or drop a pinfire cartridge! Despite the inherent risks of carrying these volatile rounds into battle, both the U.S. Ordnance Department and the Confederate Army purchased thousands of Lefaucheux revolvers during the war, and over 1 million cartridges. President Lincoln personally commissioned Marcellus Hartley, a partner in the New York firearms importing firm of Schuyler, Hartley & Graham to supply the Union Army with Lefaucheux (pronounced *lue-foe-sho*) pistols and pinfire ammunition in 1862. The Union Army received 1,900 pinfire revolvers through Hartley, and purchased another 10,000 under direct contract during the war. The Confederacy followed suit as well as having the South's most potent revolver, the 9-shot .44 caliber LeMat (also produced in France) refitted to chamber pinfire cartridges. From 1861 to 1865 the Confederate States of America purchased as many as 2,500 Lefaucheux revolvers, which became the fourth most commonly used sidearm throughout the Civil War, surpassed only by the Colt, Remington, and Starr percussion pistols.

Left: Converting percussion guns to fire metallic cartridges became a crucial task at Colt's in the early 1870s. Pictured are three variations on the 1860 Army: At top a Richards Type II conversion c1872, center a Richards Type I c.1871-72, and at bottom, an authentic copy of a rare c.1869-1870 Long Cylinder 1860 Army conversion in a Mexican engraving motif with eagle and snake ivory grips. (Roger Mucherheide collection and author's collection)

Right: The first Colt conversions were built in 1871-72 using the 1860 Army and the Richards patent for conversion to metallic cartridge. The less produced of the first series were those with 12-stop cylinders. (R.L. Millington collection, photo by Dennis Adler)

This rare Louis D. Nimschke engraved S&W Model No. 2 is fitted with pearl stocks. Note the original ammo box of .32 caliber rimfire cartridges. Wild Bill Hickok had a S&W Model No. 2 in his vest the day he was murdered in Deadwood, South Dakota. (Roger Muckerheide Collection)

Remington & Sons, Colt's largest competitor, was facing the same problems after the Civil War, excess inventory of percussion guns and the growing demand for cartridge firing revolvers, which were limited to imported guns and those built by Smith & Wesson, which held the patent for the breech loading bored through cylinder. Remington agreed to pay a royalty of $1 per gun to acquire the licensing rights 1868. This gave Remington a three year sales advantage over Colt's which would not offer a cartridge conversion until 1871. (J.D. Hofer collection, photo by Dennis Adler)

Smith & Wesson produced the first American made cartridge firing revolvers. The .32 caliber rimfire Model No. 2 was introduced in 1861 and was popular among Union officers and enlisted men as a personal sidearm during the Civil War. Engraved examples were rare. The S&W revolvers featured a unique "tip-up" barrel design. The barrel pivoted upward and the cylinder was removed from the base pin for loading and unloading. (Roger Muckerheide Collection)

Marcellus Hartley handled the majority of Union requisitions for imported firearms. A key figure in American industry (importing pinfire arms and ammunition before, during, and after the war), he was also responsible for establishing the Union Metallic Cartridge Co., one of only three American firms known to have manufactured and marketed pinfire ammunition in any quantity.

The First American Pistol Cartridge

As the eleven Southern States were seceding from the Union, (1860-61) Daniel B. Wesson (of Smith & Wesson) was perfecting a self-contained, .22 caliber rimfire metallic cartridge (essentially the same .22 caliber short rimfire bullet still used today), for which S&W received a patent in 1860. Wesson and his partner Horace Smith had also wisely acquired the exclusive rights to the 1855 Rollin White patent covering the manufacture of a bored through cylinder, a design in which Samuel Colt had shown little interest when White (a former Colt employee) first presented it to him. With the White patent, S&W would have a monopoly on the manufacture of cartridge revolvers in the United States until 1869.

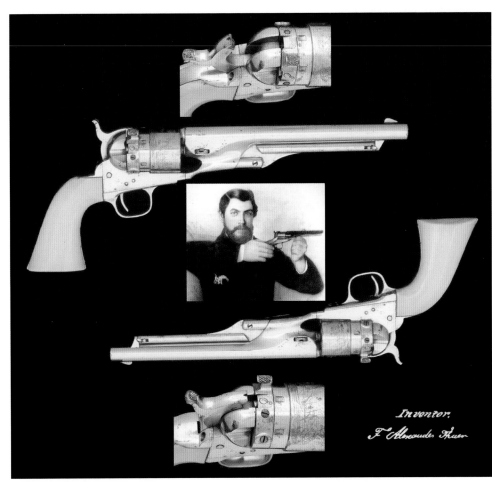

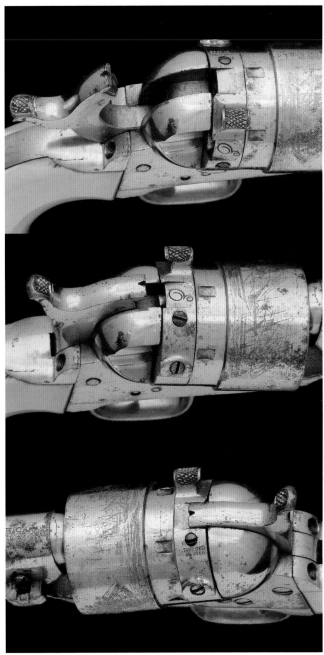

The Thuer alteration c.1868 was most commonly seen on the 1860 Army model, which was chambered for .44 caliber Thuer centerfire cartridges. The elegant design of the Colt Army lent itself well to F. Alexander Thuer's conversion ring and cylinder, which with the exception of the boss or thumbpiece did little to alter the appearance of the pistol. (Roger Muckerheide Collection)

The most complicated part of the Thuer mechanism was the breech ring itself. It contained a rebounding firing pin, and an ejector mechanism, noted by the elegantly scripted "E" to the right of the boss. A third position on the ring, located between the fire and "E" detents, provided a hammer rest as a safety, however before the gun could be discharged, the boss (or thumbpiece) had to be moved back into the firing position. It wasn't an ideal solution, but it worked. Note the patent date stamped on the breech ring. (Roger Muckerheide collection)

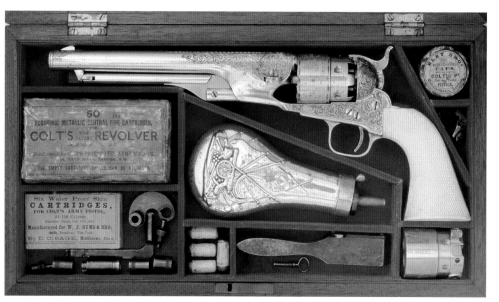

A considerable number of Thuer models were factory engraved; perhaps to increase sales after the initial bloom was off the rose. This 1860 Army is cased with both cylinders (the Thuer is in the partition usually reserved for the percussion cylinder). A deluxe cased example complete with a box of Thuer cartridges and paper cartridges for the percussion cylinder, nickel finished revolver also has checkered ivory grips. (Photo courtesy R. L. Wilson)

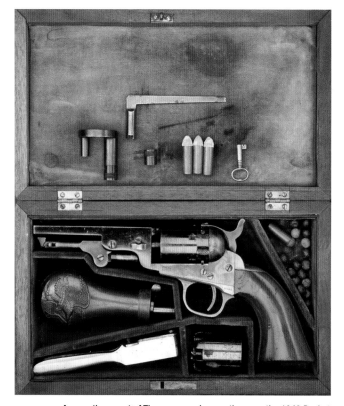

Among the rarest of Thuer conversion are those on the 1849 Pocket Pistol. This cased example with 4-inch barrel has the conversion ring and cylinder attached. A percussion cylinder was always supplied with the Thuer conversions so that the gun could be quickly switched back to cap-and-ball use. The patented Thuer loading tools and three cartridges are displayed in the lid. (Photo courtesy R. L. Wilson)

When the extension on Colt's patent for a revolving mechanism expired, Smith & Wesson quickly introduced their first cartridge-firing revolver in January 1857. The S&W Model No. 1 was a 7-shot, .22 caliber rimfire pocket pistol. An improved Second Issue model was introduced in 1860, by which time S&W had sold more than 11,000 .22 caliber cartridge revolvers!

The Smith & Wesson revolvers became extremely popular during the Civil War; however their small caliber prevented them from being approved for military use by the U.S. Army Ordnance Department, even though S&W had added a larger 6-shot, .32 caliber version, the Model No. 2, in 1861. The medium frame Model No. 2, with either a 5 or 6-inch barrel, was in such demand throughout the war that the factory had a three-year backlog of orders! Officers and infantrymen frequently carried the No. 2 as a back up pistol. Between 1861 and 1874 a total of 77,155 were sold.

Despite the prolific number of cartridge firing revolvers imported from Europe, Colt and Remington percussion revolvers remained the dominant sidearms of Union and Confederate forces. By 1868, however, the true heirs were about to set foot upon the stage as the Rollin White patent neared the end of its duration.

Colt's and Remington had been marking time for more than a decade, neither willing to challenge S&W and White. Following Samuel Colt's precedent with the revolving cylinder, White had applied for a patent extension in 1868 but the Commissioner of Patents had refused his request. White then appealed to Congress which drafted a Bill (S-273) "An act for the relief of Rollin White" that passed both houses but was returned unsigned by President Ulysses S. Grant. White's failure to get an extension opened the floodgates for the development of both the metallic cartridge and breech-loading revolver in the United States.

The most elaborate Thuer conversion known, serial No. 185326/I.E, this silver-plated example with hand carved ivory grips, gold washed cylinders, hammer, and rammer plunger, bears the fine engraving of Cuno A. Helfricht c.1871. All of 20 years old at the time, he followed in his father's footsteps at Colt as a contract engraver. More work began coming the way of Helfricht's shop in 1869 following Gustave Young's departure from Hartford. Young moved to Springfield, Massachusetts and set up his own engraving business. Within a few years Cuno Helfricht would rise to the position of Colt's chief engraver. With work like this, it is easy to see why. (Dr. Joseph A. Murphy collection)

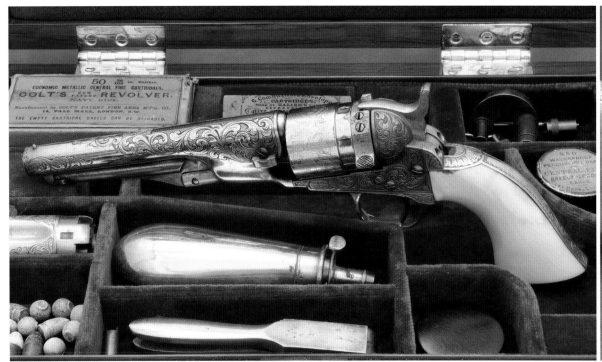

One of the finest 1862 Police Thuer conversions known, this example was engraved by L. D. Nimschke. An interesting combination of silver and gold, the barrel and frame feature nearly full coverage in the vine scroll style accented with a fine punch dot background that became a Nimschke trademark. The gun is cased with the original half fluted and rebated percussion cylinder (also engraved), a bag-shaped James Dixon & Sons/Sheffield powder flask, paper cartridges for the percussion cylinder and a box of patented Thuer metallic cartridges. (Dr. Joseph A. Murphy collection)

Samuel Colt had no idea what he had done when he turned down Rollin White's offer for the patent rights to the bored through cylinder in 1855. He would never know the importance the metallic cartridge would play in the last years of the Civil War, or the dire repercussions his decision would have on Colt's after the war.

In 1865 both Colt's and Remington found themselves with an abundant surplus of cap-and-ball revolvers, Colt's in particular, having been the primary supplier of arms to the U.S. military. As firearms technology advanced from the use of loose powder, cap, and ball to the metallic cartridge, this precipitated a need to move vast inventories of percussion arms that were becoming obsolete. It was only now that Sam Colt's unfortunate decision began to weigh in.

When the Colt's patent expired, Smith & Wesson, Remington, and other American manufacturers immediately began production of revolvers, however, no one but

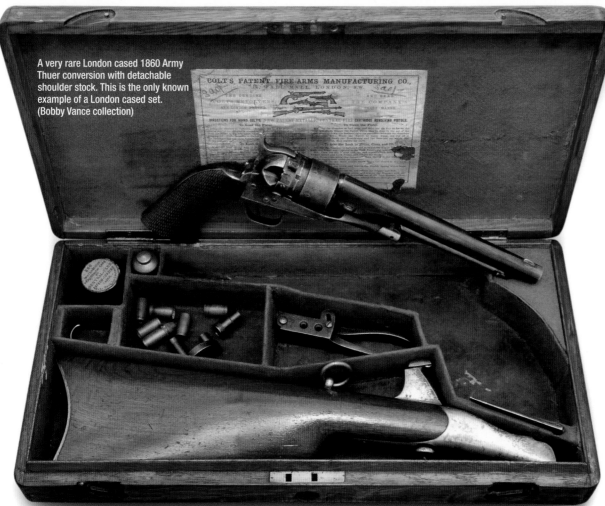

A very rare London cased 1860 Army Thuer conversion with detachable shoulder stock. This is the only known example of a London cased set. (Bobby Vance collection)

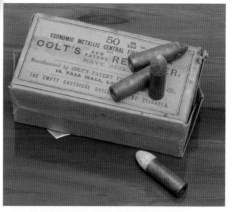

It is interesting to note that the Thuer cartridges, primarily manufactured and sold by Colt's, were centerfire, whereas early metallic cartridges for Colt conversions and 1871-72 Open Tops were rimfire. The reason for this is that Thuer cartridges were intended for reloading and centerfire was the logical choice since new primers could be easily seated in the reclaimed brass shells. (Thuer cartridge boxes stated: *"The Empty Cartridge Shells can be Reloaded."*) Another benefit of the Thuer conversion was that all models, including Pocket Pistols, fired six rounds, thus the smaller Pocket revolvers gained an extra shot when converted—an advantage even the later Richards and Richards-Mason models did not offer. (Dr. Joseph A. Murphy collection)

The Thuer breech ring was designed to fit into place against the recoil shield, with the ratchet (machined on a collar-shaped extension from the breech of the cylinder) passing through its center to engage the hand. As with percussion cylinders, the Thuer breech ring and cylinder combination were held in place by the center pin (arbor), barrel and wedge. The Thuer cylinder was bored completely through, but since it could not be loaded from the breech, due to the collar and the taper of the chamber, its design did not violate the White patent. The cylinder chambers had a tapered bore that accommodated the shape of the cartridges, which were slightly narrower at the rear to ease loading with the rammer. The Thuer conversion ring as it faced the recoil shield shows the firing pin to the left and the ejector pin to the right. When the hammer struck the ejector pin, it acted upon a lever (facing side) that "kicked" the empty casing out of the cylinder. (Bobby Vance collection)

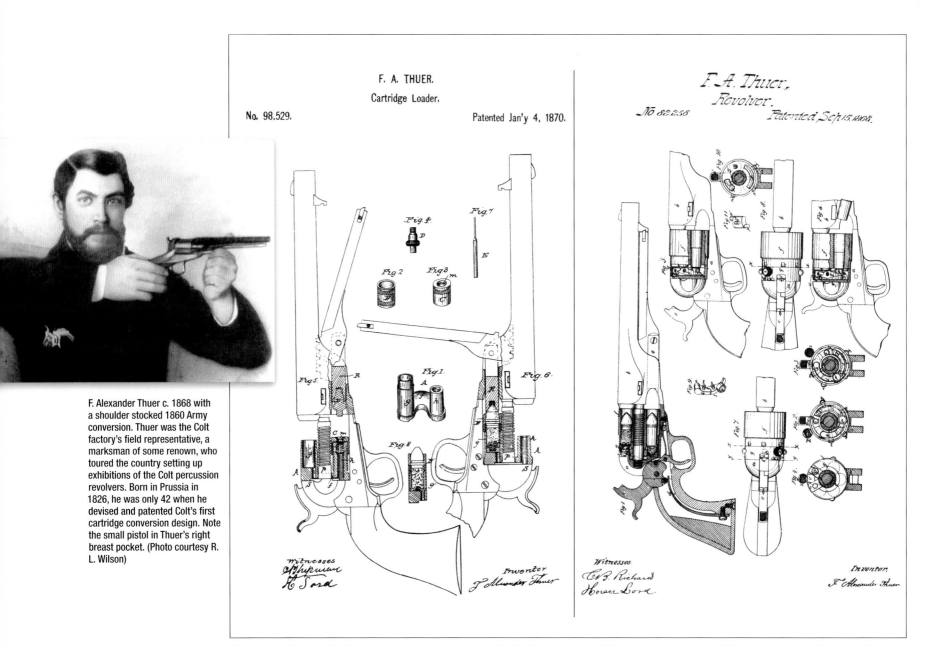

F. A. THUER.
Cartridge Loader.

No. 98,529.

Patented Jan'y 4, 1870.

F. A. Thuer.
Revolver.

No 82,258.

Patented Sep. 15, 1868.

F. Alexander Thuer c. 1868 with a shoulder stocked 1860 Army conversion. Thuer was the Colt factory's field representative, a marksman of some renown, who toured the country setting up exhibitions of the Colt percussion revolvers. Born in Prussia in 1826, he was only 42 when he devised and patented Colt's first cartridge conversion design. Note the small pistol in Thuer's right breast pocket. (Photo courtesy R. L. Wilson)

Thuer received his patent for his conversion system on September 15, 1868. The patent covered the rather extensive design of the conversion ring, which housed the firing pin and cartridge shell extractor, or more precisely, ejector. The design, as noted in the close-up view of Fig. 6., utilized two interlocking levers set into motion by the hammer to "boot" the empty cartridge casings out of the cylinder chamber.

An example of the evolution of Colt conversions is evidenced by this pair: an 1851 Navy converted to the Thuer alteration and an 1865 Pocket Model of Navy Caliber chambered for .38 rimfire, with the Richards-Mason cartridge conversion, c. 1873. The Pocket Model shown has a loading gate (many did not) and no ejector. (Photo courtesy R. L. Wilson)

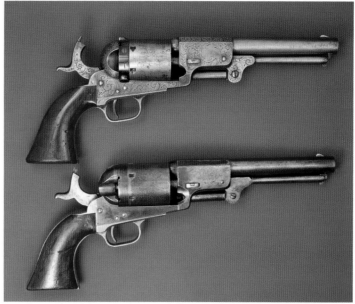

Colt's had experimented with cartridge conversions while the White patent was still in effect. Pictured is a very rare Third Model Dragoon (in the 12300 or 12400 serial number range) converted to fire .44 Thuer centerfire. Note the fine donut style scroll engraving with panel scene on the barrel lug. The gun at the bottom was a factory experimental conversion No. 15703, chambered for .44 caliber rimfire. This example from the John R. Hegeman collection, features a specially manufactured cylinder of two-sections and a channeled recoil shield to allow loading and unloading without the need of removing the cylinder. (Photo courtesy R. L. Wilson)

Smith & Wesson could manufacture cartridge-firing revolvers utilizing a breech loading, bored through cylinder.

Various attempts by other gunmakers during the war to circumvent the patent were quickly thwarted by S&W and White, who aggressively pursued all violators. S&W's legal battles over patent infringements totally impeded the development of cartridge firing revolvers in America for more than a decade.

Smith & Wesson continued to dominate the small caliber market until the introduction of the landmark .44 caliber Model Number 3 American in 1870, followed by the .44 Russian, the legendary Schofield, and New Model Number Three, all of which featured S&W's pioneering top-break design and automatic cartridge ejector.

For Colt's, the period from 1865 to 1869 was an interesting turn of events. The Hartford, Connecticut arms maker was now the one on the receiving end of an unbreakable patent. Just as Samuel Colt had prevented any American company from manufacturing revolvers until his patent expired, Smith & Wesson, and E. Remington & Sons (through a licensing agreement providing S&W with a $1 royalty per gun), were the only U.S. manufacturers permitted to build a breech-loading, cartridge-firing revolver, and Remington wasn't granted these rights until 1868. Aside from the somewhat Machiavellian approach taken F. Alexander Thuer and Colt's to circumvent the legal limitations of the Rollin White patent, Colt's was forced to wait, and did not introduce a breech-loading revolver until 1871.

Prior to the expiration of the White patent, Colt's had experimented with bored through cylinders on a variety of percussion models, a Third Model Dragoon chambered for the .44 caliber Henry rimfire cartridges, a small caliber 1849 Pocket pistol, an 1860 Army (a design that would later influence the 1871-72 Open Top), and an 1861 Navy chambered for .38 caliber cartridges. Most were viable designs, none, however, could be manufactured for sale. The only

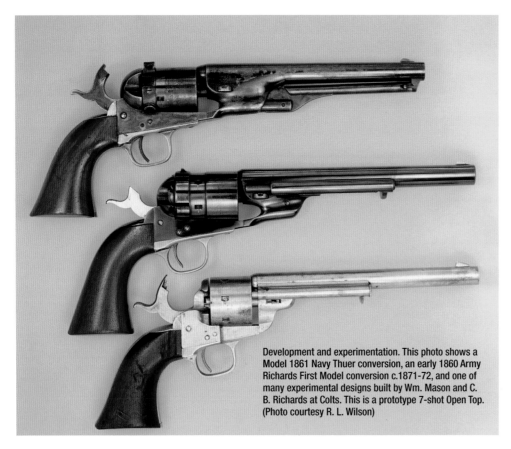

Development and experimentation. This photo shows a Model 1861 Navy Thuer conversion, an early 1860 Army Richards First Model conversion c.1871-72, and one of many experimental designs built by Wm. Mason and C. B. Richards at Colts. This is a prototype 7-shot Open Top. (Photo courtesy R. L. Wilson)

capable of being loaded from the front, the principal object of the said invention being to produce a device by which a revolver adapted for the use of loose ammunition can at a small cost be changed, so that cartridges having primed metallic shells may be used."

In theory, the Thuer alteration was a brilliant design, however in practice, it would prove to be less than ideal, but for Colt's it was the only way to offer a cartridge revolver without being challenged by S&W. Beginning in 1869 the Thuer conversion gave Colt's a competitive product in a marketplace that had been dominated by Smith & Wesson for a decade, and following the licensing agreement with S&W in 1868, even more so by Colt's oldest competitor, E. Remington & Sons.

The Thuer mechanism (as shown in the patent drawings) was a fairly straightforward design that could be adapted to any Colt cap-and-ball revolver and was produced in sizes to fit all Colt frames. Regardless of the model, the operation was basically the same, and relatively simple compared to the intricacies of loading a percussion revolver.

Colt sales literature described the loading procedure as follows: "Bring the hammer to half cock. See that the boss or projection on the ring in the rear of the cylinder is moved in position to the *right* of the hammer. Hold the pistol in the left hand, muzzle upwards, thumb and fore-finger grasping the cylinder, hammer to the left, butt resting on the breast. Insert the cartridges and ram them *home* in the usual manner."

It seemed to be a very practical and efficient means of loading. The self-contained black powder cartridge was far easier to handle than loose powder, ball, and percussion cap and ramming the cartridges into the chambers no more complicated. Extracting the spent shell casings, however, was. And here lied the problem with the Thuer conversion.

The cartridge ejection procedure as described in the instruction manual: "Move the boss on the ring in rear of the cylinder to the *left* of the hammer. Then cock and snap the pistol until all of the shells are ejected. Then move the boss on the ring back to the *right* of the hammer, and the pistol is ready for reloading." This process could be compared to the hand ejection of spent shells from a bored through cylinder, and the time to accomplish either task was likely about the same. Emptying the Thuer, however, seemed a more laborious task since the gun had to be cocked and fired six more times, assuming that the cases were ejected on the first snap. The manual noted that "...should the *first* blow fail to eject the cartridge; it should be repeated."

way for Colt's to legally circumvent the White patent was to find a means of loading a metallic cartridge other than at the breech. Enter F. Alexander Thuer, a Colt employee since 1849, an inventor, and a factory marksman who spent much of his time traveling the country demonstrating Colt percussion revolvers. Thuer's way around the White patent was avoid the use of a bored through cylinder. Each cartridge was loaded from the front of the cylinder using the rammer, as one would load a lead ball. In September 1868 Thuer received patent No. 82258 for a metallic cartridge conversion system that did not infringe upon the Rollin White patent. Thuer assigned the patent to Colt's Patent Fire Arms Manufacturing Company and production of the Thuer alteration (the term used in Colt Journals and correspondence) began late in 1869.

Somewhat generic in its legal description, the Thuer conversion was intended for a "…pistol or rifle which has a revolving chambered breech or cylinder

This beautifully engraved, nickel plated Long Cylinder 1860 conversion is an authentic copy handcrafted by R.L. Millington of ArmSport LLC using a Colt model from the 3rd generation. Millington followed the same procedure as the originals, replacing the percussion cylinder with a longer, bored through cylinder. The engraving by Conrad Anderson was based upon original patterns taken from an 1860 Army engraved in Mexico c.1872. The Mexican eagle and snake ivory grips on this original specimen also inspired the striking carved ivory stocks on this gun, which were done by Dennis Holland in Lubbock, Texas, and Dan Chesiak in Naugatuck, Connecticut. The final finishing and nickel plating was completed by Erin Armstrong at A&A Engraving in Rapid City, South Dakota. The period correct holster was handcrafted by Jim Lockwood of Prescott, Arizona.

Chambered as some of the late Long Cylinder conversions were in .44 Colt centerfire, the author has had no qualms about putting the gun through its paces, along with another copy crafted by Millington.

On the plus side for the Thuer, when a box of preloaded cartridges was not available, one could use the patented Thuer cartridge loader to make bullets, reusing empty cases fitted with a fresh primer, a measure of black powder, and a cast conical lead bullet. The Thuer loading tool, patented January 4, 1870, used the cylinder pin to hold the loading dies, and the rammer to first seat a new primer in the case and then the bullet. In a worst-case scenario, the Thuer breech ring and cylinder could be easily removed and the percussion cylinder replaced. The Colt Thuer, (like the later Remington Pocket, Police and Rider models), was two guns in one and came cased with both percussion and cartridge conversion cylinders.

The Thuer alteration was offered on the 1849 Pocket, 1851 Navy, 1861 Navy, 1860 Army (the premier version), Pocket Pistol of Navy caliber, and the 1862 Pocket Police. Dragoon revolvers and Sidehammer pistols and rifles were also manufactured in small numbers, but are usually considered as experimental models.

With thousands of surplus Civil War revolvers and parts on hand, Colt's began converting many of its own guns, first to the Thuer, then Richards, and later Richards-Mason designs between 1872 and 1873. There was an advantage to converting old guns, aside from reducing inventory, by 1873 a cartridge conversion was more affordable than Colt's all-new Single Action Army, less than half the price. For around $5 Colt's would even convert a customer's percussion pistol to use metallic cartridges,

A comparison between the Long Cylinder conversion and an 1860 Army percussion model reveals the minor, yet efficient changes made to convert the cap-and-ball guns to metallic cartridges c.1869-1870. Aside from modification to the hammer to create a firing pin, a change in cylinders, and scooping out the right recoil shield for loading, the 1860 Army retains its general appearance, even the loading lever, which no longer has a purpose.

and an independent gunsmith would probably have done it $3 or less. R. L. Wilson notes that Colt factory records indicate a total of 46,100 cap-and-ball models were either converted to or built as cartridge revolvers, in addition to those converted in the field.

By the 1870s the demand for cartridge conversions was growing. With the completion of the transcontinental railroad in 1869, the post-war move West, and with it, battles with Indian tribes enraged by the encroachment of the white man, Colt revolvers in the hands of settlers, lawmen, gunfighters, cattlemen, prospectors, and even Indians was becoming de rigueur.

Despite the fundamental practicality of the design, the Thuer was not a particularly successful gun. As R. L. Wilson noted in *The Book of Colt Firearms*, "Several points had been against the Thuer becoming a popular product in the Colt line: The tapered cartridge, the special loading tools, and the easily fouled conversion ring all contributed to the poor sales showing." Interestingly, the majority of Thuer alterations known to collectors are in very good condition—"proof," wrote Wilson, "that most were seldom used."

One of the most intriguing factory conversions, and a gun that adds considerable credibility to the Long Cylinder conversions, is this experimental 1861 Navy chambered in .38 rimfire. Like the Long Cylinder conversion, this gun has the right recoil shield scooped out to assist in loading and unloading, and does not have a loading gate. Of further interest is the fact that the cylinder was cut down from both ends (notice the cut through the patent date and roll engraving), and fitted with a breechring similar to later Richards-Mason design. The gun also has an ejector housing similar to the C.B. Richards patent for the First Model 1860 Army conversions. Note that the percussion hammer was retained and strikes an offset (rimfire) firing pin seated within the breechring. (Dr. Joseph A. Murphy collection)

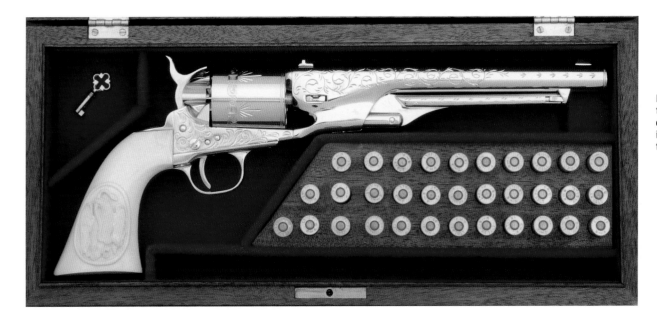

Based on a number of period examples, all of the best features of the 60 known Long Cylinder conversions were adapted to this one-off copy, including the dovetailed rear sight mounted on top of the barrel.

The Long Cylinder Colt 1860 Army Conversion

While Colt's was in the midst of depleting its Civil War inventory, a number of other approaches had been experimented with, including one idea that simplified the conversion process to the lowest common denominator. This was known as the "Long Cylinder" conversion, which simply did away with the percussion cylinder, replacing it with a longer, bored through cylinder, channeling the recoil shield on the right to allow loading and manual ejection of cartridges, milling off the step in the frame associated with the Army's rebated cylinder, and fitting the face of the hammer with a firing pin. One might regard it as a simpler version of the 1871-72 Open Top models, the first all-new cartridge gun to come from Hartford. The question about the Long Cylinder conversion is…did Colt actually do it?

According to the late R. Bruce McDowell, a pioneering researcher in the history of the Long Cylinder conversion, the design approach dealt strictly with making the 1860 Army suitable to fire metallic cartridges. The original percussion hammers were used with their noses re-machined, forming an offset rimfire firing pin at the left of the hammer face. The original guns were designed to fire the .44 Henry rimfire, as were the 1871-72 Open Tops. Long Cylinder conversions typically retained their percussion loading lever, plunger, and latch, though they no longer served any purpose. Both three-screw and four-screw Army frames were used. There were numerous design changes as manufactur-

ing continued which accounts for four known variations. Among the various changes was the addition of a barrel-mounted rear sight dovetailed in approximately $3/16^{th}$ of an inch in front of the forcing cone, or at the very end of the barrel address. Some examples, but not all, have a hammer stop, either welded or pinned within the hammer channel; newly manufactured long cylinders without the roll engraved battle scene; and converted cylinders with the rear section turned down to a ratchet stem, then built up with a ring welded to the cylinder and re-bored to the size of the cartridge case. There are no known examples with loading gates, though at least one is known to have had a Richards Type I ejector housing fitted. Surviving examples indicate that the majority of Long Cylinder models were nickel plated.

Considering that the Long Cylinder was a conversion in the first place, it is interesting to note that some of the guns were converted a second time when centerfire ammunition became available. On these examples the hammers were re-machined to accommodate a firing pin, or simply replaced with a new hammer, and the hammer stop reshaped. The majority of examples have the original 8-inch 1860 Army barrel, though some have been documented with barrels shortened to as little as 5-inches.

According to McDowell, there are several schools of thought on the origins of the Long Cylinder conversions. One theory is that the majority of the guns were built by Colt's as "experimental" models and produced in limited

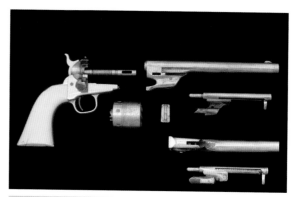

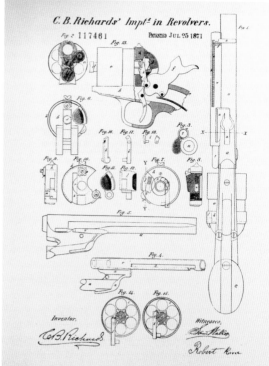

Charles B. Richards' July 25, 1871 patent for the First Model cartridge conversion covered all of the changes required to make Colt's 1860 Army into a cartridge firing revolver. The highly complex design, revealed by the disassembled gun, shows the breechring, cylinder modification, the milling of the barrel required for the ejector housing, as well as the housing and barrel (in two views, side and bottom), illustrating the assembly and fitting. (Roger Muckerheide collection)

numbers. Other opinions are that they were built prior to the expiration of the White patent to compete with the .46 caliber rimfire Remington Army conversions, which is unlikely considering Remington's predilection to litigate any violations of the White patent. Still another theory is that the guns were built for the U.S. Ordnance Department, either by Colt's or directly under Colt's supervision. There is, however, one other opinion that has long been considered the most likely: that the guns were built in the late 1860s and early 1870s in one or more gun shops or factories that had no association with Colt's (such as B. Kittredge & Co. and Schuyler, Hartley & Graham), or that they were hand built in Mexico from surplus 1860 Army parts. Considering the variations in assembly numbers on many examples, the mixing of parts with different serial numbers, and the variety of finish work from gun to gun this latter theory is highly plausible.

As McDowell finally concluded, "There appears to be no possibility that Colt was involved with the Model 1860 Long Cylinder revolver, based on the following reasoning. (1) The stamping dies used for the assembly numbers are larger and of a different typeface than those used by Colt on revolvers or conversions: (2) Though double-finger rotating arms are used on some Long Cylinder specimens, they are welded parts and welding was not practiced by Colt. (3) The mixing of serial numbers on most, but not all Long Cylinder cartridge revolvers was not a general practice of Colt. Unmatched serial numbers were only found on the U.S. Richards Conversions because of the rush to complete them for the U.S. Ordnance Department, which demonstrated no concern over numbering."

Further questions arise regarding the general quality of workmanship on many Long Cylinder models, which are not up to Colt's standards, and then there is the fact that most experimental Colts were neither blued nor nickel plated, but left in the white.

So where did the Long Cylinder Colts come from? The prevailing theory is that the 60 known examples were built outside of the Colt factory, by an individual or individuals between the late 1860s and 1873-1874. Whether or not they were built in Mexico remains one of the unsolved mysteries surrounding the rare Long Cylinder conversion that may never be solved.

The C. B. Richards Conversion

If you look closely at the Thuer patent drawing you will see two names at the lower left, the witnesses, Horace Lord, and C. B. Richards. In 1871, Charles B. Richards, a prominent inventor and Colt's Assistant Factory Superintendent, designed the first production Colt conversion, which was for the 1860 Army. He was granted patent No. 117461 in 1871 for *Improvements in Revolvers.*

As described by Richards in the patent text, "My invention relates to that kind of revolver which has a chambered breech or cylinder. It has for its object to provide a compact and cheap form of this kind of arm, which shall be fitted for the convenient use of a flanged metallic cartridge, and it is particularly useful as furnishing a means of converting a revolver constructed and intended for loose ammunition into one adapted for the kind of metallic cartridges which are loaded into the chambers from the rear."

The C. B. Richards patent was assigned to Colt's and intended for the alteration of the 1860 Army to .44 caliber central fire cartridges, a process that began commercially in 1872, a year after the introduction of the new Colt .44 rimfire Open Top model designed by Richards and William Mason, Colt's Superintendent of the Armory from 1866 to 1882.

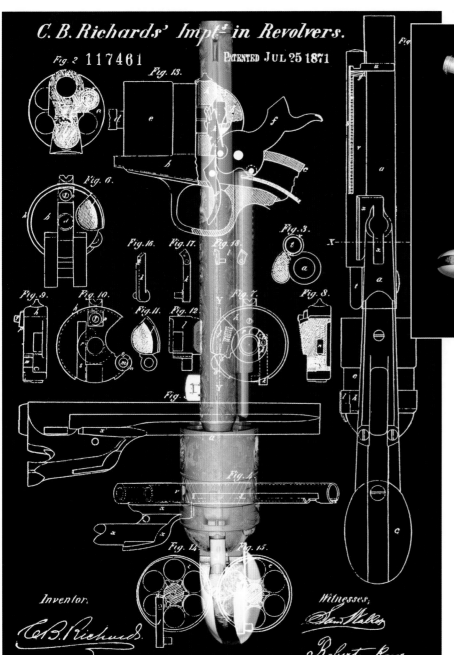

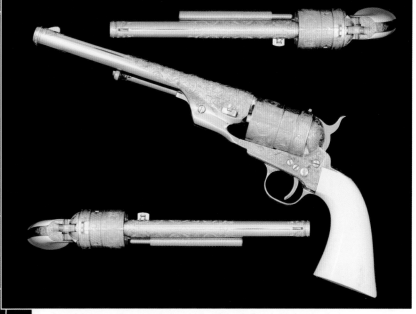

One of the more elegant variations of the Richards Type I, this handcrafted copy was created by R.L. Millington and engraver Conrad Anderson for a client. The engraving and combination of nickel and gold were copied from an original example. (Private collection)

The original Richards conversion commonly referred to as the Type I or First Model utilized a breechplate with a rebounding firing pin. The breechplate was combined with a newly manufactured cylinder or a cap-and-ball cylinder with the percussion portion cut away and the chambers bored completely through, and a new ratchet cut to engage the hand. The conversion also required removing 3/16th of an inch from the face of the recoil shield into which the breechplate (also referred to as the conversion ring) was seated and secured by the cylinder pin. The breechplate measured 0.49 inches in thickness x 1.675 inches in diameter with a channel slightly larger than the size of the cylinder bore cut out of the right side to facilitate the loading and ejection of cartridges from the breech end of the cylinder. On all Richards conversions this channel was protected by a hinged loading gate attached to the breech ring. The right side of the recoil shield was also channeled for cartridge loading, however on some experimental models, and on later Richards-Mason Pocket conversions the loading gate was frequently omitted, leaving the cylinder chamber exposed.

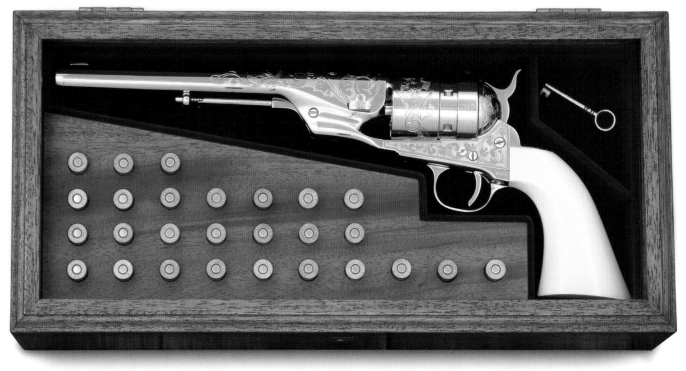

The author's engraved, nickel plated, and ivory gripped Richards Type I in a custom presentation box of the period, handcrafted by Pennsylvania furniture maker Duncan Everhart.

The final alternation to the 1860 Army required the hammer face to be ground flat in order to strike the firing pin. The sum of these modifications were irreversible and thus ruled out the refitting of the gun with a percussion cylinder. This was a disadvantage upon which Remington capitalized in the early 1870s with their popular two-piece cylinders. A simple switch back to the percussion cylinder allowed the use of loose powder, cap, and ball in the same gun.

One of the most complicated and costly components of the Richards conversion were the cartridge ejector assemblies. The newly fabricated housing (containing the ejector rod, spring, and ejector head) was attached to a metal plug that fit into the channel previously used for the loading rammer. The lug and right side of the barrel just above the rammer channel were notched to accommodate the ejector housing, which was secured by the loading lever screw passing through the lug from the left side. This process required a great deal of machining and hand labor.

Distinguishing characteristics of the Richards Type I conversion ring are the integral rear "V" sight cast into the top of the breechplate, the internal firing pin, and a 1/32nd of an inch overlap of the cylinder at the breech. When viewed from the side, the Type I breechplate shrouds the back of the cylinder, whereas on

later Richards-Mason conversions there is a clear separation between the face of the conversion ring and the cylinder breech.

Priced at $15.00, the Richards 1860 Army was produced c. 1871 to c. 1878 and it is estimated that 9,000 examples were manufactured by Colt's in the serial number range #1 to #8700 (excluding Richards-Mason arms from approximately #5800 through #7900 and conversions of percussion guns returned to the factory). Richards' numbers are also in the percussion series, from as early as serial #167,000 to #200614.

In addition to factory production models (those originally built as cartridge revolvers) and factory conversions, many 1860 Armies were converted to the Richards style on the frontier. A skilled gunsmith could copy the design. And many did. This was one of the key scenes in Tom Selleck's film *Last Stand at Saber River*, when his father-in-law presented him with a handcrafted 1860 Army conversion done in the Richards style.

The majority of Richard Type I conversions used the traditional six stop cylinder, either converted from a percussion cylinder or newly manufactured. Among the rarest examples of the Richards are those with 12 cylinder stops, the

Distinguishing characteristics of the Richards Type I conversion ring are the integral rear "V" sight cast into the top of the breechplate, the internal firing pin, and a 1/32nd of an inch overlap of the cylinder at the breech. When viewed from the side, the Type I breechplate shrouds the back of the cylinder, whereas on later Richards-Mason conversions there is a clear separation between the face of the conversion ring and the cylinder breech. Colt's produced two styles of breechrings, one with an internal spring tensioned loading gate, and a second using an external spring. Those with the external springs are easily recognized by the screw in the lower portion of the ring.

additional set having been intended to serve as a safety, by locking the cylinder between chambers. Although the design worked, one had to make certain that the cylinder was firmly set on the stop otherwise it could easily rotate back to a loaded chamber. The 12-stop safety system proved more or less as effective as the slots cut between chambers on Remington percussion cylinders, and the safety pins on earlier Colts, which similarly functioned as a hammer rest safety. The principal difficulty with the 12-stop design (as with the six-stop conversion cylinders) was that the bolt slots occasionally broke through when the percussion chambers were enlarged to accommodate .44 centerfire rounds. They also had a tendency to wear through over time and many surviving examples have one or more broken bolt slots. Ironically, the cylinder locking notches on the

12-stop rarely broke through because they were cut between the chambers.

McDowell's theory on the failure of the 12-stop cylinder design is perhaps the most likely. It could, if not properly set or with wear to the fingers of the lock bolt, cause the action to jam. And a gun that could possibly jam because of the cylinder design was a liability few could afford in the Old West.

In 1871 the U.S. Ordnance Department had ordered the conversion of approximately 1,200 U.S. issued Model 1860 Army percussion revolvers to the Richards design. Colt's handled the alterations in Hartford. Every gun within the Ordnance Department order was stamped with a new conversion serial number located beneath the original factory stamping. This usually consisted of a two or three digit number with an A suffix. The new numbers were

By 1872 there was no shortage of cartridges on the market for Colt conversions. Pictured are examples manufactured by the Winchester Repeating Arms Co., The United States Cartridge Company, Union Metallic Cartridge Company (later to own Remington), and Frankford Arsenal in Pennsylvania. (Dow and Russelle Heard collection)

Left: Pictured is an excellent example of a rare U.S. model Richards Type I conversion c.1872 with Springfield Armory proofs. It is shown with a period single loop holster and a belt converted from a Civil War carbine sling. (Dow and Russelle Heard collection)

The rarest of the Richards Type I conversion were those with 12 bolt cylinder stops. The extra set of stops was intended to serve as a safety between loaded chambers. Before Colt's began making new cartridge cylinders for the Richards and later models, the percussion cylinders were bored through and the chambers expanded to accommodate the .44 caliber cartridges. Often, the bolt stops either broke through or over time wore through. It is not uncommon to see this on early Richards conversions. (Dow and Russelle Heard collection)

A trio of Richards Type I conversions recreated in every detail by renowned Colorado gunsmith Robert L. Millington of ArmSport LLC in Eastlake, CO.

The gun used for the engraving pattern on the author's copy of the Colt Long Cylinder, is this striking c.1872 Richards Type I conversion engraved in Mexico and fitted with traditional eagle and snake ivory grips. Quite a number of early Colt conversion found their way south of the border in the 1870s and were engraved in similar styles. (Roger Mucherheide collection)

165

Nickel plating was popular on cartridge conversions, inasmuch as early examples returned to the factory for modifications had to be refinished. Nickel was also a durable finish more resistant to the ravages of black powder. The gun is shown with a period holster and cartridge belt. (Photo courtesy Greg Martin Auctions)

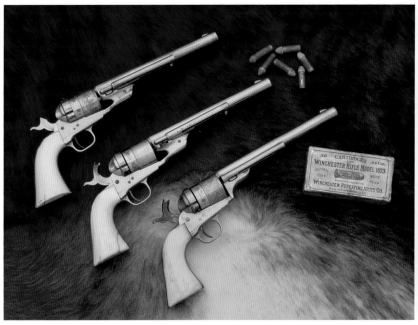

stamped on the barrel lug, cylinder, breech ring, loading gate and ejector rod arm. The military conversions were also stamped with **U.S.** either forward of, or just above the wedge on the left side of the barrel. On later conversions the A suffix was eliminated, only the loading gate and breechplate were numbered, and the conversion number was stamped either above or below the original serial number. Springfield Armory inspector marks "**A**" (O. W. Ainsworth) were present on all military conversions, and both three and four screw (the latter variation designed for a shoulder stock) Army models were modified. The breechplate and loading gate, however, altered the contour of the recoil shield, narrowing the slots originally used to anchor the shoulder stock yoke. Thus a conversion could not use the shoulder stock. The U.S. Richards were issued and used by the Cavalry well into the 1880s, by which time the Colt Single Action Army and various S&W models made them obsolete. Good examples of the U.S. models are hard to find because of the wear and tear they experienced in military service. Civilian models, however, are relatively common.

The civilian Richards models bore new serial numbering as well but without the A suffix, **U.S.** stamp or government inspector's mark seen on the military versions. The majority of civilian First Model Richards conversions had six-stop cylinders, as did most engraved specimens, and *all* nickel-plated conversions. There are no known examples of a nickel-plated Richards Army conversion with 12 cylinder locking notches. That said it is interesting to note that both the Union Metallic Cartridge Company and U.S. Cartridge Co. used a 12-stop Richards conversion to illustrate the labels on their cartridge boxes!

These Series I Richards conversions are broken down into four primary categories: the first production done in 1871 to convert military percussion revolvers to metallic cartridge; those converted at the Hartford factory using left over percussion inventory; models built at Hartford with newly manufactured cylinders, and the 12-stop variation.

The Second Model Richards Conversion

The Richards Type I proved an expensive undertaking for Colt's due to the complexity of the breechplate design, internal

The three principal variations of the 1860 Army conversion. From top to bottom, Richards Type I, Richards Type II, and Richards Mason. Between the Type I and Type II, the changes were confined to the breechring design and hammer. The Type II (center in close-up) shows the opening in the breechring for the firing pin. The Type I (left) had a rebounding firing pin within the breechring. The Type II allowed the use of percussion "V" notch hammers fitted with firing pins. The Type II was essentially the same breechring and hammer design that would be used on the new Richards-Mason conversion (right) introduced c.1872-73. (Roger Mucherheide collection)

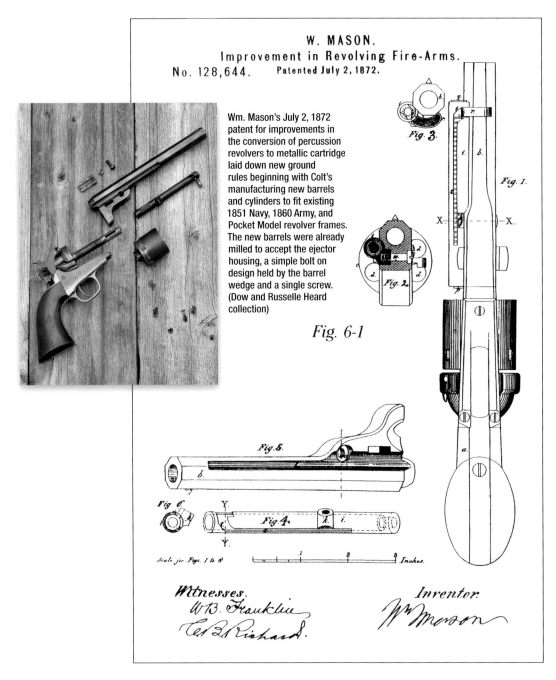

W. MASON.
Improvement in Revolving Fire-Arms.
No. 128,644.   Patented July 2, 1872.

Wm. Mason's July 2, 1872 patent for improvements in the conversion of percussion revolvers to metallic cartridge laid down new ground rules beginning with Colt's manufacturing new barrels and cylinders to fit existing 1851 Navy, 1860 Army, and Pocket Model revolver frames. The new barrels were already milled to accept the ejector housing, a simple bolt on design held by the barrel wedge and a single screw. (Dow and Russelle Heard collection)

Fig. 6-1

rebounding firing pin, and the number of steps necessary to modify the barrel, and assemble and mount the new ejector housing.

In comparison to the simple Remington New Model Army conversions, the Richards Type I was a far more dashing and innovative design worthy of the Colt name, but it was also becoming clear to Colt's management that a less costly approach was necessary. In 1872, William Mason introduced an improved design that simplified the conversion process. Mason's *Improvements in Revolving Fire-Arms* was patented on July 2, 1872. In the interim, however, Richards introduced a second version utilizing a new Mason-designed breechplate and a firing pin riveted to the hammer. Often called the Transition Richards or Type II, this second variation, produced c.1872, reduced production costs, though it still retained the cartridge ejector of the Type I. The short-lived Type II depleted remaining inventory while Colt's prepared to introduce the all-new Richards-Mason line, which would be expanded to include the 1851 Navy, 1861 Navy, and Pocket pistols beginning in 1872-73.

The dates for both the Richards and the Mason patents July 25, 1871 and July 2, 1872 appeared on the left side of the frame on all Transition Richards conversions. Only produced for a short time they are among the rarest of Colt cartridge conversions.

Richards-Mason Conversions

Simplicity is defined as, "the state, quality, or an instance of being simple," a fairly broad interpretation that suits a variety of objects and individuals. It is the second definition, however, that exemplifies William Mason's 1872 patent for *Improvements in Revolving Fire-Arms*, "Freedom from complexity." Mason took a more pragmatic approach to this design. While Richards' 1871 patent for *Improvements in Revolvers* was based on the 1860 Army, Mason chose one of Colt's oldest models as the foundation, the 1851 Navy. A simple gun evolved from the earliest Dragoons it was the most prolific and popular revolver then in existence.

Mason's design was not based solely on the conversion of 1851 Navy revolvers but as the patent drawings illustrate, production utilizing newly manufactured components for the barrel, cylinder, and breechplate. What was to become the Richards-Mason conversion was a combination of three U.S. Patents, No. 11746 (July 25, 1871, by C.B. Richards), No. 119048

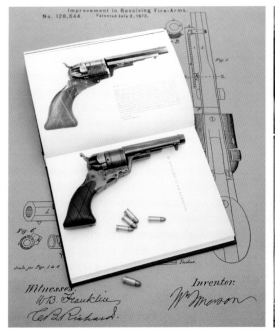

(September 19, 1871, by C. B. Richards), and No. 128644 (July 2, 1872 by William Mason, assigned to Colt's). Specifications of the latter called for "an efficient means of rotating the breech; also, for the application to the pistol of a conveniently-arranged shell ejector." This was to be the principal feature of both percussion conversions and newly manufactured cartridge models utilizing percussion parts. While that may sound the same, the applications were entirely different.

Factory production of the Richards-Mason cartridge models encompassed Colt's entire range of percussion revolvers, but just as with the Richards conversions, it began with the 1860 Army, this time utilizing remaining inventory (frames and internal parts), combined with new production barrels, cartridge cylinders, and the Mason breech ring and ejector.

The key to Colt's reduction in assembly costs was a new S-lug barrel design, manufactured with a channel for the ejector housing, and a recess (forward of the wedge opening) into which a threaded stud on the Mason ejector housing was inserted and fastened to the lug by a screw passing from the right side of barrel.

The second cost cutting measure was the Richards-Mason breech ring, which was cut away at the top, providing either a tapering hole through which a hammer-mounted firing pin could pass for centerfire models, or an off center notch on the left, for rimfire cartridges. This new design also eliminated the costly Richards Type I rebounding firing pin and integral breech ring rear sight, thereby allowing the use of original percussion-style hammers with the "V- notched" hammer sight.

All 1860 Army conversions were chambered for .44 caliber centerfire cartridges. This was an interesting choice considering that the new 1871-72 Open Top, which *preceded* the Richards-Mason Army into production, was based on an 1860 Army-style frame, (without the rebated cylinder step cut) but chambered exclusively for .44 caliber Henry rimfire cartridges! Thus in 1872 Colt's had two entirely different large caliber cartridge models in production.

Not regarded as a conversion, the 1871-72 Open Top model was Colt's first all-new cartridge revolver. The design did away with the need for a breechplate and cut down cylinder, and that

An open loading gate shows how much of the recoil shield had to be cut away for a loading and unloading channel. The depth was such that the cylinder ratchet was exposed. (Dow and Russelle Heard collection)

Navy Caliber Pocket Models were popular with engravers because the octagon barrel lug flats provided more surface area for engraving. (Dow and Russelle Heard collection)

It is estimated that of the 2,200 Richards-Mason 1861 Navy models built, 1,200 were percussion pistols returned to Colt's for conversion. Serial number ranges for percussion models are below 10356 (most with four digit serial numbers) the majority of which were returned by the U. S. Navy Ordnance Bureau in 1873, 1875, and 1876 for alteration on contract.

Navy-Navy conversions were martially marked, the same as 1851 Navy-Navy models. The left side of the frame was stamped **COLTS** on all conversions, and

PATENT

–PAT. JULY 25, 1871 .–
–PAT. JULY 2, 1872 .–

on most examples. As with the 1851 Navy-Navy conversions, the patent dates on 1861 Navy-Navy models were stamped to the immediate right of, or slightly over printing the **COLTS/PATENT** marking. On factory produced cartridge models the two line patent dates were added to the left side of the frame and the **COLTS/PATENT** stamping eliminated.

The barrel addresses on all 1861 Navy models, regardless of whether a percussion conversion or original metallic cartridge model read:

– ADDRESS COL. SAM_L COLT NEW-YORK U.S. AMERICA –

The 1861 Navy was easier to manufacture since Colt's had an abundant supply of barrels, thereby eliminating the time and expense of producing new conversion barrels. This had become necessary for the Richards-Mason 1860 Army and 1851 Navy conversions after Colt's remaining Civil War inventory of these pieces had been depleted, while frames remained abundant.

For 1861 Navy cartridge conversions the barrel loading lever and plunger channels and lever latch dovetail were plugged and machined to blend into the surrounding surfaces. A channel was milled into the right side of the barrel for the ejector housing and a hole drilled and counter-bored for the mounting stud and screw.

The 1861 Navy conversions, like their 1851 counterparts, were produced in three variations: those converted from original percussion revolvers, factory built examples utilizing remaining percussion inventory, and those converted outside the Colt factory.

As had been the case with the 1851 Navy conversions, both internal spring and external spring loading gates were used on the 1861 Navy models, the latter noted by the stem of the spring leaf being screwed into the side of the frame below the gate. Earlier models were fitted with external springs and succeeded by the internal spring design as production continued into the 1870s. Colt's exhausted its old inventory of percussion hammers in mid-1872, after which new

or the Hartford address:
– ADDRESS SAM_L COLT HARTFORD CT. –

The Hartford address is usually seen on percussion models converted in the serial number range 74000 to 101000. Later percussion models and original cartridge models were stamped with the Type II address:
– ADDRESS COL. SAML COLT NEW-YORK U.S. AMERICA –

The Other Navy

The 1861 Navy makes the most elegant of all Colt cartridge conversions. More than 2,000 were produced, about 400 chambered for .38 caliber rimfire and 1,800 for centerfire rounds, the latter beginning after August 1873 when .38 caliber central fire cartridges became readily available. Notes R. L. Wilson, "[In addition] about 100 rimfire and 100 centerfire revolvers are estimated to have been field conversions. As a rule of thumb, pistols in the U.S. Navy marked serial number range [approximately numbers 1500 through 9800] are centerfire, as are specimens in the Colt factory produced series in the range number 1400 to 3300. Colt factory produced series revolvers from number 1 through approximately 1400 are usually rimfire."

hammers with distinctive bordered and underlined knurling on their spurs were used on Navy conversions. The new conversions also had a larger diameter hammer screw. All later models bore the two line patent date, which was stamped on the left side of the frame.

The 1861 Navy factory conversions have 7-$\frac{1}{2}$ inch barrels with slightly crowned muzzles. Field conversions were sometimes fitted with shortened barrels measuring 5-$\frac{1}{2}$ inches, a popular length for lawmen and those feeling the need to clear leather a little faster.

An interesting and often confusing stamping on most Navy conversions is the .36 caliber mark on the left side of the triggerguard flat, which is a holdover from the percussion era and was not changed when Colt's started producing original .38 caliber cartridge models. It is not unusual to see **.38** stamped over the **.36** on some conversion triggerguards.

With both centerfire and rimfire versions produced, it is important to note that there were two different styles of centerfire firing pins in use on the 1861 Navy. The more common is known as the cone-type, which was threaded into the hammer face, whereas the narrow blade-type pin, cut into the hammer face and secured by two lateral rivets, is seen less often. All rimfire conversions were for the civilian market and all military conversions were centerfire.

One of the most popular models of its time, the 1861 Navy remains a highly desirable Colt conversion among present-day collectors. Nickel or silver plated examples are prized and engraved and cased models extremely rare. Most were produced by Schuyler, Hartley and Graham of New York City, and engraved by Louis D. Nimschke.

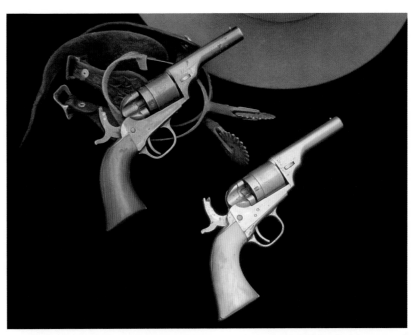

The most popular percussion Pocket Pistol and conversion was the Model 1849. The frames were used with new Round Cartridge Barrels and new cylinders all the way through the early 1880s. The easiest model to build, the 1849 conversions did not have loading gates, and most came with the short 3-$\frac{1}{2}$ inch barrel. Nickel finishes and ivory grips were common. (Dow and Russelle Heard collection)

Conversions for Small Frame Colts
The Richards and Richards-Mason Pocket Pistols

There were certain individuals who, because of their nature or line of work, preferred to carry smaller, lighter weight revolvers, often concealed in a vest or trouser pocket, or kept close at hand in a small California Pattern holster. The cartridge conversion Pocket Pistol became a favorite among lawmen as well as an assortment of nefarious characters: gamblers, highwaymen, and desperados desiring a "hide-away" gun; a gun no less deadly than its medium frame counterpart, as most were chambered for .38 rimfire or centerfire cartridges. The Pocket Pistol was also a favored equalizer for women; good women, bad women, and some very bad women. Thus the small, 5-shot, .38 caliber Police and Navy, 1849 Pocket, and even a Paterson conversion or two, had been woven into the fabric of the Old West by the mid 1870s.

R. L. Wilson notes, that for collectors, Colt Pocket Pistols comprise the most exasperating and complex group of cartridge conversions. "Serial num-

ber ranges encountered are three—the range of the Navy, Police, and 1849 Pocket, and a special range [of new production or original metallic cartridge models] from #1 through approximately #19000. Furthermore, several basic barrel types were employed; loading gates and ejection rods may or may not be present; iron and brass straps were used; barrel and frame markings vary; *et cetera, ad infinitum.*"

There are almost as many variations as there are guns, chambered for both rimfire and centerfire rounds, with barrel lengths of 3-inches, 3-$\frac{1}{2}$ inches, 4-$\frac{1}{2}$ inches, 5-$\frac{1}{2}$ inches and 6-$\frac{1}{2}$ inches.

In all, approximately 25,000 Colt Pocket Pistols were either manufactured as original cartridge models or converted to metallic cartridge at the same time Colt's was manufacturing the 1873 Peacemaker, the New Line Pocket revolver, and the Double Action Lightening models.

"From a review of the above facts," notes Wilson, "it is obvious that Colt's had over produced on percussion parts, and was not about to see these wasted

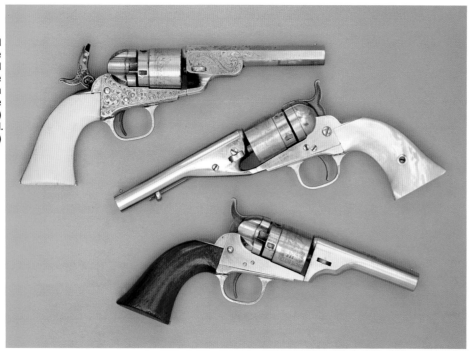

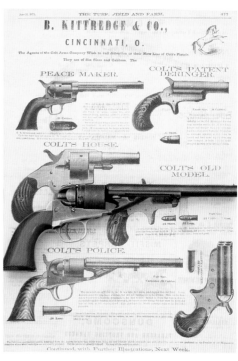

The three principal Pocket Model cartridge conversions; Navy Model with octagon barrel, Police Model with conversion barrel, and Pocket Frame (Navy, Police, or 1849) with the new S-Lug barrel. (Photo courtesy R. L. Wilson)

Far right: A Police conversion sits atop a newspaper ad c.1875. The price for the guns was $14. (Roger Muckerheide collection)

as scrap." Thus Colt's proliferation of Pocket Pistols extended well beyond any other percussion conversion models.

Pocket conversions break down into three fundamental categories: 1862 Police, 1865 Pocket Model of Navy Caliber (the so-called Pocket Navy) and newly manufactured Round Cartridge Barrel models. This provides a starting point for cataloging a variety of individual variations produced either as new cartridge revolvers or percussion conversions between 1873 and the early 1880s.

The first category, manufactured between 1873 and 1875 in an estimated total of 4,000 examples, is the 1865 Pocket Model of Navy Caliber with either 3-inch or 4-1/2 inch octagon barrel. The Navy conversions were 5-shot percussion revolvers, re-chambered for .38 caliber rimfire (although a few are known to have been reconverted to .38 centerfire).

The Navy conversions did not have cartridge ejectors, and were produced both with and without loading gates. The rebated cylinders bore the traditional roll engraved stagecoach holdup scene, and barrels were marked with the Type II address. New production Pockets had the two-line patent dates stamped on the left side of the frame, whereas original percussion conversions bore the earlier **COLT'S PATENT** stamp. However, some small frame conversions had no markings at all.

The second variation of the Navy featured the Mason cartridge ejector and an octagon percussion barrel turned round. It was produced in both .38 Colt Long centerfire and rimfire versions, and available with 4-1/2, 5-1/2, or 6-1/2 inch barrels. With the octagon barrel turned round, a distinctive barrel lug contour, and Mason ejector housing, the round barrel Pocket Navy conversions are the least common of all Richard-Mason Pocket models. It is estimated that no more than 2,000 were manufactured.

The 1862 Police model was another ideal candidate for conversion to the metallic cartridge. Approximately 6,500 conversions were produced between 1873 and 1875 and offered in either .38 rimfire or .38 centerfire. The conversion process was almost identical to that of the Navy. The loading lug and rammer channels were plugged, along with the loading lever latch dovetail. Percussion barrels in 4-1/2, 5-1/2, or 6-1/2 inch lengths were milled to fit the Mason patent ejector, the cylinders cut down and bored through, and the frame fitted with the Richards Type IV conversion ring (for small frame revolvers).

Interestingly, the majority of Police conversions, those built between 1872 and 1874, were assembled with round, rebated Navy-style cylinders, and chambered primarily for rimfire cartridges.

The original half-fluted 1862 Police percussion cylinders had proven less adaptable to conversion than the round, rebated Navy cylinders, which could better tolerate the higher pressures generated by cartridge loads. Additionally, when the supply of original 1862 Police percussion cylinders was exhausted, it was easier and less costly for Colt's to utilize one cylinder design for all Pocket models. With few exceptions, the round, rebated Navy cylinder was then used on *all* late model Pocket Pistol conversions. (This does not include original percussion models sent to Colt's for conversion, in which case the half-fluted cylinder would have been reused).

One version that left no one in doubt as to its origins was the new Round Cartridge Barrel Pocket Pistol with ejector and loading gate. Produced from 1873 to 1875, this compact, 5-shot revolver was fitted with a new production S-Lug barrel available in lengths of 4-$\frac{1}{2}$, 5-$\frac{1}{2}$, and 6-$\frac{1}{2}$ inches, and chambered for either .38 rimfire or .38 centerfire calibers. All Round Cartridge Barrel models were stamped with the

COLT'S PT.F.A. MFG.Co
HARTFORD CT. U.S.A.

barrel address and the Richards-Mason patent dates were stamped on the left side of the frame.

Another variation of the Round Cartridge Barrel revolver was fitted with a 3-$\frac{1}{2}$ inch barrel, no ejector, or loading gate and built on the Police, Navy and 1849 frames.

As mentioned earlier, the Model 1849 was the most popular Colt percussion pistol ever produced, a favorite of miners and sod busters during the California Gold Rush, the most commonly carried "back up" gun among Union and Confederate soldiers during the Civil War, and in the 1870s the most enduring of all Colt cartridge conversions.

Most conversions in the 1849 serial ranges (approximately #274000 to 328000, an estimated 4,000 guns) were produced from 1876 to 1880. These are extremely interesting specimens because the 1849 was originally chambered for a .31 caliber lead ball, whereas the 1862 Police and Navy were originally .36 caliber. Yet when they were converted to metallic cartridge, the 1849 models were chambered the same as Police and Navy models: .38 caliber. During the conversion, the 1849 Model frames were notched (stepped) to permit the use of a new .38 caliber rebated cylinder. All 1849 conversions retained the **.31 CAL.** stamp on the left side of the trigger guard shoulder, though many were re-stamped with an **8** overprinting the **1**.

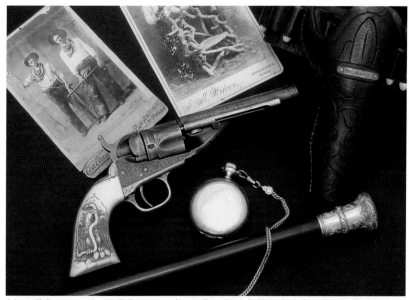

A beautifully engraved early Police conversion attributed to L.D. Nimschke. Carved eagle and snake ivory grips add the finishing touches. Chambered for .38 centerfire (they were also available in rimfire), the gun is accompanied with a hand tooled holster and belt by Freund & Bros. (Calvin Patrick collection)

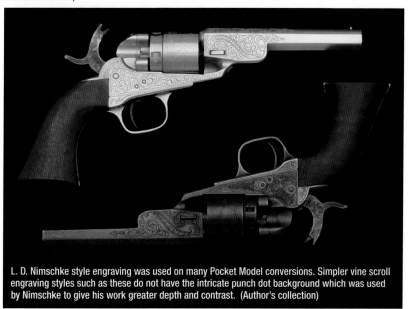

L. D. Nimschke style engraving was used on many Pocket Model conversions. Simpler vine scroll engraving styles such as these do not have the intricate punch dot background which was used by Nimschke to give his work greater depth and contrast. (Author's collection)

It took Colt's more than a decade to deplete its inventory of percussion frames, during which time new cylinders and barrels were produced to continue production of cartridge models based on Civil War era guns. Even with the advent of the Single Action Army in 1873, and later models such as the 1877 Lightening double action revolver in .38 and .41 caliber, demand for the less costly and just as reliable conversion models remained high into the late 1870s, and for the Pocket Models until 1882-83 when Colt's finally ran out of parts. (Dow and Russelle Heard collection)

Having been the best-selling Colt percussion model ever built, there were an abundance of 1849 frames and parts on hand well into the 1870s. This was the most compact and lightest weight of all Pocket Pistol conversions. More reasonably priced than other models, owing to its simple construction (no loading gate or ejector), it remained in production through the early 1880s.

Production of Pocket conversion parts spanned two distinct periods: between 1871 and 1875, and again as percussion inventory began to dwindle, from 1877 to 1879. Models produced throughout both periods are distinguished by a number of specific characteristics. Dished lugs and plugged loading lever channels on Navy models clearly indicate a percussion conversion, whereas any Navy model with a solid lug barrel is an original metallic cartridge pistol. All Police conversions had percussion barrels with the loading lever channels and lever catch dovetail plugged and refinished to blend with the surrounding surfaces. These were produced from existing percussion inventory.

Barrel addresses on both Police and Navy models were either the single line address:

ADDRESS COL. SAML COLT NEW-YORK U.S. AMERICA.

or original two-line address:

ADDRESS SAML COLT
HARTFORD CT.

This trio of Police Models shows an original half fluted rebated cylinder conversion and two later conversions done with the Navy Caliber roll engraved rebated round cylinder. All there are rimfire models. (Dow and Russelle Heard collection)

Far left: The Old West was populated by some rough characters on both sides of the law, and Colt's small frame conversions were popular to both lawmen and the lawless. Pictured with their period holsters are, clockwise: an 1862 Police in .38 Colt rimfire; another Police model holstered; a nickel plated Navy Model with turned round barrel and ivory grips; a Navy conversion with the Round Cartridge barrel; and an 1862 Police. (Calvin Patrick collection)

The new S-lug round cartridge barrels or turned round barrels bore the later two-line address:

COLT'S PT. F.A. MFG. Co
HARTFORD. CT. U.S.A.

A fourth variation covers those models built in England, which bear the London address:

ADDRESS SAML COLT
LONDON

Solid lug Round Cartridge Barrels were produced after the supply of percussion 1862 Police and Navy barrels were exhausted, sometime around 1874. They were manufactured in 3-¹/₂, 5-¹/₂and 6-¹/₂inch lengths with total production estimated at 7,500 between 1874 and 1879.

Turned round barrels were originally octagon percussion barrels re-machined by Colt's for the Pocket Navy conversions and offered in barrel lengths of 4-¹/₂, 5-¹/₂ and 6-¹/₂ inches. It is not exactly clear why Colt's chose to do this, but turned round barrel production overlapped the introduction of the solid S-Lug Round Cartridge Barrels, thus it could be assumed this was done to deplete the remaining percussion barrel inventory by making them look similar to the new Round Cartridge barrels. Approximately 1,200 to 2,000 turned round barrel models were produced c.1873-74.

The design of Pocket Pistol loading gates, when loading gates were fitted, followed those of the Richards-Mason 1851 Navy and 1861 Navy, using both internal and external spring designs. Breechplates also followed the large frame configuration, with a convex/concave fit to the recoil shield, and replacement of the single tooth percussion revolver hand with the new double tooth conversion hand.

Pocket model hammers were incised to seat either a rimfire pin on the left side of the hammer, or a wedge-type pin notched into the hammer face for centerfire models. The firing pins on both versions were secured to the hammer by two rivets. On a few centerfire conversions a cone-type firing pin screwed into the hammer face was also used, however, the wedge-type is the most commonly seen. The majority of Pocket Pistols appear to have been chambered for rimfire cartridges.

As previously mentioned, most Pocket Pistols had both patent dates stamped on the left side of the frame, while conversions from percussion pistols bore the **COLT'S PATENT** or **COLTS PATENT** frame stamping. On later production Navy models with the 4-1/2 inch barrel and 1862 Police and original metallic cartridge models, the Richards-Mason patent dates are stamped without the dashes:

PAT. JULY 25. 1871.
PAT. JULY 2. 1872.

Two more variations of the 1862 Police, an early turned round percussion barrel (top) with its distinctive lug profile, and a later model fitted with a new Richards-Mason patented S-lug barrel. (Dow and Russelle Heard collection)

Far right: Another Colt from south of the border, this one a converted c.1865 Pocket Model of Navy Caliber chambered in .38 rimfire and fitted with the external spring loading gate. It is pictured with a rather interesting holster, a quarter flap Mexican holster featuring yucca or cactus fiber embroidery. Once again the very popular carved eagle and snake ivory grips. (Dow and Russelle Heard collection)

On turned round barrel Pocket Navy models and on all solid lug barrel models, the patent dates appear with the dashes in front of and behind each date, however, without the period after 1871.

- PAT. JULY 25. 1871 -

- PAT. JULY 2. 1872. -

It should be further noted that on some late production Model 1862 Police and Navy conversions, and on cartridge revolvers with ejectors and loading gates, that the top patent date stamp was the same as seen on early Single Action Army revolvers.

PAT. SEPT. 19. 1871.

PAT. JULY 2. 1872.

As with the turned round Navy barrels, there is no documented explanation for this change in manufacturing. The **SEPT. 19. 1871** patent date appeared on early Peacemakers approximately within the serial number range of 25 to 22000, which according to *Colt's Dates Of Manufacture* by R. L. Wilson would cover the period from 1873 to 1876.

Pocket Pistols, perhaps by the nature of their smaller size, were more often engraved and finished with nickel or silver plating than large frame Colt conversions. Some of the finest embellishments appear on Colt Police and Navy models, both from the percussion era and throughout the 1870s and 1880s.

The Pocket Pistols rang down the curtain on the cartridge conversion era, being both the last percussion models introduced by Colt's and the last to be converted for the metallic cartridge. For more than a decade the Richards-Mason patents broadened Colt's entire product range by making available a cartridge conversion for every percussion model built from the 1851 Navy to the 1865 Pocket Model of Navy Caliber. For those venturing West in the 1870s, a Colt cartridge revolver became one of the most important of all worldly possessions.

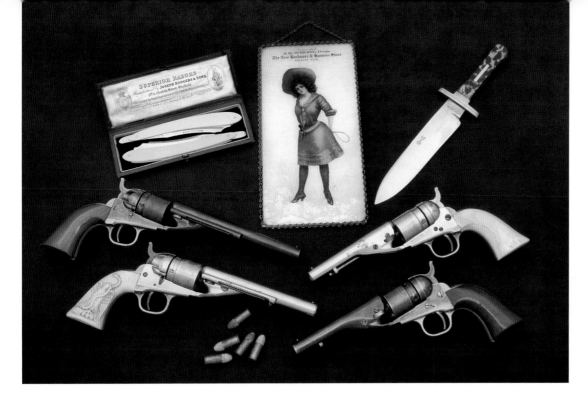

At six foot two, with reddish brown hair, a broad mustache and penetrating blue eyes, which he later remarked were actually hazel, Stoudenmire favored liquor, women, and dancing, and had little trouble making both friends and enemies alike. After a year serving with the Texas Rangers as a Second Sergeant in the famed A Company, he drifted from town to town finally migrating to the Texas Panhandle with his brother-in-law and former Texas Ranger, Stanley M. "Doc" Cummings. After briefly operating a sheep ranch, by 1881 Dallas, Doc and Virginia Stoudenmire Cummings were heading for El Paso.

In 1881, El Paso was a struggling border town. Law, what there was of it, was mostly a succession of City Marshals allied with one outlaw faction or another, the proverbial wolf guarding the hen house. Stoudenmire's imposing build, short temper and quick gun hand had already created something of a reputation in Southern Texas and the Mayor pro-tem of El Paso, along with the city aldermen, believed that a man like Stoudenmire could be the answer to their problems. Early in 1881 he was installed as City Marshal against the wishes of some aldermen who believed he was as dangerous as the criminals they sought to rid themselves of, and in some respects they were right. Stoudenmire himself admitted in an 1882 newspaper interview, "I have had a number of difficulties in my life…but my troubles have always been on the side of law and order…" He characterized his mistakes as those of the head, "not of the heart."

Every Town Marshal who had preceded him had done little to enforce any laws and most had been drunks, including Stoudenmire's immediate predecessor William "Bill" Johnson. His first job as the new Marshal of El Paso was to dismiss Johnson, who usually hung out just a few steps away from Frank Manning's saloon. The Mannings were clearly on one side of that line dividing law abiding citizens from criminals. The outlaw base of operations for horse thieves and cattle rustlers around El Paso was the Manning ranch owned by brothers James,

A Man And His Colt Conversions – The Life and Times Of Dallas Stoudenmire

The line that divided lawmen from the lawless was often indistinguishable on the Western Frontier and Dallas Stoudenmire walked that line until he was murdered on the streets of El Paso in 1882.

A Southern Gentleman born in Macon County, Alabama in 1845, Dallas Stoudenmire regarded the carrying out of the law as purely black and white, and though he had his own demons, when challenged by scofflaws, drunks, rustlers, and gunmen, he dispensed quick justice from the muzzles of two 1860 Army revolvers converted to fire .44 caliber metallic cartridges.

The pair of Richards-Mason Colts was a gift from a friend. Stoudenmire had one modified, removing the ejector housing from the right side of the barrel and having the length cut down from 8-inches to 2-⁷/₈ inches. This gun he carried in his left trouser pocket. Being left handed it was a quick draw gun without either an ejector or front sight to snag on his clothes. The other Colt with 8-inch barrel was carried butt forward in his right pocket for a cross draw. Stoudenmire preferred to carry his brace of side arms in this fashion, rather than use a conventional holster.

John, and Frank. Another brother George Felix "Doc" Manning, a practicing physician, joined them in 1881. Together they controlled most of the trafficking in stolen cattle, and owned the Coliseum Saloon and Variety Theater on El Paso Street.

In a drunken stupor Bill Johnson refused to hand over the keys to the jail to Stoudenmire, who loomed menacingly over the man. Johnson finally pulled a ring from his pocket and began fumbling. Losing his patience Dallas shouted "Damn you, I want them now!" then he grabbed Johnson shook him violently and tore the key ring from his hand. The ex-Marshal stood dumbfounded and embarrassed by this public dressing down. Dallas had unknowingly made an enemy not only of Johnson but of the Manning brothers, who had supported Johnson's appointment to City Marshal.

Stoudenmire began patrolling El Paso's streets daily, his tall figure clothed in dark trousers, vest and frockcoat, a shining badge on his lapel and the

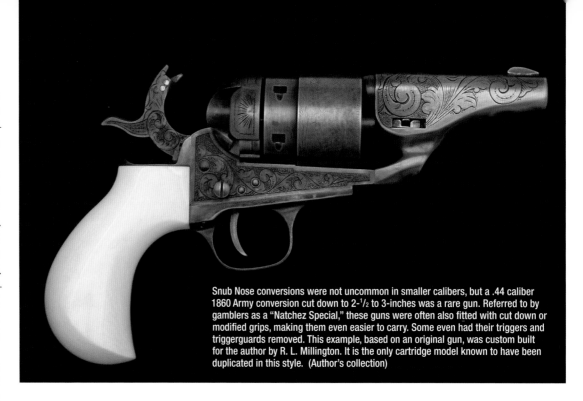

Snub Nose conversions were not uncommon in smaller calibers, but a .44 caliber 1860 Army conversion cut down to 2-1/2 to 3-inches was a rare gun. Referred to by gamblers as a "Natchez Special," these guns were often also fitted with cut down or modified grips, making them even easier to carry. Some even had their triggers and triggerguards removed. This example, based on an original gun, was custom built for the author by R. L. Millington. It is the only cartridge model known to have been duplicated in this style. (Author's collection)

pair of Colts in his pockets. He was a man who could not be bought or bribed, and already there was talk that things were going to have to change around town. Killers and ne'er-do-wells peered over saloon doors and wondered about their future. Until now there had never been any real law in El Paso.

Doc Cummings and Virginia started a new career opening The Globe Restaurant on El Paso Street, which soon became the finest eatery in town. While Dallas was having lunch one afternoon at The Globe, a fight broke out on the street between Constable Gus Krempkau and two other men. In a matter of moments gunfire erupted and Krempkau lie dying in the street. Dallas came bolting through the restaurant door, Doc Cummings right behind carrying a scattergun. Stoudenmire took aim and fired at Krempkau's assailant but his first shot missed and hit an innocent bystander. The second round landed squarely in the head of its intended target, cattle rustler John Hale. George Campbell, another miscreant and former El Paso Marshal, who had instigated the shootout, watched as Stoudenmire shot Hale down. He drew his own gun to warn him off but before he could say a word Dallas dropped him with a single shot. The whole affair had lasted no more than a minute from beginning to end. The Manning brothers regarded Campbell and Hale as friends and took their being gunned down by Stoudenmire personally. It was high time, they decided, to assassinate El Paso's hardnosed new lawman!

They enlisted Bill Johnson as a dupe in their plan, plied him with whisky and urged him to seek revenge for losing his job and being cuffed by Stoudenmire in public. The events unfolded over a period of hours on Sunday, April 17, 1881. An anonymous message was received by the Marshal notifying him to get out of town "or be dead before another sun rises over the city." He laughed it off but that evening changed his usual routine for patrolling El Paso's streets. After his usual drink or two at The Globe he began his walk, only this time with Doc Cummings at his side packing a brace of pistols in his pockets as well. Stoudenmire suspected any attempt on his life would take place close to the Manning's saloon.

Johnson was sitting in the shadows across the street from the Coliseum Saloon with a scattergun in one hand and a bottle of courage in the other. As Stoudenmire and Cummings approached, Johnson got too anxious and fired prematurely, missing both men, who wheeled around and together put eight bullets into the ex-City Marshal before the echo of the shotgun blasts had faded. The Manning brothers however, had not put all their faith in Johnson. Moments later shots rang out from the vicinity of their saloon. To everyone's surprise, rather than seeking cover, Stoudenmire turned and charged straight across the street at his attackers, both guns blazing away. His would-be assassins, perhaps in awe of such bravado, decided to retreat.

In the hail of lead Dallas had been shot; a stray bullet hitting him in the heel. He was helped to the side of the street while Cummings retrieved a rifle and gathered a vigilante committee to clean out the assassins in the Manning's saloon. "Let's go kill the damn sons-of-bitches," he roared. But there was no one left to kill. They all had fled.

Stoudenmire was taken to the Ranger Camp where he spent a week recovering from his injury. In the interim the Texas Rangers swept in to preserve law and order until the Marshal returned on April 24. Stoudenmire's deputies were mostly ex-Texas Rangers who came and went with regularity, the only one who stayed on was James B. Gillett, who assisted in solving several cases of robbery and murder in El Paso.

In early February 1882 both Dallas and Gillett came down with influenza and were confined to bed. Though he was up in a few days, Stoudenmire was feeling weak and the doctor suggested he take some time off and recuperate fully in Columbus, Texas. This transpired while Doc Cummings, who had been temporarily deputized to help track a suspect into Mexico, was out of town. When he returned to find his brother-in-law away and Gillett still incapacitated, he took it upon himself to police El Paso. This was the beginning of the end. His grudge with the Manning brothers, who Doc correctly believed had been behind the attempt on Dallas's life, overrode his better judgment and he headed for the Coliseum Saloon where he goaded Jim Manning into a gunfight. When it was over, Cummings lay dead on El Paso Street with Manning claiming self defense. Doc had been shot twice, yet Manning's Colt had only been discharged once. The Coroner's jury concluded that Cummings had been shot once by Jim Manning, and once by a person unknown. But most everyone knew the person unknown had to have been Manning's bartender David King. Manning was charged with murder and Doc Cummings was laid to rest on February 18, one week before Stoudenmire was to return. The murder case never came to trial.

The death of Doc hit Dallas hard. He was more than a brother-in-law; he had been his best friend. Bent on revenge, Stoudenmire began drinking heavily and making threatening comments in public to the Manning brothers. When El Paso City Councilman Noah Flood, a former San Francisco Prosecuting Attorney, tried to "instruct" the Marshal in big city law enforcement, Dallas picked up the alderman and drop-kicked him out of his office onto the street.

One Sunday morning the Right Reverend Mr. Tays reflected on the drinking habits of the City Marshal in his sermon, which so angered Stoudenmire that he emptied both his revolvers into the steeple bell that night awakening the entire town. His heavy drinking finally caught up with him in March when he was too sick with alcoholic jitters to perform his duties. The city council quickly moved to temporarily replace him with Deputy Marshal Gillett. Stoudenmire returned in April but his problems with the aldermen were just beginning. It had been un-

One of a handful of portraits known of U.S. Deputy Marshal Dallas Stoudenmire, this picture was taken in El Paso c.1881 while he was serving as town Marshal. Always well dressed, he preferred to carry his guns in his pockets, which were said to be leather lined. His favorite was a cut down Richards-Mason 1860 Army with an S-lug barrel, no ejector and no front sight. (Photo of Dallas Stoudenmire courtesy University of Oklahoma Western History Collection)

covered that he was also a U.S. Deputy Marshal, which was in conflict with his position as City Marshal. On his behalf Stoudenmire defended this by explaining he was only given the position so that he could carry a six-shooter in the territory of New Mexico. Nevertheless, the faction of the council that already had enough of Stoudenmire used this infraction as a means to vote him out of office. A new City Marshall, W. W. Mills was nominated by the council and seconded. But before a moment passed, Dallas Stoudenmire was also nominated by another member of the council and this too was seconded! They were deadlocked. The tie was broken by the Mayor, who voted for Stoudenmire.

One might have thought Dallas would be on his best behavior after that but his drinking and the feud with the Manning brothers continued. On May 27, 1882 the city council again convened to ask for his resignation. Two days later a sober and calm Dallas Stoudenmire resigned as El Paso's Marshal. The position was filled by Deputy Marshal James B. Gillett. While everyone heaved a sigh of relief they had no idea what was about to happen. Dallas was not really out of a job, not financially, as Doc had left him The Globe Restaurant, and not legally, on July 13, 1882 he was appointed United States Deputy Marshal for the Southern District of Texas, with headquarters in El Paso!

Dallas spent part of his time as a U.S. Deputy Marshal in the territory of New Mexico and on occasion working for the Santa Fe Railroad to prevent and detect train robberies. At a reception hosted by the Santa Fe in Hot Springs, New Mexico, in September 1882, Stoudenmire was asked about his difficulties being the Marshal of El Paso, Texas.

"I was pretty nigh single handed against the town," he told them, "and everybody trying to get the drop on me to kill me. It got so that if a man had a charge in his gun he wanted to get rid of, he'd wait around the corner and fire it into me. I don't mind a shooting scrape when it comes; it was the suspense that wore on me. I never knew when I might be attacked unawares. It might happen in a railroad train or anywhere that I chance to be. I've had the offer of two different city marshalships this week. I don't know what I'll do about them. Go back to El Paso maybe when I get straightened up." Go back to El Paso is what he did and it was to be the last thing he would ever do.

Dallas returned to El Paso on Sunday night September 17, 1882. He had been drinking all day and was coming into town to serve a warrant. He went

Stoudenmire had four law enforcement careers, first as a Texas Ranger with A-Company, then U.S. Deputy Marshal and City Marshal of El Paso, Texas, and finally as a U.S. Deputy Marshal for the Southern District of Texas. He once said, "I was pretty nigh single handed against the town and everybody trying to get the drop on me to kill me." The letter under the gun was written by Stoudenmire's sister Virginia protesting the acquittal of his murderers, and that of her husband and Stoudenmire's best friend, Doc Cummings in 1882. Virginia Stoudenmire Cummings believed that the killings had been planned.

Dallas Stoudenmire's cut down Richard-Mason was chambered for .44 Colt cartridges.

Locked in a struggle with Doc Manning, Dallas Stoudenmire had already been shot twice, and as he tried to gain the upper hand Doc's brother Jim came up from behind, drew a snub nose revolver without a trigger and fanned a single shot toward Stoudenmire. He missed, but before Dallas could react, Manning moved closer and shot him in the head almost at arm's length. Jim Manning was acquitted of murder because there were no witnesses except his brother, who saw nothing. Hideaway guns of this design were not uncommon among the most nefarious of Old West villains.

the Acme Saloon and ordered whiskey. Bartender . Brooks looked at Dallas and said "Why don't you ome and get in bed?"

No, I'm not going home," replied the Marshal, "in I'm going to stay up all night."

fter leaving the Acme he walked past Frank Man- 's place and stopped. He peered inside to see if the ted man was there, he wasn't, so he strolled back e Acme and poured another drink while Brooks ed the day's receipts. After closing the saloon he ked with Stoudenmire to Abbie Bell's parlor house, re they talked for awhile until Dallas decided to go d spend what was left of the night.

y morning the Manning brothers were aware that idenmire was back in El Paso and they were prepar- for a fight. Dallas headed down to the Acme around n and took a seat in the back, so he had a clear view he door. Frank Manning entered and went up to bar, ordered a drink for himself and bought one for ks, who knew what was sure to happen. "I don't t any trouble in my saloon," he said to Manning. At that Dallas rose and ked out of the Acme brushing past Frank Manning. But a few minutes later eentered followed close behind by Doc Manning. With two of his enemies he room his anger began to grow and he left once more, this time heading n the street to the Gem Saloon. Entering in a jovial mood as his hangover n the night before began to fade, he jumped up on the bar and danced along ength and then said to no one in particular, "Them sons of bitches have put a job to kill me this evening." The patrons responded with curiosity and cern, mostly for their own well being.

fter a few minutes in the Gem he headed down the street to the Pony Sa- n. It might have occurred to bystanders by now that Stoudenmire was look- for someone, and it obviously wasn't the Manning brothers. In fact, he told Jones, Brooks' partner in the Acme Saloon, that he wasn't looking for a t with the Mannings at all and was merely in El Paso to serve a warrant on eone else. When Jones returned to the Acme he told Brooks and the Man- g brothers, who were more or less relieved, neither really wanting a gunfight Stoudenmire.

hat evening Dallas asked Brooks and Jones to accompany him to the Coli- n Saloon so that everyone could take a drink and shake hands. Doc Man- was playing billiards when Stoudenmire entered, and he glanced over

pleasant enough, quickly erupted into an argument Jones stepped in pushing the two men apart to quell dispute, but it was too late. Doc Manning drew his and began firing over Jones, who dropped to the fl preventing Dallas from getting off a shot. Manni slug hit Stoudenmire in the left arm. The long barre Colt which was only half drawn went spinning ac the floor. Dallas reeled backwards toward the d as Manning fired another shot, this one with a fa powder charge had less force but still pounded i Stoudenmire's chest knocking him completely outs the saloon. The bullet, however, struck a wad of pap in his shirt and a locket with a picture of his sister ginia. Manning pursued Stoudenmire onto the bo walk ready to fire again but Dallas drew the snub n Colt and fired a shot into his assailant that took out use of his right arm and sent Doc's gun flying into street. Manning lunged at Stoudenmire grabbing l around the arms to prevent him from getting off a ond shot and as the two men grappled Jim Mann

came running up. He drew a snub nose revolver without a trigger and fan a single shot toward Stoudenmire. He missed, but before Dallas could r Manning moved in closer and shot him in the head almost at arm's len Stoudenmire's snub nose Colt fell from his hand as he collapsed. Doc Mann pounced on the dead man's body and began beating him furiously with his gun until he was pulled off by Marshal Gillett and Texas Rangers J.M. De and Ed Scotten. Gillett placed the Manning brothers under arrest for murd

The Coroner's jury could not find a witness that actually saw Jim Mann fire the shot into the Marshal's head and it was determined that he was ki by "…a shot fired from either a .44 or .45 in the hands of party unknown." El Paso District Attorney proceeded with the murder charges anyway bu separate trials the Manning brothers were found not guilty.

All that remains of Dallas Stoudenmire are photographs taken of the M shal in El Paso, the snub nose Colt and the locket that might have saved his had Jim Manning not been there to finish what he had started back in A 1881, the murder of Dallas Stoudenmire.

Our special thanks to Bob Millington of ArmSport LLC for recreating the Stoudenmire Colt and Jar H. Earle, Texas A&M University, for his pictures of the original Stoudenmire Richards-Mason revolv Primary research was conducted through the University of Oklahoma, the El Paso Public Library, the book Dallas Stoudenmire El Paso M shal by Leon C. Metz published in 1969 by University of

The 1871-72 Open Top could be regarded as the gun between the guns. Intended as a new model, being chambered only in .44 Henry rimfire deemed it from the day it ... to be dead. (Rock ...

Chapter Seven
The 1871-72 Open Top
Colt's first all-new Single Action Revolver

The Open Top was new, innovative, and virtually obsolete the day it was introduced. In Colt's haste to produce a new cartridge revolver upon the expiration of the S&W Rollin White patent, the company chose to build a model based on the venerable 1860 Army frame but with an all new barrel and cylinder design. And chamber it for what in 1871 was the most abundant metallic cartridge then in use, the Civil War surplus .44 Henry rimfire. The Henry, upon which Oliver Winchester would build his fortunes, had been used extensively during The War Between The States, and the .44 rimfire cartridges manufactured by the tens of thousands. A revolver designed to make use of those affordable war surplus cartridges seemed inspired. And for a brief time it was.

As with nearly every cartridge revolver developed by Colt' throughout the early 1870s, the Open Top bears the signatures of Charles B. Richards and William Mason. Confusion and misconception have always surrounded this historic Richards and Mason six-gun because the Open Top was neither a transitional model nor a cartridge conversion, it was a new design intended by Mason to be Colt's first original cartridge model. Its introduction in fact, preceded that of the Richards-Mason percussion conversions, and both types were produced concurrently in 1872.

Colt's experimented with several variations of the Open Top design, including models chambered for .44 centerfire, .38 centerfire, and .32 rimfire cartridges, the latter two variations often referred to as "Baby Open Top" revolvers, as they were assembled on a smaller frame, about the size of a Police or Navy model.

Although Wm. Mason and C. B. Richards built a number of experimental Open Tops in Colt's model room, the only example put into production was chambered for .44 Henry rimfire cartridges. There was a good rationale for this decision, aside from the availability of ammunition. There were also thousands

An 1871-72 Open Top played a role in one of Tom Selleck's best westerns, Louis L' Amour's *Crossfire Trail*, where Selleck's character Rafe Covington, carried this cut down 5-1/2 inch model with ivory grips. There were three identical guns used in the movie, and a fourth built for the author. All four were finished by Kenny Howell, the armorer on all of Selleck's westerns, including *Last Stand at Saber River* and *Monte Walsh*. (Author's collection)

Colt's 1871-72 Open Top was a unique design preceding the introduction of the Richards and Richards-Mason cartridge conversions. Chambered for .44 Henry rimfire cartridges, the Open Top was the first production cartridge revolver manufactured by Colt's Patent Fire-Arms Mfg. Co. A total of approximately 7,000 were produced from 1871 to 1873. (Dr. Joseph A. Murphy collection)

of solid war surplus Henry rifles, thus Colt's had decided upon a revolver that could share its ammunition with the Henry rifle. While this appears to be logical, it becomes somewhat paradoxical as in less than a year Colt's had the Richards 1860 Army conversion available chambered for .44 centerfire, a cartridge preferred over the .44 Henry rimfire by the U.S. military. Despite the availability of Henry ammunition, the Open Top was out of production by the summer of 1873, whereas the Richards and Richards-Mason Army conversions chambered for .44 centerfire cartridges would be produced until 1878. The Open Top then, was the only production casualty of the cartridge conversion era – an ironic turn of events. It would be unfair to call the 1871-72 Open Tops a failure. The limited production of approximately 7,000 examples has made them a highly collectible Colt model.

At a glance, the Open Top resembles the Richards-Mason Army, fitted with the later solid S-lug barrel, but can be quickly distinguished by the integral rear sight cast into the top of the barrel at the breech, and the full-length non-rebated .44 caliber cylinder.

Open Top barrel addresses were: — **ADDRESS COL. SAML COLT NEW-YORK U.S. AMERICA** — on all but very late production guns.

Elaborate decoration for the 1871-72 Open Tops often featured engraving by L.D. Nimschke or in the Nimschke style. Ivory grips were another feature seen frequently on Open Tops. This example, serial No. 3256 was shipped to H&D Folsom Arms Co. in New York on July 11, 1874. It is fully deluxe engraved in the Nimschke style of the 1870s by Ben lane, Jr., who also hand carved the Mexican eagle and snake ivory grips. (Dr. Joseph A. Murphy collection. Holster by Jim Barnard, Trailrider Products, Littleton, CO.)

Prototype model 1871-72 Open Top built on the Model 1860 Army revolver. Serial No. 3, the gun has an 8-inch barrel, rebated cylinder and is chambered in .44 Colt centerfire. This is the exception to all of the rules concerning the Open Top models. (Dr. Joseph A. Murphy collection)

Another exception chambered for .44 Colt centerfire, the Open Top with 5-¹/₂ inch barrel featured in Tom Selleck's film *Crossfire Trail*. (The gun was made for the movie by Kenny Howell, the copy of the holster by Jim Barnard, Trailrider Products. Author's collection)

The Open Top did not require a conversion ring as the breech area was machined directly from the recoil shield, making the loading gate a separate assembly mounted to the frame by a screw at the base of the gate. Similar to the Richards and Richards-Mason cartridge conversions, 1871-72 Open Tops utilized both the internal and external loading gate spring designs, the latter noted by the bottom of the spring leaf being screwed to the frame just above the trigger screw.

The general configuration of the Open Top frame was that of the 1860 Army without the step required by the Army's rebated cylinder. All factory-produced Open Tops had 7-¹/₂ inch barrels, although a number are seen with 5-³/₈ inch or 5-¹/₂ inch barrels cut down by their owners or by gunsmiths for retailers who wanted to offer something a little different. Shortened barrels were favored by frontier lawmen as they allowed for a quicker draw, often the difference between life and death in the untamed cow towns of the 1870s. Colt's, however, did not build any Open Top with a barrel length other than 7-¹/₂ inches.

Most of the parts for the Open Top frame and lock mechanism were interchangeable with the Richards-Mason 1860 Army conversions, and the Mason-style cartridge ejector was used as well. There were two versions

A pair of early Open Tops, one with a nickel finish (quite popular at the time) and ivory grips, and a magnificently engraved example with carved eagle and snake ivory grips. The close-up shows the rimfire firing pin riveted to the hammer. Also note the double patent dates on the frame, – PAT. JULY 25, 1871. – and – PAT. JULY 2, 1872. –. (Nickel gun Roger Muckerheide Collection and engraved gun George Jackson Collection)

of the Open Top, distinguished principally by the size of the grips. On early models, the shorter 1851 Navy-size grips were used with brass grip straps, whereas on later production the heftier 1860 Army stocks were fitted with steel grip straps. Of course, there are variations, and often at Colt's whatever was at hand was used.

There was some degree of consistency in Open Top factory stampings. All models had **.44 CAL** stamped on the left triggerguard shoulder and barrel addresses were:

— **ADDRESS COL. SAML COLT NEW-YORK U.S. AMERICA** — on all but very late production. The last examples bore the **COLT'S PT. F.A. MFG. CO. HARTFORD. CT. U.S.A.** address. And all Open Top pistols had the **COLTS PATENT** stamp on two lines on the left side of the frame.

Although the Open Top was a new design, it suffered the same disadvantages as earlier Colt revolvers: an open frame and separate barrel pinned to the cylinder arbor. Stiff competition from Remington, which had introduced a solid frame revolver back in 1858, compounded by the U.S. Ordnance Department's rejection of the Open Top as a military sidearm, finally compelled the company to abandon Samuel Colt's original design, and develop a solid frame model to compete with Remington.

As R. L. Wilson noted in *The Book Of Colt Firearms* "Bearing in mind the rejection of the Open Top by the U.S. Ordnance Department, Colt's engineers, particularly William Mason, worked feverishly to develop the successor to the Open Top…The Single Action Army was a natural evolution by combination of the best design features of the percussion, conversion and Open Top models with the necessary alterations dictated by military needs and the properties of the metallic cartridge ammunition. In 1872 the Colt Peacemaker was adopted by the U.S. Army, following a vigorous and highly competitive series of tests." The Open Top's fate was sealed.

Although Colt cartridge conversions remained in production for another decade, it was the failure of the Open Top that changed Colt's fortunes for the better. With William Mason returning to the drawing board to design an entirely new gun, Colt's would introduce as an 1873 model, the most successful Single Action revolver in American history, the Peacemaker.

This example of the Open Top with the external spring loading gate is pictured with a saddle and pommel bag-holster. (Dow and Russelle Heard Collection)

Throughout the 1860s and well into the 20th century, the most elaborately engraved Colts were those done by Charles Lewis Tiffany and Tiffany & Co. His New York firm was responsible for some highly embellished militaria beginning in 1863. Schuyler, Hartley and Graham began cataloging Tiffany-style grips in 1864 and offering them on engraved Colt revolvers. By the time the Colt Open Tops were being produced in 1871-72, engraved examples (usually by L. D. Nimschke) fitted with Tiffany grips were regarded the *ne plus ultra* of embellished firearms. The battle scene motif (one of several Tiffany designs) is the most commonly seen, if the word "common" can even be applied to a Tiffany Colt. Both of the examples shown are contemporary handcrafted copies of original Open Top Tiffany models sold through Schuyler, Hartley and Graham in the 1870s. (Private collection)

Chapter Eight
The Peacemaker
Reinventing the Colt Single Action Revolver

In one of the earliest 20th century books written about the history of Colt's, *A History of the Colt Revolver* by Charles T. Haven and Frank A. Belden with Stephen V. Grancasy (in 1940 the Curator of Arms and Armor for the Metropolitan Museum of Art), the authors described the Single Action Army by its original factory classification, the "New Model Army Metallic Cartridge Revolving Pistol." A rather cumbersome description popularly shortened to "Peacemaker" around 1873, the new Colt was also known as the "Frontier Six-Shooter." The military often used the contraction SAA. No matter what name was used the new Colt was destined to become the most successful and longest-lived design in firearms history.

The earliest technical description of the Single Action Army illustrated the differences from previous Colt single action revolvers. "The front of the frame was connected to the standing breech by a top strap over the cylinder, and the barrel was screwed into it. The cylinder was held in place by a removable pin passing through it and working in and out of the front of the frame under the barrel." Interestingly, this same wording could have been used verbatim in 1858 to describe the Remington Army Model revolver. The only technical differences was in styling and in the use of a bored through cylinder and metallic cartridges rather than percussion cap, loose powder and ball. Colt had, in effect, built a better Remington. The architect of this new gun was none other than Colt's Su-

In this artificially aged photograph the author portrays one of the many frontier lawmen who were forced into a showdown with gunfighters or criminals. A 5-1/2 inch Colt Peacemaker was often the preferred gun of choice for City Marshals and Sheriffs. (Photographed at Old Bedford Village, Bedford, Pennsylvania)

Left: Not long after the Peacemaker was issued to the U.S. Cavalry, George Armstrong Custer and the 7th Cavalry engaged Sitting Bull at Little Big Horn. Custer's entire regiment was wiped out. Pictured is a U.S. issue Model 1873 Single Action Army, however, from a period just after Little Big Horn. Very few of the guns from that battle were recovered. Custer himself was likely not even carrying a Colt on that fateful day. (Robert and Judy Millington collection)

An early Single Action Army, serial number 9076 (manufactured 1874), in .45 caliber. This is the standard configuration for the SAA with a 7-$\frac{1}{2}$ inch barrel, blued and case hardened finish, and walnut grips. This gun also has an extra cost German silver front sight. (Dr. Joseph A. Murphy collection)

Early model SAA with two line patent dates. Also note the **45 CAL** stamping on the triggerguard shoulder.

perintendent of the Armory, William Mason, who received a patent for his design on September 19, 1871. A second patent was issued on July 2, 1872 and a third on January 19, 1875. Since almost all of the first deliveries of the SAA were to the Ordnance Department, the civilian market had yet to realize the benefits of the new Colt revolver in 1873-74. Most individuals were carrying either Civil War era revolvers, Richards or Richards-Mason conversions in 1873. Few outside of the military even had a chance to see a Peacemaker.

There was a sense of both elegance and simplicity in Mason's design. Aside from frame, barrel, cylinder, and grips, the mechanics of the Peacemaker were confined to only nine parts: mainspring, hammer swivel, hammer, short sear, short sear spring, long sear, lifter with spring (operates the lifter and long sear), trigger, and trigger spring. The remaining components of the SAA were cylinder pin and retaining screw, triggerguard and backstrap, hammer roller and hammer screw, hammer cam, hand (pawl), bolt, trigger, firing pin, and ejector assembly. The exterior bore three screws in the frame (one of which was the hammer screw), the retaining screw for the cylinder arbor, and the backstrap (2) and grip strap (1) screws. When one piece grips were replaced by two-piece grips a grip screw was added to the parts list. The government continued to order SAA revolvers from 1873 to 1891, accounting for some 37,000 guns. Their longevity in service was such that no more than 2,000 were returned to the factory for refinishing, and that was in 1895-96. The government arsenal at Springfield reconditioned another 14,900 SAA in 1898, most of which were altered by the armory to barrel lengths of 5-$\frac{1}{2}$ inches.

Over the past 135 years since Single Action Army manufacturing began late in 1872, there have been very few changes to the fundamentals of the Wm. Mason design, those principally concerning improvements in ease of operation and certain variations in frame and backstrap design to accommodate special models. With only a brief period between World War II and 1955, when the Peacemaker was temporarily discontinued[1], it has been built by Colt's longer than any other revolver manufactured anywhere in the world, and remains to this day the indisputable icon of the American West.

Early Single Action Army models, also known as black powder frame models, used a retaining screw in the face of the frame to keep the cylinder pin in place. In order to take the cylinder out for cleaning the screw had to be removed first.

[1] According to R. L. Wilson and The Book of Colt Firearms, Colt's sold SAA models to the British during the war, and from 1947 to 1960 (overlapping the start of postwar production) Colt's built approximately 300 revolvers from prewar parts in the serial number range 356000 to 357000, these representing the final pre-World War II production of the Peacemaker.

The 1873 Single Action Army brought Open Top production to a hasty conclusion, but did not ring down the curtain on the cartridge conversion era, which continued until the 1880s. The legendary Peacemaker remained in production from the time of its introduction in 1873 until 1940! It was brought back in 1956 and contemporary Colt SAA models are still being built to this day. This beautifully aged Peacemaker from the 1880s is shown with a period saddle and holster. (Dow and Russelle Heard Collection)

Nickel plated finishes were first offered in 1877 as a second standard finish. This example with 4-³/₄ inch barrel has rare hand carved mother-of-pearl snake and eagle grips. (Dow and Russelle Heard Collection)

W. MASON.
Revolving Fire-Arms.

No. 158,957.

Patented Jan. 19, 1875.

Fig 6
Fig 5
Fig 3
Fig 4
Fig 1
Fig 2
Fig 7
Fig 9ª
Fig 8

Witnesses.

Wm. Mason.
Inventor
By Atty.

The Wm. Mason patent for the Single Action Army, serial No.158,957, is dated Jan. 19, 1875. This appears as the third patent date stamp on models built from 1875 until 1890 when it was changed to a two line patent date showing **PAT. Sept. 19. 1871** and **Jan. 19. 1875.**

An exceptional U.S. Martial Colt SAA with U.S. Ordnance inspector markings of Henry Nettleton and John E. Greer, Captain, U.S.A. c.1878. This .45 caliber model, serial number 48953, is in 98 percent original condition. The inspector's cartouche can be clearly seen in the grip panel JEG. The opposite panel is stamped HN. This gun was part of a shipment of 100 SAA models sent to the U.S. government on July 30, 1878. An example in this rare original condition can command upwards of $40,000 today. (Photo courtesy Greg Martin Auctions)

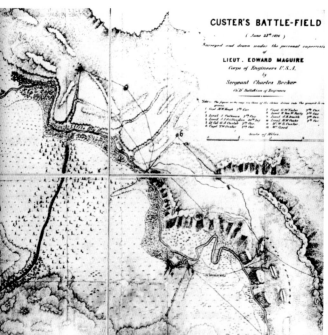

A map of the Custer battlefield drawn up to help understand what transpired shows the vast area that was covered. With the 7th Cavalry divided into three brigades, neither Major Marcus Reno nor Capt. Frederick Benteen's men could have heard the fighting taking place at Little Big Horn. Even if they had stayed together, their combined force of some 600 men would not have stood a chance against the 3,000 to 5,000 Indian warriors under Sitting Bull's command.

Far left: One of the most misunderstood characters in American Frontier history, George Armstrong Custer is often portrayed as egocentric, callous, and even foolhardy. Of the three only the latter may have truly applied to Custer; but a tendency to be foolhardy, or in one's own mind gallant, is quite often the bedrock of courage. (Photo courtesy George A. Custer Museum of the Monroe County, Michigan, Historical Museum)

Photographic proof that Custer and the 7th Cavalry were among the first to be issued the new Colt Single Action Army, this picture was taken in 1873 during the Yellowstone Expedition. Custer is holding a map while his chief scout, Bloody Knife points out their position. Both Bloody Knife and the second scout, next to Custer's dogs, are holding Peacemakers. (Photo courtesy George A. Custer Museum of the Monroe County, Michigan, Historical Museum)

With the Single Action Army having passed Ordnance Department trials at Springfield, the government placed an order for 8,000 Colt revolvers to be issued to the United States Cavalry in 1873. In his summation of the National Armory trials, John R. Edie, Captain of ordnance wrote: "I have no hesitation in declaring the Colt's revolver superior in most respects, and much better adapted to the wants of the Army than the Smith & Wesson." It is Important to note that both the S&W c.1874 (as improved by Major George W. Schofield) and later New Model Remington c.1875 cartridge revolvers were also adopted for use by the Cavalry, but the Colt Single Action Army remained the dominant sidearm of the military for the remainder of the 19th century.

By 1874 the Single Action Army had been distributed among U.S. Cavalry regiments, including the 7th Cavalry under the command of George Armstrong Custer. One of the most misunderstood characters in Civil War and American Frontier history; he is often portrayed as egocentric, callous, and even foolhardy. Of the three only the later may have truly applied to Custer; but a tendency to be foolhardy, or in one's own mind gallant, is quite often the bedrock of courage. That was an attribute Custer proved to have in abundance during the War Between the States, advancing through the ranks ahead of many of his classmates and even superiors, from Lieutenant, after graduating from West Point in 1861, to Captain by 1862, and after first being passed over for the rank of Colonel early in 1863, at age 23 he was given a field promotion to Brigadier General in June. By the end of the war he had been promoted to Major General.

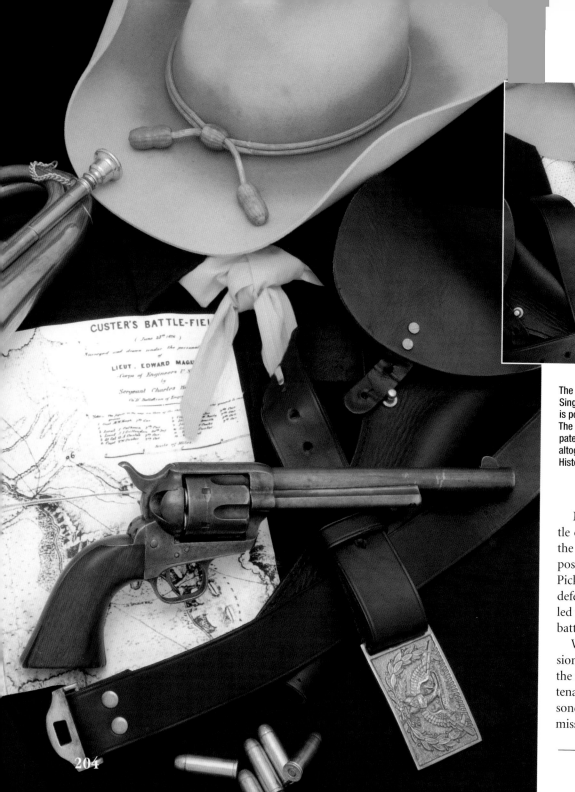

CUSTER'S BATTLE-FIEL

(June 25 1876)

Surveyed and drawn under the personal

of

LIEUT. EDWARD MAGU

Corps of Engineers U.S.

by

Sergeant Charles B

The majority of soldiers at the battle of Little Big Horn were armed with the new Colt Single Action Army and the Trapdoor Springfield Carbine. This U.S. marked example is post Little Big Horn and bears the three patent dates on the left side of the frame. The guns issued to the 7th Cavalry, with few exceptions would have had the two line patent dates as they were issued in 1873 and perhaps additionally in 1874. It is altogether possible that some newer guns c.1875 could have been at Little Big Horn. Historians have noted the serial number ranges of "Custer Battlefield Guns."

Many Civil War historians believe Custer's audacity in the Battle of Gettysburg, where he led the first known cavalry charge of the war, riding head on into Confederate General J.E.B. Stuart's position below Cress's Ridge and stalling his crucial assault during Pickett's Charge, may have contributed to the Confederate Army's defeat at Gettysburg. Custer's later skirmishes with Southern forces led to the death of Stuart, the Confederacy's chief of cavalry, at the battle of Yellow Tavern on May 11, 1864.

With the war over, in the spring of 1866 Custer's field commission as Major General of Volunteers automatically reverted back to the regular army rank of Captain. In July he was promoted to Lieutenant Colonel of the newly formed 7th Cavalry which was garrisoned at Ft. Riley, Kansas. Thus began George Armstrong Custer's mission on the Western Frontier.

Philadelphia was astir with the excitement of anticipation as a whole nation, well prepared by months of publicity, awaited the May 10, 1876, opening of the International Exposition in Fairmont Park to celebrate the nation's centennial year of Independence. The great event was opened by the President of the United States and the Emperor of Brazil. As thousands waited to enter they could see, close by, the vast Main Exhibition Building. Beyond were the towers and expanse of Machinery Hall, the Gothic "barns" of Agricultural Hall, the arabesque architectural intricacies of Horticultural Hall, the art galleries of Memorial Hall, and twenty-four state and many other buildings-236 acres of exhibits and exhibition grounds. Colt prepared specially engraved Single Action Army models for their pinwheel display of 18 guns. This beautifully engraved example is shown on an original scarf sold at the 1876 Exhibition, and with a Visitor's Guide, Pocket Photo Album, a special "Package" ticket, and Centennial awards. More than eight million admissions, from this country and abroad-the population of the United States was forty million-were counted at the fair during the six months it was open, from May 10 through November 10. It was perhaps the greatest extravaganza ever staged in the State of Pennsylvania. A little over a month after the Exposition opened, Custer's 7th Cavalry would be wiped out at the Little Big Horn. (Dr. Joseph A. Murphy collection)

By 1867 the Indian campaigns had begun after settlers and travelers were repeatedly attacked or murdered by roving bands of Cheyenne and Sioux warriors. In the beginning Custer had no desire for war with the Indians but as America began its expansion west it soon became a military matter and the 7th was drawn into the increasing fragility of the government's treaties with the Indians.

His first attempt to bring about some degree of peace, by sitting in council with Chief Pawnee Killer in the spring of 1867, brought no positive results, and not long after a military party of 10 troopers turned up missing. Among those in the group carrying communications from General Sherman to Lt. Col. Custer, was Sioux Chief Red Bead. Custer's chief scout, William Comstock and his party of Delaware Indians went looking for the missing troopers and found their arrow riddled bodies, along with that of Chief Red Bead. It had been the Sioux, along with a few Cheyenne warriors, who had attacked and killed them. This was the answer to Custer's forbearance with Pawnee Killer. Though the soldiers had all been mutilated almost beyond recognition, Red Bead was untouched except for his scalp, which had been removed from

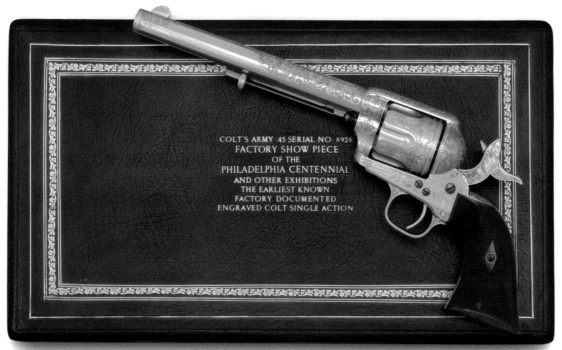

The 1876 Centennial Exposition Colts were, at the time, the most highly engraved Colt Single Action Army Revolvers ever done. This example, serial No. 8928/E, has been specially cased for preservation by Dr. Murphy.

his head and left lying next to his body, as if to warn other Sioux of the consequences for siding with the white soldiers.

Custer oversaw the burial of Lieutenant Lyman S. Kidder who had led the party, and then continued on to his assignment at Ft. Wallace, Kansas. When he arrived he found the garrison in disarray, the fort under almost constant siege by Indians, low on supplies, and men suffering from an outbreak of cholera. The disease had begun spreading on June 28, the day Major H. C. Merriam's cortege, unaware of the illness some of its men were carrying, left Fort Harker for the Southwest, and as it went distributed the fatal disease it carried to every fort and camp at which it stopped.

With no telegraph and the stages running but once a week, there was no hope for quick communications, thus Custer chose another course. Concerned for the safety of his wife who was at Ft. Riley, he turned over command of Ft. Wallace to Major Joel Elliott, and ordered his officers to select 12 men with the best horses from each company for a journey to Fort Harker. With 75 of his

best mounted cavalrymen Custer began a 200 mile ride to report on the situation at Ft. Wallace. The detachment first arrived at Fort Hays, a distance of 150 miles, which they covered in only 55 hours. Custer then left most of his contingent at Ft. Hays to rest their exhausted mounts and continued on to Ft. Harker. Arriving in the middle of the night, he reported to the commanding general, A.J. Smith. He then requested permission to continue on to Ft. Riley to see that his wife was safe. General Smith was sympathetic in such matters and the next morning Custer set out by train.

Truth be told, George Custer had made his share of enemies, both in the military and in government. His decision to leave his command at Ft. Wallace and head for Fort Harker, though without doubt the correct decision in Custer's mind, greatly angered General Grant, as well as General Smith, who thought better of his nighttime decision the next morning. He ordered Custer to return immediately to Ft. Wallace. Custer did not, at least in the expedient way Smith expected, and on his return trip to Ft. Wallace, Custer was placed

Three of the guns from the 1876 Centennial, each showing a different theme portrayed in the engraved panel scenes on their frames. Most of the SAA exhibition guns, 18 of which were set in a central pinwheel, were fitted with ivory grips. The gun in the middle was later presented to Robert A. Pinkerton. The display cabinet from the Centennial Exhibition showed a great many Colt models available in 1876. Note the Buntline with skeleton shoulder stock in the lower right corner of the case. The Centennial engraving is attributed to Cuno A. Helfricht and his shop at Colt's. (Dr. Joseph A. Murphy collection)

under arrest when he stopped at Ft. Harker. A general court martial was convened at Ft. Leavenworth on August 27th 1867. He was charged with absenting himself from his command at Ft. Wallace and conduct to the prejudice of good order and military discipline in his handling of the trip from Ft. Wallace to Ft. Harker. Contradictory stories were told at Custer's hearing, that the post was in better shape than Custer claimed and certainly did not now consider itself besieged. There was food for a month and there was no cholera. Though Custer contended otherwise, he was convicted of all the charges brought against him and suspended from rank, pay and command for one year.

Despite being a Lt. Col., Custer's comportment was still that of a General, as was the degree of respect he received from his men, and though his superiors believed he needed disciplining they were not about to take his case any further. General Grant approved the sentence as it stood, though he commented on its

leniency. For George and Libbie Custer it was perhaps the best thing that could have happened. They returned to their home in Monroe, Michigan and he began writing his memoirs, got reacquainted with old friends, and spent time hunting and fishing. This peace lasted until September 24th, 1868.

The Indian campaign had not gone well during Custer's absence. Skirmishes with Indians were on the rise and Cheyenne raids led by Chiefs Roman Nose and Medicine Man were becoming more daring and deadly. Generals Sherman, Sully and commanding General Phillip H. Sheridan (one of Custer's great supporters) all wanted him to return to Ft. Hays, Kansas. Taking up the call to duty Custer bid Libbie farewell and arrived at Fort Hays six days later. What he found was another war.

The Indians were more adept at plains warfare and with their fleeter, smaller ponies it was easy for them to escape their pursuers and virtually disappear. Cav-

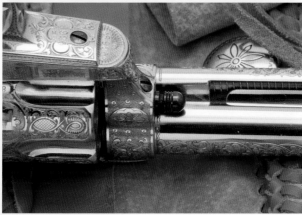

alry horses were larger and heavier, the soldiers laden with gear. After reviewing the situation Custer determined that the Cavalry should wait, hone its skills for plains warfare and not proceed until winter came. This no doubt surprised those in command, but his rationale was sound. Do what the enemy does not expect. Warfare in winter is difficult, but for the cavalry, which had fought through the winters during the Civil War, it was not untried. The Indians, on the other hand, would be less likely to travel, congregating along streams, and their horses would be weaker with less to eat. General Sheridan told Custer, "I rely on you in everything, and shall send you on this expedition without orders, leaving you to act entirely on your own judgment."

By that December, Custer's 7th Cavalry had routed the Indians camped along the Washita River just south of Fort Hayes, Kansas, and east of the Texas Panhandle in Oklahoma. He had attacked with the full force of the Seventh, destroyed their villages, and killed more than 100 warriors, including Chief Black Kettle, freed white prisoners, and captured other Indians including squaws and children, who he ordered left unharmed. Taken into custody they were paraded in full dress before General Sheridan at his headquarters on December 2nd, led by Osage Indian guides chanting war songs, the 7th Cavalry's sharpshooters, and then Custer, his officers and men. As in the Civil War, he knew how to run a campaign. He knew how to win.

Though he had relieved much desperation from the lives of settlers in Kansas, it was just the beginning. Now there came a division between peaceful Indians who had perhaps too much faith in the white fathers, and those who had none. The establishment of reservations was to locate friendly Indians in known areas, since soldiers outside these defined reservations had no way to distinguish between friendlies and hostiles. Custer had also taken into custody, under a flag of truce, head Chiefs Satanta and Lone Wolf, but their warriors had fled. Custer then suggested a bold plan to General Sheridan.

One of the Exposition display guns, serial number 8926, was refitted with carved steer head ivory grips. The engraving theme on the frame of this gun was the hunting of lions and tigers portrayed in a Greek Mythological style, with a naked hunter and huntress on horseback armed with only a club and a spear, respectively. The price for the gun, supplied from Henry Folsom & Co., was $46.60. (Dr. Joseph A. Murphy collection)

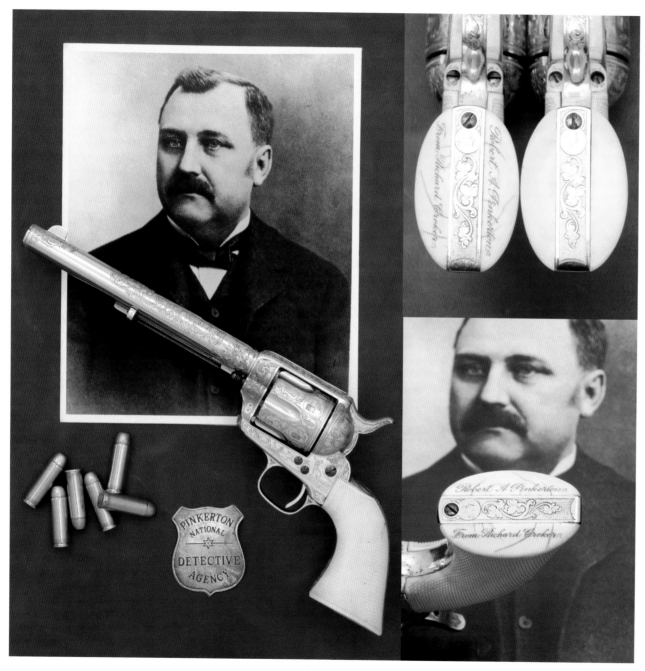

He asked permission to take a small force of only 40 men and scouts to seek out the remaining Indians, but with a second, larger force in reserve. Custer's party, he explained to Sheridan, would be regarded as too small a contingent to be intent on attack yet large enough to dispel any thoughts the Indians might have of murdering them. It was his intent to convince the remaining warriors that he had no desire for further bloodshed and they should follow their Chiefs' example and surrender. This venture might well have ended his life long before the Little Big Horn, but once again his determination, and perhaps luck, prevailed.

He first found the Arapahos and convinced them to return to the reservation without incident. Within a week he had tracked the Cheyennes, who were holding two white girls captive. Custer and his interpreter approached the Indians under a flag of truce and were guided by several warriors to their village. He first ascertained that the two girls were there and alive, and then proceeded to convince more than 50 warriors and their chiefs to accompany him back to his camp for a council meeting. While there, the remaining Indi-

The Exposition gun presented to Robert A. Pinkerton of the Pinkerton National Detective Agency, was part of a sequentially numbered set of guns in the Exposition, Nos. 51546 and 51547, the latter presented to Pinkerton by Alderman Richard Croker, the Democratic leader of New York's East Side. (Dr. Joseph A. Murphy collection)

ans began to quietly prepare their departure, much the same as had happened with Satanta and Lone Wolf, but this time Custer had placed sentries in positions to observe their village and once informed of the activity sent for 100 additional men to be quietly brought up from the rear. Once in place Custer stood up, unbuckled his gun belt and dropped it to the ground. He told them he had no desire for bloodshed. But he now had their encampment surrounded by soldiers. And so Custer's plan played out. He said one of the Chiefs could return to the village with his demands. This transpired as expected and after a few days, and the threat that the remaining Chiefs would forfeit their lives if Custer's requests were not met, the Cheyennes returned the captured girls. Custer then asked for their surrender and an agreement to move their village to Sheridan's headquarters at Camp Supply. This too was agreed. He had accomplished what was seemingly impossible and without firing a single shot or causing the loss of a single life.

With the Kansas Plains under control Lt. Colonel Custer was free to live a more leisurely life, spend time hunting and finally enjoying the company of his wife Libbie at Sheridan's headquarters. He had, unfortunately, also become something of a Frontier celebrity and was frequented by visitors from the east coast and even from abroad who wanted to meet the legendary Indian fighter.

The Custers moved from Camp Supply to Ft. Leavenworth in October 1869 and then the following spring to Fort Hayes, where the 7th Cavalry would once again patrol the plains. There was little to do, however, and by 1870 dignitaries were arriving with regularity, hoping for the opportunity to go buffalo hunting with Custer. And he was more than happy to oblige them.

Among Custer's more famous hunting trips was one in January 1872 when he was requested to lead a buffalo hunt for General Sheridan and Grand Duke Alexis of Russia. The government pulled out all the stops for the Czar's son, including the commissioning of Buffalo Bill Cody as one of the guides.

After their first hunt Custer was asked to accompany the Grand Duke, who had taken a liking to his affable style. They traveled to Denver, Colorado, and from there the diplomatic party went on to Topeka, Kansas, St. Louis and finally Louisville, Kentucky. Following a lavish party for the Grand Duke, Alexis invited Custer to come to New Orleans and tour the waiting Russian fleet before his departure. Custer had unintentionally become a statesman. But any political aspirations he might have imagined were quickly forgotten when the 7th Cavalry was sent back to the Frontier in March 1873. This time, Custer's command would take him to the Dakota Territory and his first task would be to protect the surveyors of the Northern Pacific Railway, which like the white man was expanding across America.

What came to be known as the Yellowstone Expedition[2] began in July 1873. The Dakota Territory was so rugged that Custer had to dispatch two companies to advance and clear a

[2] The expedition was so named for the Yellowstone River which flows from North West Wyoming, through Yellowstone Lake and North East through Montana into the Missouri River in Western North Dakota. Excerpted from Dennis Adler's article "Custer's Last Guns" published in Guns of the Old West magazine.

A page from the Henry Folsom & Co. sales document of October 15, 1877, which lists some of the guns from the 1876 Exposition, sold afterward. The serial numbers are in the left hand column. (Dr. Joseph A. Murphy collection)

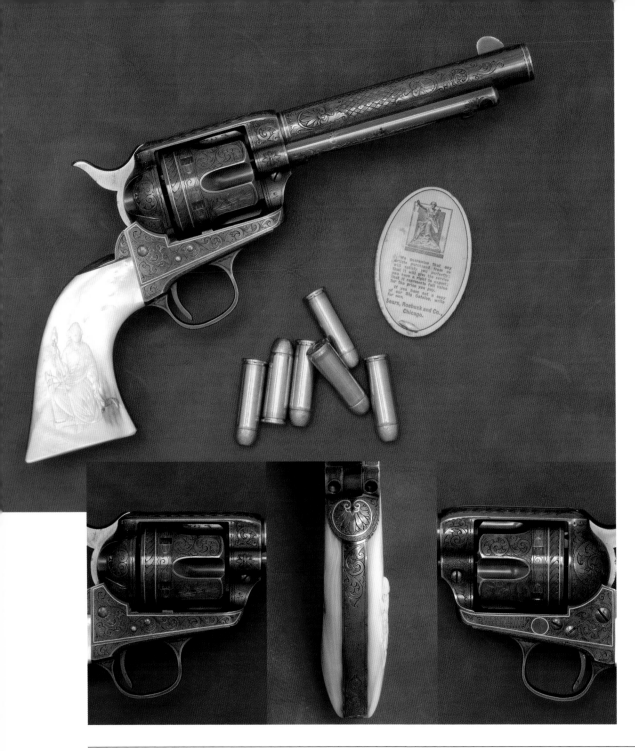

path for the main command and survey team. After a month they encountered their first hostiles. Custer and 90 of his men in advance of the main body were attacked by several hundred Sioux. The experienced 7th made quick work of them, inflicting heavy losses before the attackers gave ground, but two of Custer's men were lost, his Veterinary Surgeon, and a trader traveling with the 7th were caught between the main command and Custer's advance party. Neither man was armed.

Custer pursued the remaining Sioux several days later and finally engaged them along the Yellowstone River. The Indians lost more than 40 warriors in the skirmish and Custer had his 11th horse shot out from under him. After that the survey team was not harassed for the remainder of their 95 day expedition, which concluded on September 14th.

Two years before Little Big Horn, Custer and the 7th had been ordered to prepare an expeditionary force to explore the Black Hills region of the Dakotas. More than 43,000 square miles of the Black Hills had been ceded to the Sioux as reservation lands by the treaty of 1868. Few white men had ventured there, but by 1873 the westward expansion was pushing at the borders of the Black Hills.

Custer left Fort Lincoln on July 2nd along with General G. A. "Sandy" Forsyth and Lieutenant Fred Grant, the President's son. In Custer's party were two of his trusted guides and the youngest Custer

One of the most famous pre-World War II Colt Single Action Army revolvers, serial No. 172485, is known as the "Sears" Single Action. The profusely engraved and gold inlaid 5-1/2 inch model was made for Sears, Roebuck & Co. in October 1897, and was later featured in their 1901 catalog for $50. The gun was accented with mother-of-pearl grips featuring a carved likeness of Columbia, the Goddess of Liberty. Another distinctive feature of this gun is the frame, which is blued rather than color casehardened. This gun was in the Mel Torme collection for many years changing hands in the late 1970s for six figures. The next owner was Connecticut gun collector John Solley. In the March/April 1983 issue of *Man at Arms* magazine, it was proclaimed as one of the most beautiful Colt Single Action revolvers ever made. (Dr. Joseph A. Murphy Collection)

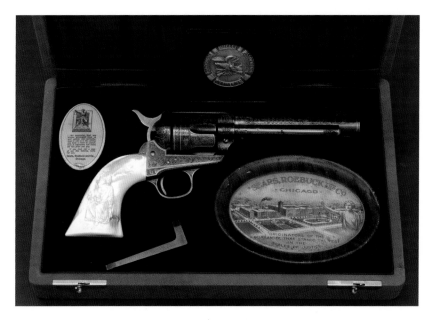

brother, Boston. The expeditionary force consisted of over 1,000 men, 1,900 horses, cattle, and 110 covered wagons with supplies. It would have been hard for the Sioux to miss them. Surprisingly, they met no resistance heading into the interior of the Black Hills, seeing only smoke signals and a few Indians watching them from a distance. Throughout the two-month expedition Custer had no encounters with the Sioux, except for a short visit with Chief One Stab, who was invited to Custer's camp to receive gifts of food, coffee and sugar. In exchange One Stab spent several days as a guide for the expedition. The Black Hills, as Custer would report, contained an abundance of game, pasturage, pure water, and timber. It was the purest of lands, and the Sioux had made it their home. Then gold was discovered.

Custer had noted, though with no great emphasis, that gold appeared to be plentiful in the streams they crossed while exploring the Black Hills, but when the newspapers got word of gold, their headlines ignited the greatest fever of enthusiasm since the days of the '49ers. There was an almost immediate disregard for the sanctity of the Indians in the Black Hills of Dakota, and even with the threat of arrest by the military for trespassing, they still came. Even when arrested, after they were released they came again. As prospectors continued to encroach on the Sioux reservation tensions increased.

In May 1875 Richard A. Roberts, whose brother-in-law, Col. George W. Yates, was with Custer's 7th Cavalry came to visit Fort Lincoln and participate in the

second Black Hills expedition. It was, however, called off by Washington, a great disappointment to Custer and his men. Roberts, the grandson of former Pennsylvania Chief Justice John Bannister Gibson, returned to Fort Lincoln again in April 1876 to work as Custer's civilian secretary. A graduate of Lafayette College, with a Bachelor of Philosophy degree, he was also employed by the *New York Sun* to write about events unfolding on the Frontier. Of Custer Roberts wrote, "The whole regiment with one or two exceptions seemed imbued with the spirit of its commander, and in fact so close was he to his officers, that when off duty one would be led to think that all were brothers, and happy brothers at that. The General [a title of respect he received from his men even though his official rank was Lt. Col.] was passionately fond of dogs, and his kennels at the back of his quarters or house were filled with the finest breeds of fox and stag hounds, or gazers who ran entirely by sight. The stag hounds were the largest and the finest at the time in this country and were pure Scotch. His stable contained noble and fine bred horses and a thrill of pleasurable sympathy would pass through me, as I have seen him pat his favorite horses, Dandy and Vic, and heard their responsive whinny, and watched the potential of spirit flash from their eyes to his. Animals, like children, seldom err."

Since fall 1875 there had been growing unrest among the Sioux Nation and it was only a matter of time until the dam broke and all of the work that had been done to secure peace with the Indians would come undone. General Sherman had noted in an official report, "…Sitting Bull, who had never yet in any way recognized the United States Government…except by snatching rations occasionally [should] cease marauding and settle down as the other Sioux have done at some designated point." That "point" was January 1876. Hostile Sioux warriors inhabiting Missouri and Yellowstone had been ordered to return to their reservations by the end of the month, and when they did not, the Army's hand was forced.

In the midst of preparing for a campaign against Sitting Bull, Custer was requested to appear in Washington to testify before the Committee on Expenditures, in the House of Representatives. This had nothing to do with the forthcoming expedition but was concerned rather with improprieties at Frontier trading posts, something that Custer had previously commented upon. Unfortunately, this hearing wasn't so much about the cost of goods as it was a means of stoking the coals of a political fire in Washington. Custer had become a highly visible pawn in an attempt by Representative Heister Clymer, the Committee's Chairman, to vilify the Republican Secretary of War, William Belkamp. Custer told the Committee only what he knew of the problems at trading posts and of the exorbitant prices many soldiers in the 7th Cavalry had to pay, but his statements were damaging both to Secretary Belkamp and to Orville Grant, the President's brother, both of who had become involved in the sale of post traderships.

The Buntline Special is a mixture of fact and fiction, a tale that has been told for more than a century. Colt's did in fact build the first examples with barrels of 10, 12 and 16 inches in length beginning in 1876. The story goes that successful dime novelist Ned Buntline, actually a writer named Edward Zane Carroll Judson, presented the 16-inch models to famed lawmen Wyatt Earp, Charlie Bassett, Neal Brown, Bat Masterson, and Bill Tilghman. Buntline was friends with Buffalo Bill Cody and even joined his Wild West Show for a time. He is shown in the photo seated to the right of Cody. Standing at Cody's left is famous Wild West showman and sharpshooter "Texas Jack" Omohundro. The guns shown are from Colt's 2nd Generation Buntlines which were built beginning in 1957. In the 1993 movie *Tombstone*, Kurt Russell as Wyatt Earp, carried a 10-inch Colt Peacemaker in the pivotal shootout at the OK Corral.

The former General of the Army and now President, Ulysses S. Grant already had little fondness for Custer, and his testimony against both a member of his cabinet and his brother provoked even more contempt. After the hearings he refused to see Custer when he called at the White House. Upon returning to Fort Lincoln, he was informed that he would not be permitted to command the 7th Cavalry in dealing with the Sioux uprising. The order had apparently come down from the President through General Sherman. This so enraged Custer that he wired the President requesting that he at least be permitted to serve with the 7th, if not command it. General Terry, in command of Fort Lincoln and the entire expedition, also sent his regards to the President suggesting that Custer's service to the 7th Cavalry "would be very valuable." When the Washington newspapers picked up on the story they labeled it "Grant's Revenge." Quickly becoming a polit-

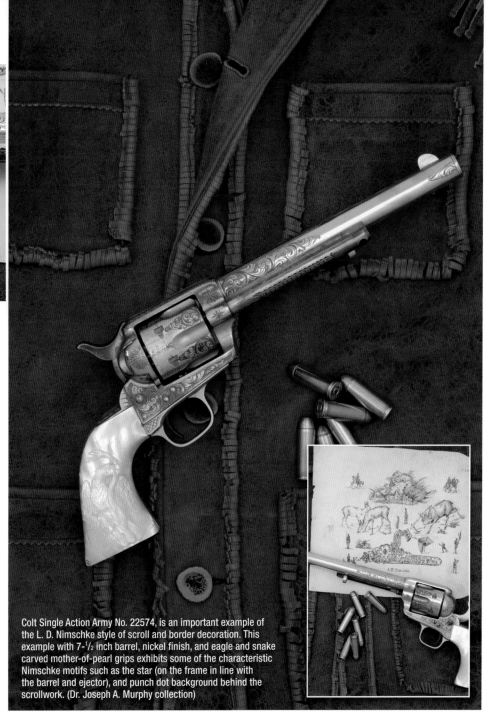

ical teapot about to boil over, Grant rescinded his order on May 8, 1876. It was the beginning of the end for George Armstrong Custer, and his brothers, Tom and Boston, all of who would die together at the Little Big Horn on June 25th, along with 222 other officers and men of the 7th Cavalry.[3]

The Army's estimates of Sitting Bull's war party were no more than 1,500 warriors, thus the 7th Cavalry rode into a conflict with the belief that they had, if not superior numbers, superior capability and firepower. Sitting Bull had in fact amassed a force of from 10,000 to 12,000 Indians, of which 3,000 to 5,000 were experienced warriors. Later reports stated that Sitting Bull's village had been nearly four miles long and at places one half mile wide. Even if Custer had not divided his forces, Lt. Col. Custer's, Major Marcus Reno's, and Capt. Frederick Benteen's entire complement of 600 wouldn't have stood any better chance.

Ironically, the horse of Custer's friend and secretary, Richard Roberts, had played out about 70 miles from Little Big Horn. Fifteen years later in his book, *Custer's Last Battle*, Roberts wrote, "Here is where I met, as I thought, the greatest disappointment of my life, that is, I had to be left behind and could not accompany the scouting party, as my pony was com-

[3] Custer had divided the 7th into three battalions at Little Big Horn; his was the only battalion that was completely wiped out. Ibid.

Colt Single Action Army No. 22574, is an important example of the L. D. Nimschke style of scroll and border decoration. This example with 7-1/2 inch barrel, nickel finish, and eagle and snake carved mother-of-pearl grips exhibits some of the characteristic Nimschke motifs such as the star (on the frame in line with the barrel and ejector), and punch dot background behind the scrollwork. (Dr. Joseph A. Murphy collection)

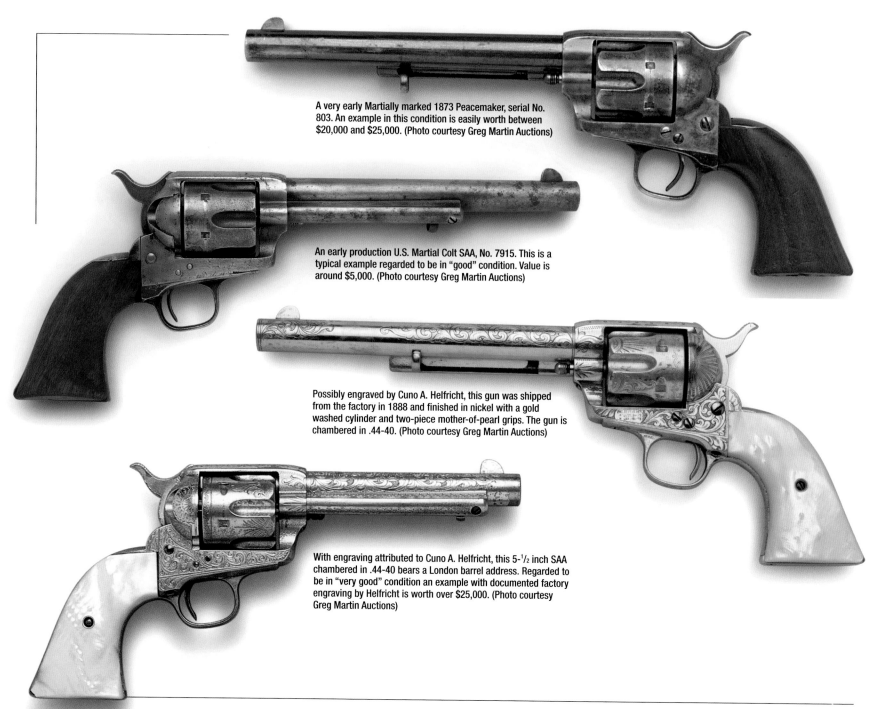

A very early Martially marked 1873 Peacemaker, serial No. 803. An example in this condition is easily worth between $20,000 and $25,000. (Photo courtesy Greg Martin Auctions)

An early production U.S. Martial Colt SAA, No. 7915. This is a typical example regarded to be in "good" condition. Value is around $5,000. (Photo courtesy Greg Martin Auctions)

Possibly engraved by Cuno A. Helfricht, this gun was shipped from the factory in 1888 and finished in nickel with a gold washed cylinder and two-piece mother-of-pearl grips. The gun is chambered in .44-40. (Photo courtesy Greg Martin Auctions)

With engraving attributed to Cuno A. Helfricht, this 5-1/2 inch SAA chambered in .44-40 bears a London barrel address. Regarded to be in "very good" condition an example with documented factory engraving by Helfricht is worth over $25,000. (Photo courtesy Greg Martin Auctions)

The SAA Sheriff's Model varied in barrel length from 2-1/2 inches to 4-inches and in increments of 3-inches (shown), 3-1/4 inches, and 3-1/2 inches. They were not fitted with ejectors. (Author's collection)

Far left: A second lease on life, this U.S. Army issued Peacemaker was reconditioned, altered to a barrel length of 4-7/8 inches and fitted with a dovetailed front sight. It has also been adapted to the 2nd type Bridgeport gun rig shown, c.1882. (Photo courtesy Greg Martin Auctions)

pletely done up and no other horse could be procured for me, so I swallowed my 'hard luck' and bade each of the officers goodbye, and shook each one by hand and saw General Custer and Col. Yates, my brother-in-law, for the last time on earth."

Of all the soldiers massacred at Little Big Horn, George Armstrong Custer was the only one not mutilated by the Indians. He was left untouched where he fell with four or five brass cartridge shells from his prized Remington Rolling Block rifle still underneath his body. Even in death, the Indians respected him. Most historical accounts claim that Custer was carrying his Colt Model "P" revolver, the Remington-Creedmore Rolling Block and a British "Bull Dog" style revolver when he was killed. None of his guns were found at the site, only the spent casings. It is now believed, however, that Custer did not carry his Colt on the expedition, but rather a Webley No.1 RIC revolver presented to him in September 1869 by C. S. Paget. An avid gun collector, the Webley revolver was absent from Custer's gun rack. [4] [5]

The Colt models issued to Custer and the 7th Cavalry were from the earliest production. Often referred to as the black powder frame, the distinguishing characteristic of the early Single Action Army is the use of a retaining screw in the bottom front of the frame, which when tightened into a groove in the cylinder pin secured the arbor in place. Removing the cylinder required taking out this screw so the arbor could be pulled forward and through the cylinder. Beginning in 1892 the retaining screw was replaced by a transverse cylinder latch, which simply needed to be depressed in order to release the cylinder arbor and allow it to slide out.

Between 1873 and 1899 Colt's made approximately 25 changes to the Peacemaker including variations in calibers, barrel lengths, front sight design, barrel address stampings, patent dates, grip design (hard rubber eagle and shield grips offered beginning 1882, changed to hard rubber without eagle and shield in 1896) and model variations specific to the SAA Target and Bisley models.

[4] "Custer's Last Handgun" by Garry James, Guns & Ammo, December 2006, G.A. Custer, His Life and Times by Glenn Swanson.
[5] Research for portions of this chapter was conducted at the George A. Custer Museum of the Monroe County, Michigan, Historical Museum, and from the books The Custer Album by Lawrence A. Frost, 1964 Superior Publishing Co.; General Custer& His Sporting Rifles by C. Vance Haynes, Sr., 1995 Western Lore Press; The Little Big Horn by Robert Nightingale, 1996; The Peacemakers by R.L. Wilson, 1992; Custer Battle Guns by John S. AuMont, 1974, The Old Army Press; and Custer's Last Battle, Reminiscences of General Custer by Richard A. Roberts, Ph. B., M. S., Monroe County Library System.

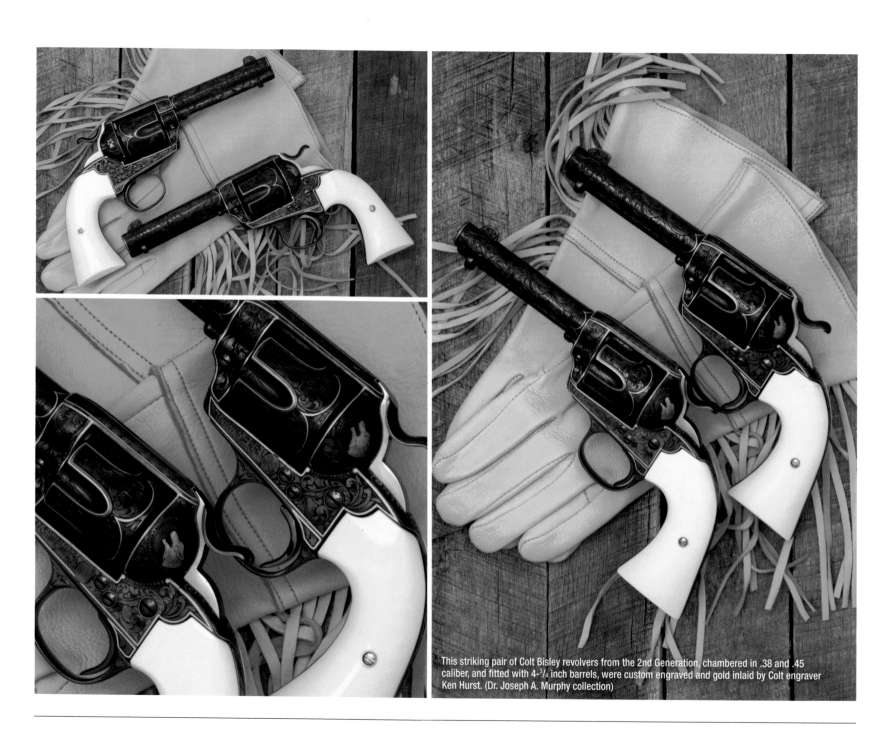

This striking pair of Colt Bisley revolvers from the 2nd Generation, chambered in .38 and .45 caliber, and fitted with 4-3/4 inch barrels, were custom engraved and gold inlaid by Colt engraver Ken Hurst. (Dr. Joseph A. Murphy collection)

William "Bill" Tilghman had one of the longest careers of any lawman. Spanning half a century he served as a U.S. Deputy Marshal, City Marshal, and Chief of Police witnessing first hand the changing American frontier from the 1870s to the Roaring Twenties. Among the guns he carried was this factory engraved presentation Single Action Army with mother-of-pearl grips. (Private collection)

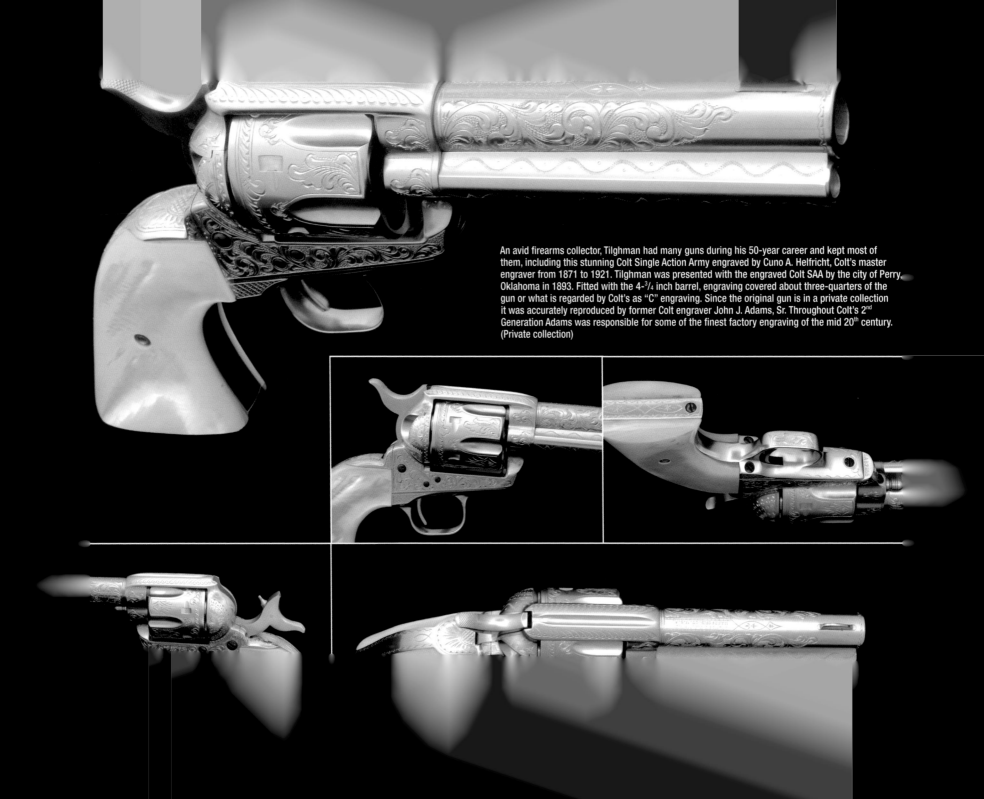

An avid firearms collector, Tilghman had many guns during his 50-year career and kept most of them, including this stunning Colt Single Action Army engraved by Cuno A. Helfricht, Colt's master engraver from 1871 to 1921. Tilghman was presented with the engraved Colt SAA by the city of Perry, Oklahoma in 1893. Fitted with the 4-3/4 inch barrel, engraving covered about three-quarters of the gun or what is regarded by Colt's as "C" engraving. Since the original gun is in a private collection it was accurately reproduced by former Colt engraver John J. Adams, Sr. Throughout Colt's 2nd Generation Adams was responsible for some of the finest factory engraving of the mid 20th century. (Private collection)

This is another 2nd Generation Colt SAA, serial No. S05304A, chambered in .44-40 and fitted with a 4-inch barrel and ejector housing. Factory "D" engraved with one-piece ivory grips, this is the shortest barrel length factory engraved model known to date. (Dr. Joseph A. Murphy collection)

One of the longest living heroes of the American West, Tilghman carried a badge and a gun for more than 50 years and had befriended such luminaries as Wyatt and Virgil Earp, Doc Holliday, the Masterson brothers, and Ben Thompson.

Born William Mathew Tilghman in Ft. Dodge, Iowa, on July 4, 1854, Bill had an adventurous spirit, leaving home at age 16 to seek his fortune. For the next decade he lived on the plains among the Indians, learning to hunt buffalo, track, and gain a respect for life and the land. He wasn't without skirmishes in his youth, and was known to have killed seven Cheyenne braves in a shootout. Bill was not an educated man in the contemporary sense, but one who learned life's lessons well and made the most of every opportunity presented him, training in those practices which make men proficient in all the crafts of the frontier.

While hunting buffalo in Kansas in 1872, he came upon a party of surveyors laying out a new town site called Dodge City. Three years later, Tilghman, although a life long teetotaler, opened a saloon in Dodge City, Kansas. In 1878 he accepted the offer of his friend, Bat Masterson, to become his deputy sheriff. Bill Tilghman's courage and honesty led to his becoming City Marshal and Undersheriff of Dodge City. He remained in Dodge until April 22, 1889, the date when Oklahoma was opened to settlement.

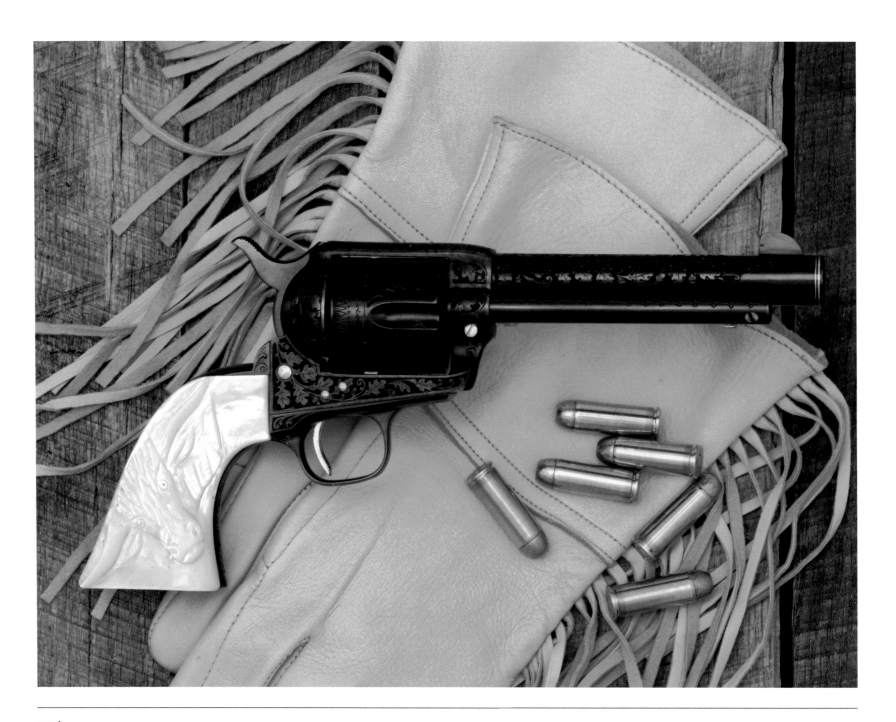

Tilghman was among the earliest arrivals in the Oklahoma territory, establishing his first home at Guthrie. Although he had wanted to try his hand at farming and cattle, his reputation as a lawman in Dodge City followed him, and in 1891 he was appointed a deputy United States Marshal, a position he held continuously for 19 years, being re-appointed by every United States Marshal in Oklahoma until 1910.

He performed his duty with a capable efficiency and courage that would be difficult to match, and those who were competent to judge him said that Bill Tilghman, while a Deputy Marshal in Oklahoma, had more criminals to contend with than any other officer of the law in the entire Southwest. Wrote lawman turned author Bat Masterson, "He was the greatest of us all."

Unlike most western lawmen, Tilghman rarely resorted to using violence and during his career killed only two criminals in gunfights. Along with his deputies, Heck Thomas and Charlie Colcord, Tilghman was largely responsible for wiping out organized crime in Oklahoma, particularly in Perry, a lawless, wide open boom town that Tilghman brought under control after becoming City Marshal in 1893.

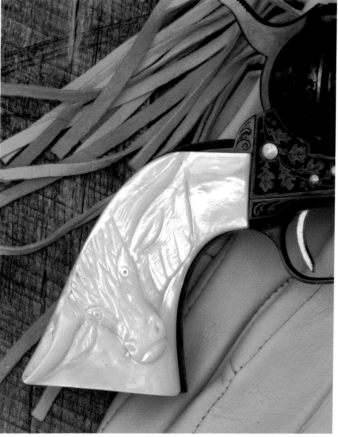

Unlike the Earps, Bat Masterson, Bill Hickok, or Dallas Stoudenmire, Tilghman was not the least bit flamboyant. He was a quiet man who dressed formally but never in anything that would draw attention. Greatly respected for his unwavering courage, it is claimed that Tilghman was paid more reward money than any other law officer in the Old West. Most lawmen, however, had far shorter careers! His most famous arrest was that of William Doolin, a notorious gang leader, robber, killer, and close associate of the Dalton Brothers. He had been working on the capture of Doolin for three years – the price on his head was a hefty $5,000 – and on January 15, 1896 Tilghman tracked him to a bathhouse in Eureka Springs, Arkansas. He took Doolin alive and transported him to the Guthrie, Oklahoma jail without the aid of handcuffs or restraints. When he arrested Doolin, the outlaw told Bill he had a small silver mug that was a present for his infant son. Tilghman, a man of kindness, saw to it that Doolin's son got the mug. Doolin was less kind; he escaped from the Guthrie County jail and went on the run again. He was later shot dead by a U.S. Marshal.

Although Tilghman owned many guns, ranging from Civil War Colts to Smith & Wesson double actions and in later years a .45 Automatic, his favorite gun was the Colt Peacemaker. Said Tilghman of his Colts, "I never missed a man I was trying to hit." It was during this period that Colt's Patent Fire Arms Manufacturing produced a beautifully engraved Single Action Army with a 4-³/₄ inch barrel, presented to Tilghman by the city of Perry. It was inscribed on the backstrap, For William Tilghman Dec. 15. 93. This fine piece was custom built in every detail from the hand carved pearl grips to the hair trigger and honed action. The engraving was done in the shop of Cuno A. Helfricht, Colt's master engraver from 1871 to 1921.

The Model P Colt Single Action Army was the most popular handgun of the American West. It was the canvas upon which most of America's greatest engravers produced their finest work. The same was true during the 2ⁿᵈ Generation. Serial No. 355870, this 5-¹/₂ inch barrel example was custom engraved and gold inlaid in a rare oak leaf pattern by William McGraw, an Ithaca Gun Co. engraver. The gun is fitted with double hand carved steer head mother-of-pearl grips. (Dr. Joseph A. Murphy collection)

Theodore Roosevelt was a true adventurer and long before he became President of the United States he had made a name for himself as a soldier, rancher, and accomplished pistolero with a fondness for Colt Single Action Army revolvers. Noted R. L. Wilson in *The Peacemakers – Arms and Adventure in the American West*, On handguns, TR summed up preferences with: "Of course, every ranchman carries a revolver, a 45 Colt or Smith & Wesson, by preference the former." In his own battery were two exquisitely engraved Single Actions one with monogrammed and carved ivory grips, the other with mother-of-pearl grips inscribed in script, Theodore Roosevelt. For this photo montage a series of pictures showing Roosevelt at different times in life, as a young soldier, with the Rough Riders, and as President were combined with copies of his wardrobe created by the clothiers at Orvis. The fully engraved and nickel plated Roosevelt SAA with monogrammed ivory grips is also a reproduction, one of a limited series produced by Cimarron F.A. Co. in Fredericksburg, Texas.

There have been many famous Colt Single Action revolvers in movies, but none as memorable as Alan Ladd's nickel plated Colt in *Shane*, one of the 10 Greatest Westerns ever made.

Alan Ladd as Shane and Jean Arthur as Marion Starrett had one of the films two emotional relationships. Marion became infatuated with Shane, and he was drawn to her gentleness and honesty. The other relationship was the bond between Shane and Joe and Marion Starrett's son Joey, played by Brandon De Wilde. The striking holster with Indian conchos, the barrel without front sight, and horse head grips made Shane's gun one of the focal points of the film. As a gunman Shane had his own particular shooting style and Alan Ladd played the part to the hilt whenever he drew his Colt, fanning off multiple shots. Both the original gun and holster have been lost, but were recreated for this book and an article in *Guns of the Old West* magazine by renowned gunsmith and engraver John J. Adams, Sr., who built the copy of Shane's Colt, and noted western holster maker Jim Lockwood, who duplicated the original Shane holster created for the 1953 film by the legendary Rod Redwing. (Shane clothing for the author created by River Junction Trade Co.)

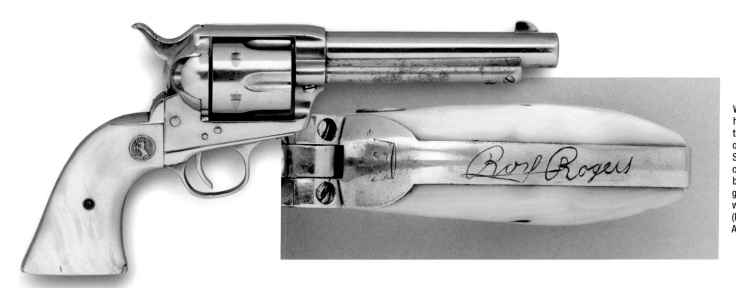

When it came to TV cowboy heroes there were many in the 1950s including the King of the Cowboys, Roy Rogers. Serial No. 168462, this .32-20 caliber SAA with 5-1/2 inch barrel and mother-of-pearl grips was probably the most watched Colt in TV history. (Photos courtesy Greg Martin Auctions)

The gun, which is still in excellent condition, also has blued screws to contrast its polished nickel finish. It remained one of his favorites and saw very little use.

After retiring as U.S. Deputy Marshal in 1910, Tilghman was elected to the State Senate from the Thirteenth Senatorial District. However, he found himself less suited to the lifestyle of a politician and in 1911 resigned from the Senate to become chief of police in Oklahoma City. He was 57 years old.

In 1915 he became interested in filmmaking and was instrumental in bringing out a moving picture entitled *The Passing of the Oklahoma City Outlaws*.[6] The scenes re-enacted under his direction were filmed in the rugged country of the old Creek and Osage Nation, where many bloody dramas in the conflict of law and order actually occurred. There was an instructive moral element in his film drama, which depicted the life of the outlaw from the first act of crime until inevitably becoming entangled in the toils of justice, and contrary to many of the characterizations of outlaws in early silent films, in Tilghman's drama they were not represented as heroes who would readily gain the admiration of young boys. Said Tilghman, "…based on a long and thorough experience with criminals…there is no such thing as an outlaw hero." Thus he was determined to make authentic Westerns, rather than the fake carrying on of Tom Mix and other Western movie stars of the day. The only problem was that no one wanted to see his non-stars in any story. The truth about real outlaws was neither exciting nor colorful, even in black and white.

His life as a tough and well respected Oklahoma lawman continued until the day he died on the evening of November 1, 1924 at age 70. At the time he was the City Marshal in Cromwell, Oklahoma, and was in the process of disarming and taking into custody one Wiley Lynn, a crooked prohibition officer who either black marketed or drank the liquor he confiscated in raids. On this day he had done the latter and Tilghman was arresting a staggering drunk Lynn for discharging his revolver into the evening sky. Bill easily disarmed him of his service revolver but suddenly Lynn pulled away from Tilghman's grip and drew another revolver he had hidden in his clothes, firing two shots almost point blank. Bill was killed instantly, his own gun still in his hand and unfired.

After his murder, Bill Tilghman's body lay in state in the Capital Building in Oklahoma City before being buried in Chandler, Oklahoma, ending the remarkable half-century career of the last good man to tame the badlands.

The 20th Century Single Action Army

Colt had long realized that no matter how many guns they designed or how many improvements were made in handgun design; no gun, revolver, semi auto, rifle or shotgun, would ever surpass the popularity of the Peacemaker. Even with the advent of Colt's semi-autos and the military's adoption of the Model 1911 as its new sidearm, the SAA remained in production throughout the early 20th century, and was used by both U.S. and British forces during World War I. Between 1900 and 1940 Colt's produced over 165,000 Single Action Army revolvers. From 1956 to 1970 another 59,000 2nd Generation models were produced. The numbers within the 3rd Generation continue to climb with no end in sight.

[6] *The film has also been listed as* The Passing of Oklahoma Outlaws.

Commissioned under the Tiffany & Co. name in 1992 and designed by Tom Watts of Tiffany & Co., this pair of handcrafted Colt 1860 Army revolvers took master engraver Andrew Bourbon six months to complete. The intricate design incorporates the use of engraving, casting, and ceramitation. They are regarded as the most intricately designed Tiffany Colts ever built, in this or any other century. Bourbon's work was supervised by R.L. Wilson, of American Master Engravers, Inc., the subcontractor with Tiffany & Co. for arms embellishments. (Dr. Joseph A. Murphy collection)

Chapter Nine

The Presentation Colts
The Gun As Art

One hardly associates Tiffany & Co. with guns, but there was a time, more than a century ago when one could just as easily purchase a fine gun as a diamond brooch at the exclusive New York City establishment.

The House of Tiffany was founded in 1837 by Charles Lewis Tiffany and John B. Young. It was known then as Tiffany & Young. When Jabez L. Ellis joined the company it became Tiffany, Young & Ellis; a boutique catering to New York and New England society. Jewelry was not Tiffany's principal line; in fact fine imported silver was their stock in trade up until 1853 when Charles Tiffany took control of the company.

The new Tiffany & Co. began manufacturing its own products in the 1850s with the help of New York Silversmith John C. Moore and his son Edward C. Moore. It was the Civil War, however, that put Tiffany & Co. into the business of producing exquisitely engraved militaria, beginning with fine presentation swords in 1861. Tiffany's clientele included Generals Ulysses S. Grant and William Tecumseh Sherman, and Admiral David G. Farragut.[1]

The War Between the States also encouraged Tiffany & Co. to venture into the field of engraved and embellished firearms for presentation, and to become the exclusive New York and New England dealer for the Henry Deringer. Colt's became a Tiffany customer during the war, as did Smith & Wesson, both of whom used silver Tiffany grips on some of their most elaborately engraved pistols.

Tiffany gripped Colts were offered in the entire range of single action models then in production. As noted by R. L. Wilson, the elaborate, cast metal grips became "…more reminiscent of the hiltings on presentation swords of the period."

Pictured on top of R. L. Wilson's book *Steel Canvas* is the last Tiffany gripped Colt produced. Known as the Heirloom Colt 1860 Army, this was the last of a limited edition created by Colt Blackpowder Arms between 1998 and 2000. The gun was engraved with 100 percent coverage in the L. D. Nimschke style, silver plated and accented with a 24Kt. gold plated cylinder, loading lever, hammer, and trigger. The guns currently demand upwards of $6,000.

[1] Steel Canvas – The Art of American Arms *by R. L. Wilson.*

The rarest of Tiffany percussion era Colts, an 1862 Police with the American eagle motif. Note the ornate butt cap. (Photo courtesy R. L. Wilson)

The master of Colt engraving and engraving as a whole for the American firearms industry in the mid to late 19th century, Louis Daniel Nimschke did much of the engraving seen on Tiffany gripped Colts sold through Schuyler, Hartley and Graham in New York.

Some of L. D. Nimschke's finest work was for Schuyler, Hartley and Graham, very likely the original source of this 1871-72 Open Top with Tiffany grips. A good number of post Civil War Colts were given the Tiffany treatment including cartridge conversions of the 1860 Army. (Photo courtesy R. L. Wilson)

Another rare Tiffany Colt, this one on a Thuer conversion of an 1861 Navy Model. The grip style used was the most popular of the Tiffany designs, the Civil War Battle Scene. (Photo courtesy R. L. Wilson)

Below: Sometimes it's hard to tell the real thing. This handsome pair of Tiffany gripped 1851 Navy Models are handcrafted reproductions done by master engraver John J. Adams, Sr. in the 1990s. Both guns are now in a private collection. Though worth far less than an original pair, their appearance and the quality of the workmanship differs little from those sold by Schuyler, Hartley and Graham in the 1860s. (Private collection)

There were three basic designs created between 1861 and 1875, and these have been given the name "Tiffany grips" by collectors, though the exact association of Tiffany & Co. with these styles is shrouded to a certain extent in uncertainty. The most popular of the three designs was the now famous Civil War Battle Scene. The American and Mexican eagle were the next most popular, and the rarest was known as "The Missionary and Child." The back of the grip had a portrait of lady justice bearing a cross, with a crouching American eagle over a shield produced in high relief on the butt cap. This unique design was commissioned by the U.S. government for use on a pair of 1862 Police models presented by President Lincoln in to Kibrisili Pasha, the governor of Adrianople North West Turkey.

All Tiffany designs had a presentation escutcheon just below the hammer (with the exception of "The Missionary and Child" and large cast butt plates usually with an American eagle, though there were other designs). The cast Tiffany grips were either silver or gold plated and occasionally a combination of both, particularly on contemporary (20th century) examples.

The Tiffany "influence" in grip design was prolific in the 1860s and well into the post Civil War era. The design, though often called "Tiffany gripped" was not necessarily an assurance that they were cast by Tiffany & Co. In fact, most were not. Historian R.L. Wilson is of the

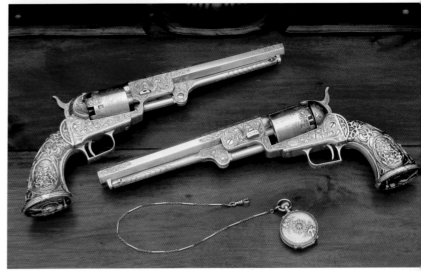

One of the finest contemporary copies of an engraved cased set of 1860 Army revolvers, in the Cuno A. Helfricht style, was commissioned for William R. Harry and engraved by John J. Adams, Sr. The set was cased in a period correct presentation box made from 100 year old mahogany by case maker Duncan Everhart. The Colt 2nd Generation accessories were finished to authentic period condition by Frank Klay.

Cartridge conversions were also given the Tiffany treatment when they were modified from Civil War era percussion revolvers. A number of Tiffany gripped guns were done on the 1860 conversions of Richards and Richards-Mason styles. This example is a contemporary model engraved and Tiffany gripped by John J. Adams, Sr. The grip design is of the Civil War Battle type with a U.S. cartouche and American eagle butt cap. The period style holster is also a handcrafted reproduction done by renowned Western holster maker, Jim Lockwood. The silver conchos on the holster and belt were hand fabricated.

John J. Adams Sr. worked for Colt as an engraver during the 2nd Generation Colt Blackpowder era. Today, Adams and his son John operate Adams & Adams in Vershire, Vermont, specializing in engraving styles of the 19th century, as well as doing contemporary engraving for Smith & Wesson. Here John Adams, Sr. works on the author's Tiffany Colt 1860 Army cartridge conversion in 2006. While more than 130 years have passed since the earliest Tiffany conversions were done by L. D. Nimschke and Tiffany & Co., the techniques of hand cutting and hand engraving are still the same. (Photos by Sarah Adams)

opinion that most of the grips were actually done by the Ames Sword Co. of Massachusetts, which also manufactured highly embellished swords for Schuyler, Hartley and Graham. In addition, John Quincy Adams Ward, the prominent American sculptor who designed the Justice and American eagle pattern Tiffany grips, was employed by the Ames Sword Co.[2]

Many of the "Tiffany gripped" Colts sold in the 1860s and 1870s were marketed through the New York retail firm of Schuyler, Hartley and Graham, which employed L. D. Nimschke and his shop as their "in-house" engraver, thus many of the finest Tiffany style Colts are Nimschke engraved. Others were done by the Nimschke shop or in the Nimschke style by other engravers hired by Schuyler, Hartley and Graham. Tiffany-style grips are also seen on Colt cartridge conversions of the 1860 Army, 1851 Navy, and Colt's Pocket Models, as well as 1873 Peacemakers and later Colt revolvers.

Contemporary Colt revolvers (including 2nd Generation percussion and Single Action Army models) were produced by Tiffany & Co. in the 1980s when the New York firm returned briefly to its late 19th century heritage, through the efforts of Colt Industries Chairman George A. Strichman, historian R. L. Wilson, and Tiffany & Co. Chairman William R. Chaney.

Custom engraved Colts are still produced today by the Colt Custom shop. Former factory engravers have also become well known sources for fine engraving in the styles of Young, Nimschke, and Helfricht, as well as their own individual styles.

Over the decades since Colt's began remanufacturing models from the 19th century and continuing its production of the 1873 Peacemaker, thousands of extraordinary guns have been produced. Many of the finest were done in the 1980s by some of the greatest engravers of the 20th century: Alvin A. White, Andrew Bourbon, Winston Churchill, Howard Dove, John

[2] Ames swords were carried by enlisted men and officers alike from obscure frontier Indian skirmishes to every famous battle fought by American military and Naval forces from the swamps of Florida and the plains of Texas in the early 1800s to the great battle fields of Europe in the twentieth century. The first presentation swords ever commissioned by Congress to honor heroes of the Mexican War were contracted to The Ames Sword Company. Excerpt from the Ames Sword Company 1829 – 1935 by John D. Hamilton. The Ames Sword Co. is still in business, headquartered in New London, Ohio.

Four variations of Tiffany gripped Colts, an 1860 Army Thuer conversion with Civil War Battle Scene grips, 1862 Police with American eagle grips, an 1871-72 Open Top with Civil War Battle Scene, and an 1873 Peacemaker with gold plated Battle Scene grips. (Photos courtesy R. L. Wilson)

Gold plating (rather than traditional silver) sets off this Tiffany grip on an 1873 Peacemaker. The engraving patterns exhibit a variety of L. D. Nimschke styles. (Photo courtesy R. L. Wilson)

J. Adams, Sr., Ken Hurst, George Spring, Denise Thirion, Leonard Francolini, and K. C. Hunt.

Today, the Colt's Custom Shop headed by George Spring; Adams & Adams (John J. Adams, Sr. and John Adams, Jr.); Andrew Bourbon; Leonard Francolini; Conrad Anderson; Denise Thirion and dozens of contemporary artisans carry on a tradition established more than 150 years ago by Samuel Colt and his guild of engravers; Gustave Young, Louis Daniel Nimschke, Cuno A. Helfricht, their families and descendants.

It is possible today to experience the same sense of pride in an engraved Colt revolver as it was in Samuel Colt's time. It is tribute to an art that, like the guns of the 19th century, has transcended time.

Among the last contemporary Colts to be commissioned under the Tiffany & Co. name this exquisite pair of 2nd Generation 1860 Army revolvers was designed by Tom Watts of Tiffany & Co. to depict a North and South theme. The handcrafted Colts took master engraver Andrew Bourbon six months to complete using a variety of traditional engraving and casting techniques, combined with an innovative process known as "ceramitation" to create the cloisonné style flags which drape over the barrels. (Dr. Joseph A. Murphy collection)

The intricate engraving, gold inlays, and faux cloisonné (real cloisonné would have cracked) combined with an exquisite bluing process has rendered a Civil War commemorative pistol set unlike any other. The Tiffany style cast gold grips are hand carved with images of soldiers, one set for the U.S. Army and one for the Confederate Army. The draping of the Union Jack and Stars and Bars over the barrels was the most difficult part of the design. The frames are outlined in gold, the inside pattern a variation of an L. D. Nimschke design.

GENERAL SHERMAN'S AD

GENERAL SHERMAN'S ADVANCE—HOWARD

PLURIBUS UNUM

WEEKLY.

TURNER'S MILL, ON THE NICKAJACK CREEK, GEORGIA.—[Sketched by T. R. Davis.]

GENERAL SHERMAN'S ADVANCE—FISH-TRAPS IN THE CHATTAHOOCHEE.—[See next Page.]

[August 13, 1864.

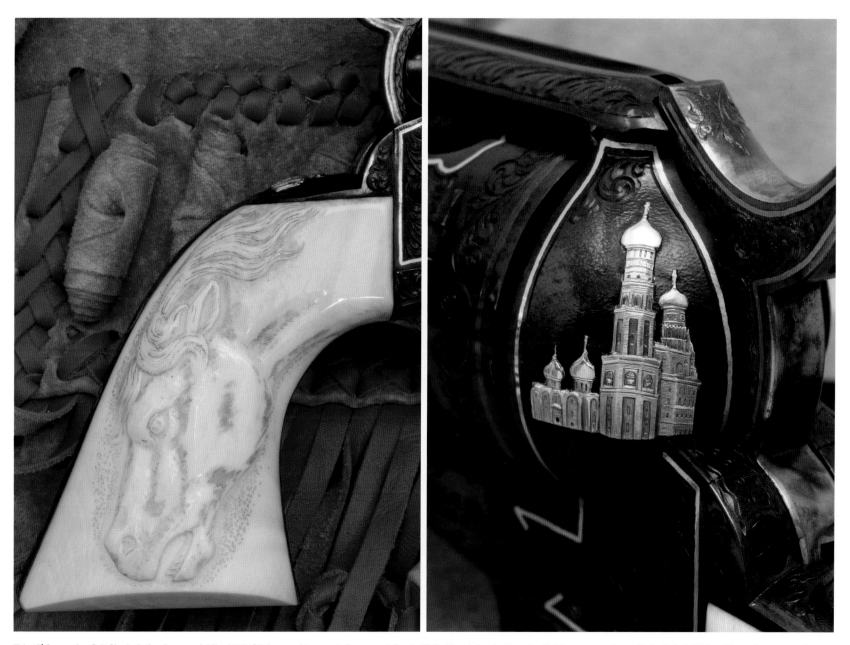

This 2nd Generation Colt Single Action Army, serial No. 23311SA, is one of two made for presentation to Nikita Khrushchev by Romaine Fielding; engraved en suite by Alvin A. White with varying scenes of Russian landmarks. (Dr. Joseph A. Murphy collection)

After singer Mel Torme parted with his Sears, Roebuck & Co. Colt in the late 1970s, he always had a little seller's remorse, which was to some degree alleviated in 1985 when he was presented with this exact copy of the gun engraved by Leonard Francolini and with grips by Alvin A. White. The 2nd Generation Colt was built as a present in appreciation of Torme's performance at a benefit concert for the Metropolitan Museum of Art's Arms and Armor Department in October 1985. The concept for the recreation of the Sears revolver was by R.L. Wilson, who had sold Torme's prized Colt to John B. Solley. On the evening of Torme's performance, at the penthouse of the St. Regis the revolver was formally presented to the legendary singer and song writer. (Dr. Joseph A. Murphy collection)

Engraved for the author by Alvin A. White and Andrew Bourbon in 1997, this 2nd Generation Colt Third Model Dragoon was the last black powder revolver engraved by A. A. White, who also hand carved the eagle ivory grips. (Author's collection)

Above: A rare cased pair of 2ⁿᵈ Generation Colts engraved by Alvin A. White and factory lettered. A very limited number of cased sets combining the 1851 Navy and Third Model Dragoon were produced by Colt's in 1983.

Left: This magnificent pair of 2ⁿᵈ Generation Walker Colts was engraved by Alvin A. White for Colt Industries Chairman George A. Strichman. The pair is now on permanent display at the Autry Museum of the American West in Los Angeles, California.

This pair of 2nd Generation Colt Single Action Army revolvers (SA48345 in .44 Special and 45684SA in .45 caliber) was engraved and gold inlaid by Howard Dove in an American Indian theme. Dove also did the scrimshawed ivory grips. (Dr. Joseph A. Murphy collection)

One of master engraver Howard Dove's finest pieces, this 2nd Generation Single Action Army is known as the California Eureka Gun. The engraving and inlay work is the finest ever done by Dove who used different shades of gold and silver combined with high relief engraving. The detail in the guns needs to be examined up close to appreciate the work that Dove put into this singular Single Action Army. (Dr. Joseph A. Murphy collection)

Another of Howard Dove's finest guns is the 7th Cavalry General George Custer Single Action Army. For this gun Dove created a modern interpretation of the 1876 Centennial Colts by engraving scenes within the frame, as Cuno A. Helfricht had done for the Fairmont Park, Philadelphia Centennial Exposition. The battle scenes depict the fight between Custer's men and Sitting Bull's war party at Little Big Horn.

PAT. SEPT. 19, 1871
JULY 2, 72 JAN. 19, 75

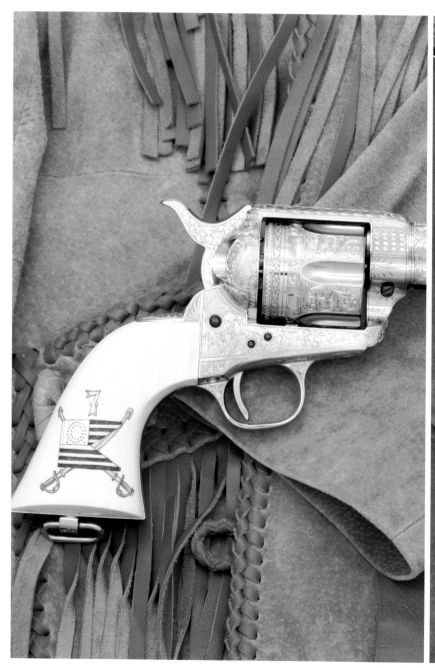

The bust of Custer on the left recoil shield is his famous pictorial pose. The balance of engraving is in the L. D. Nimschke style. The ivory grips were scrimshawed by Dove with the 7th Cavalry's flags. The entire gun is nickel plated with nitrite blue screws. (Dr. Joseph A. Murphy collection)

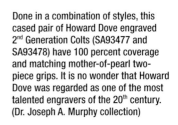

Done in a combination of styles, this cased pair of Howard Dove engraved 2nd Generation Colts (SA93477 and SA93478) have 100 percent coverage and matching mother-of-pearl two-piece grips. It is no wonder that Howard Dove was regarded as one of the most talented engravers of the 20th century. (Dr. Joseph A. Murphy collection)

Known as the Hartford Colt, this masterpiece by Howard Dove was engraved and gold inlaid with the Colt factory dome, rampant colt, a bust of Samuel Colt, and an inlay of the first Colt prototype revolver. (Dr. Joseph A. Murphy collection)

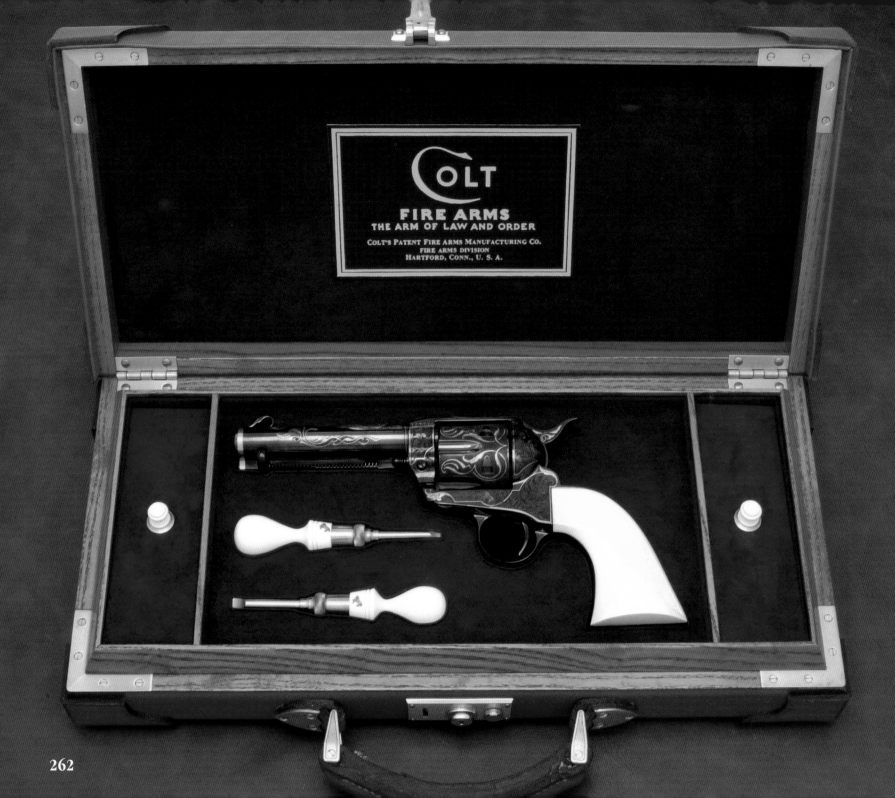

262

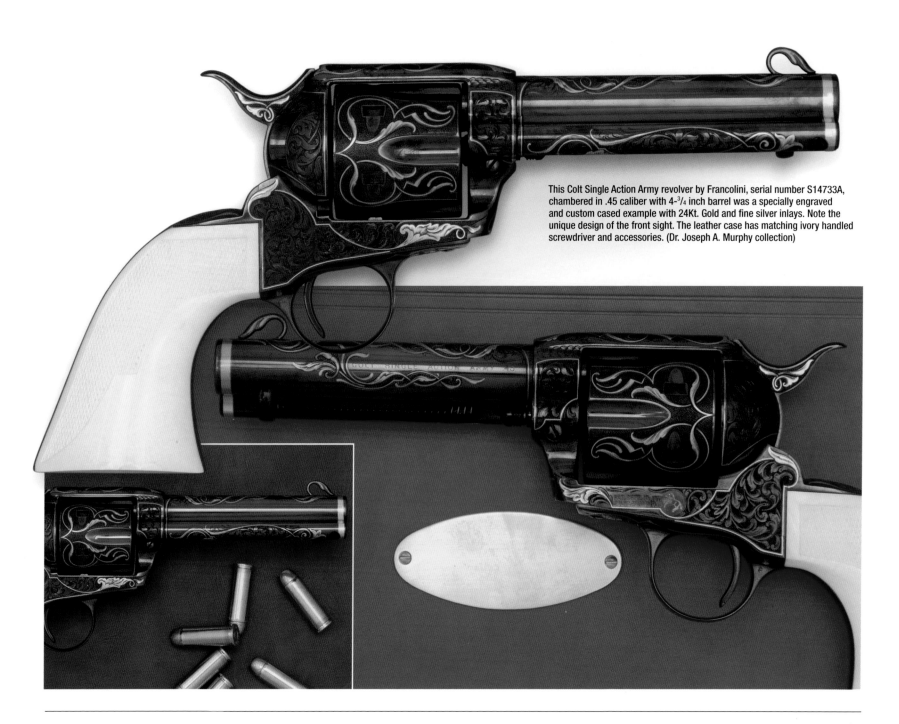

This Colt Single Action Army revolver by Francolini, serial number S14733A, chambered in .45 caliber with 4-3/4 inch barrel was a specially engraved and custom cased example with 24Kt. Gold and fine silver inlays. Note the unique design of the front sight. The leather case has matching ivory handled screwdriver and accessories. (Dr. Joseph A. Murphy collection)

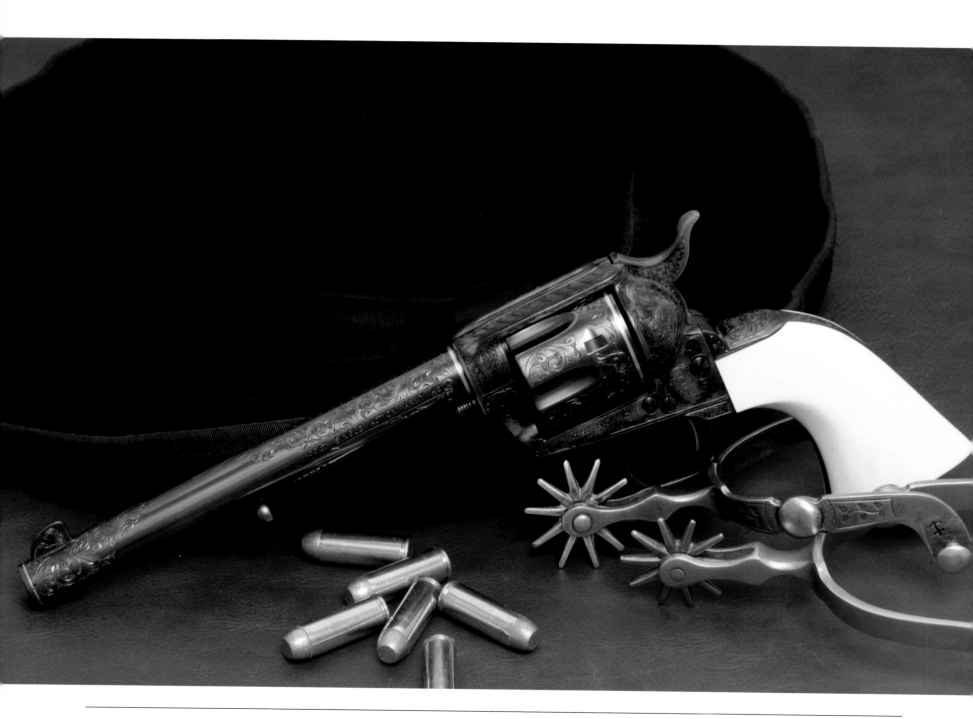

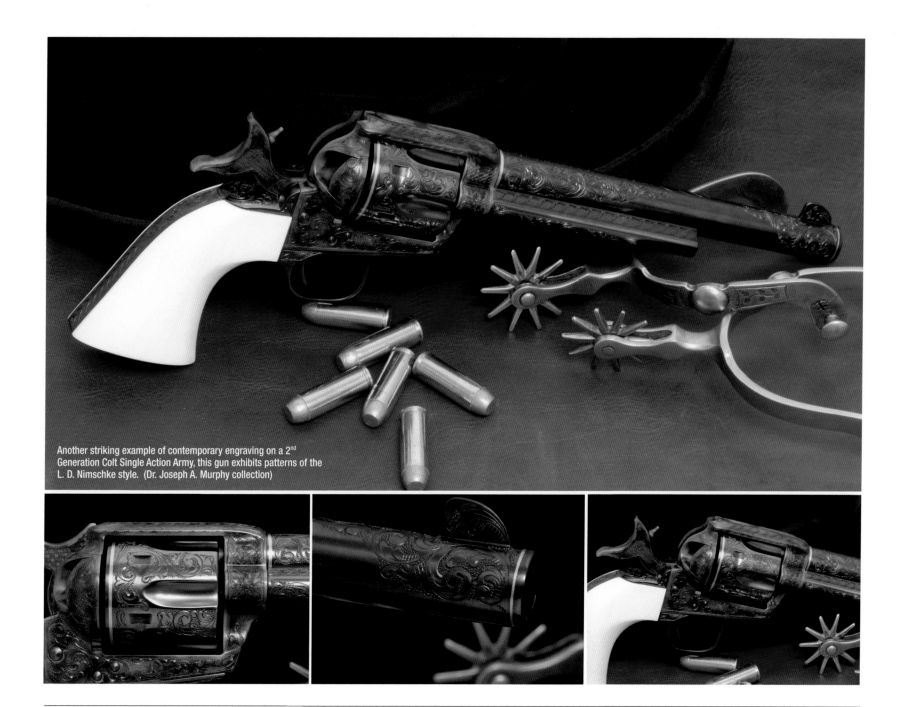

Another striking example of contemporary engraving on a 2nd Generation Colt Single Action Army, this gun exhibits patterns of the L. D. Nimschke style. (Dr. Joseph A. Murphy collection)

John J. Adams, Sr. has been engraving Colts for more than 30 years, beginning with A. A. White Engravers in 1976. A. A. White produced engraved guns for Colt's during the 2nd Generation models. Beginning early in the 1960s Adams, like the rest of the A. A. White guild, copied the designs of Young, Nimschke, and Helfricht, but Adams also has his own style as evidenced by this Adams & Adams Engraving Sampler on a 2nd Generation Colt SAA.

REWARD!

WELLS, FARGO & Co.
ese and Coppero...
ing, by one m...
(Ruplee's Brid...
coin and gold d...

For arr...
Robber...
tion of t...

ROB...
set; wei...

...c. 1, 1875.

A Mexican, ligh...
...oustache and sh...

John Adams, Sr. recreated the famous factory engraved Colt SAA presented to legendary Frontier lawman Bill Tilghman in December 1893.

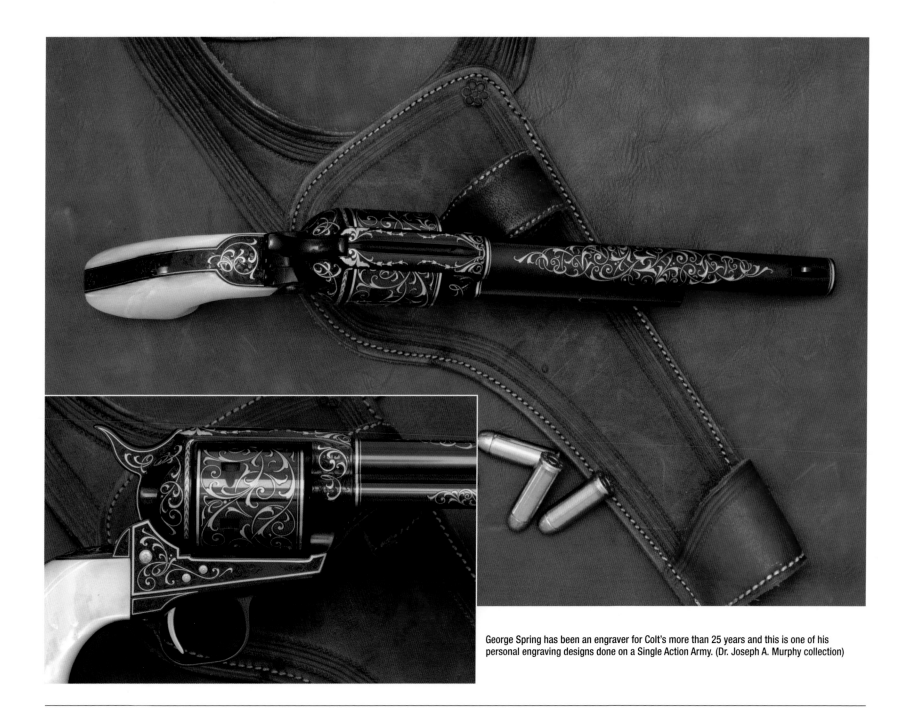

George Spring has been an engraver for Colt's more than 25 years and this is one of his personal engraving designs done on a Single Action Army. (Dr. Joseph A. Murphy collection)

Smoke Over Hartford

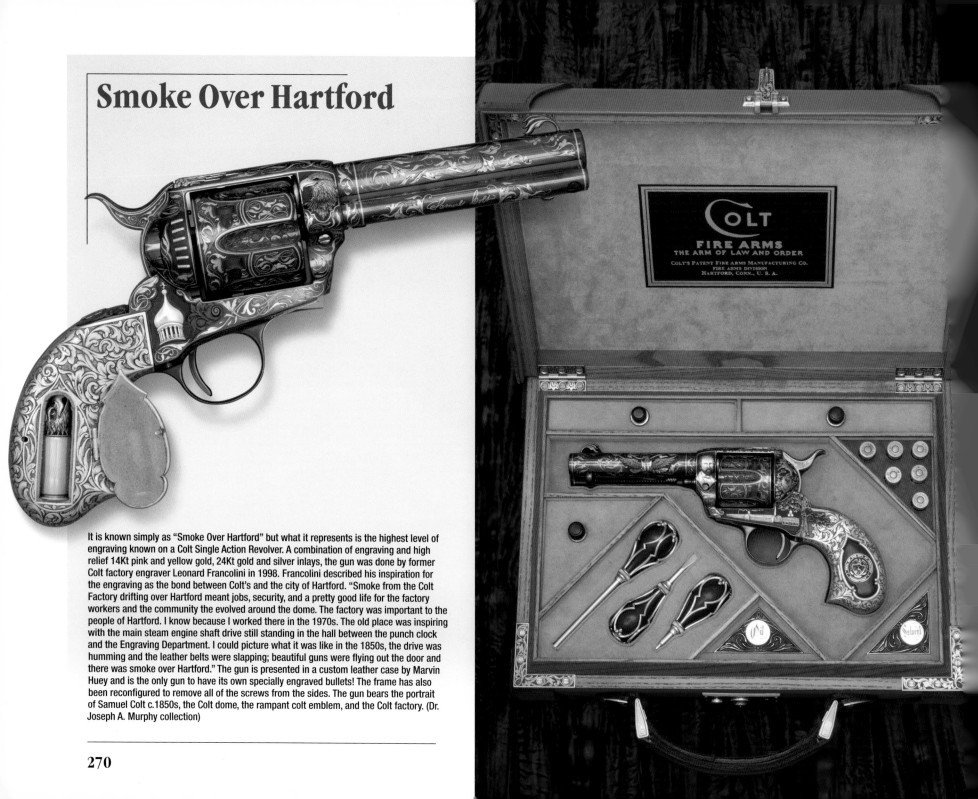

It is known simply as "Smoke Over Hartford" but what it represents is the highest level of engraving known on a Colt Single Action Revolver. A combination of engraving and high relief 14Kt pink and yellow gold, 24Kt gold and silver inlays, the gun was done by former Colt factory engraver Leonard Francolini in 1998. Francolini described his inspiration for the engraving as the bond between Colt's and the city of Hartford. "Smoke from the Colt Factory drifting over Hartford meant jobs, security, and a pretty good life for the factory workers and the community the evolved around the dome. The factory was important to the people of Hartford. I know because I worked there in the 1970s. The old place was inspiring with the main steam engine shaft drive still standing in the hall between the punch clock and the Engraving Department. I could picture what it was like in the 1850s, the drive was humming and the leather belts were slapping; beautiful guns were flying out the door and there was smoke over Hartford." The gun is presented in a custom leather case by Marvin Huey and is the only gun to have its own specially engraved bullets! The frame has also been reconfigured to remove all of the screws from the sides. The gun bears the portrait of Samuel Colt c.1850s, the Colt dome, the rampant colt emblem, and the Colt factory. (Dr. Joseph A. Murphy collection)

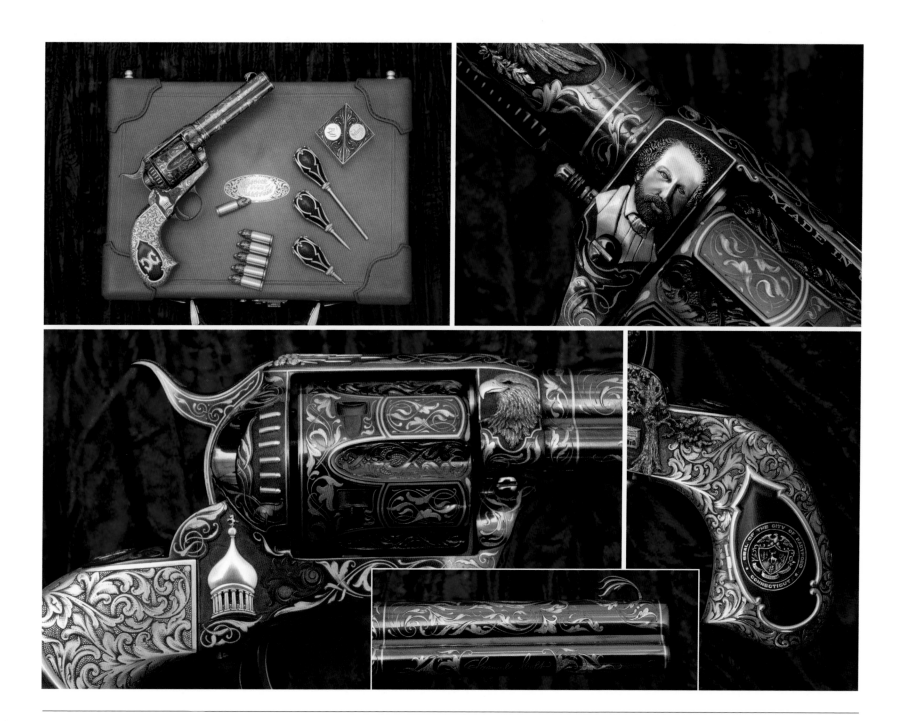

Prototype Colt revolving rifles and the prototype Revolving Pocket Pistol are one of the many special displays at the Wadsworth.

Chapter Ten
The Wadsworth Atheneum Museum of Art
Home To Samuel Colt's Private Collection

The state of Connecticut has a rich firearms heritage with New Haven having been home to the Winchester Repeating Arms Company, and Hartford the residence of Colt's Firearms Manufacturing Company. It should come as no surprise then that Samuel Colt's personal arms collection is still in Hartford, housed in the Wadsworth Atheneum Museum of Art.

When Samuel Colt's widow, Elizabeth Hart Jarvis Colt, died in 1905, she bequeathed her late husband's entire personal collection of firearms to the Wadsworth along with a memorial collection of his guns that had been assembled at the time of his death during the Civil War. A great benefactor of the Wadsworth, she also gave them a large art collection and donated money for the construction of a Colt Memorial wing.

Late in 2005 a new exhibit of the Colt collection was mounted at the Wadsworth and is being readied for a national tour after which the collection will be on permanent display. The exhibit goes on tour in March 2007. The photographs in this chapter were provided by *Man at Arms* magazine editor Stewart Mowbray from the exhibit at the Wadsworth, which opened in September 2006.

In addition to the Colt collection the exhibit features 50 additional guns from the Museum of Connecticut History, making this the most complete display ever of Samuel Colt's own firearms. The Wadsworth features Colt's study pieces of revolving firearms that pre-dated his invention; his original wooden model of an arbor pin, barrel group and hammer; a beautiful progression of prototypes by Anson Chase and John Pearson; mint condition Patersons, including a stunning Number 5 Holster Pistol with ivory grips; the curiously un-

The entrance to the exhibit leads the way through the early history of Colt's from the Paterson to the early percussion models of the 1850s and beyond. The exhibit was funded in part by a generous grant from Hartford philanthropists Melinda and Paul Sullivan.

A cast Rampant Colt, the company symbol, stands at the entrance to the exhibit.

gainly prototype Holster Pistol c.1846, presented for review to the Secretary of War, William L. Marcy, and Captain Samuel Walker; a Model 1847 Holster Pistol that may have been owned by Samuel Walker himself; experimental models galore – many beautifully decorated but remaining unfinished; pristine samples of practically every Colt firearm made up through the Civil War; metals, prizes and gifts awarded to Colt during his lifetime; and a vast array of American and European counterfeit Colts or competitor's pistols that violated the Colt's patent.

Aside from the guns, there are photos of the early Colt factory machinery, a colorful series of famous advertising paintings by George Catlin, various objects of decorative art from Armsmear (Samuel Colt's residence), and a series of panoramic, color paintings of Hartford during the catastrophic flood of 1854, showing the Colt Armory awash in flood waters. These panoramic panels were on display in Armsmear until Mrs. Colt's death in 1905, where they had been a popular conversation piece for her visitors.

"Samuel Colt: Arms, Art and Invention" is a compact exhibition. There are often eight or more guns in a display case intelligently organized so that one can compare similar examples and see their differences. The signage is excellent, not only identifying the firearms and explaining them, but also elaborating upon their role in the development of Colt's brand name product. Marketing is a key theme in this show, and Samuel Colt's advertising, promotional gifts and industrial design genius are all highlighted. Taken as a whole, it presents a narrative of Colt's career that should hold the interest of casual visitors who might not normally be interested in guns.

The layout of the display cases guides the visitor through a progression of story lines without seeming repetitive or rigid. This is difficult to accomplish with an open floor plan, where the displays are arranged in one large relatively square room rather than in a narrow hall where traffic flow is one-way and predetermined. Visitors to the Wadsworth can view the displays from a number of different starting points and in different directions, all routes still somehow making sense and telling a logical story – an elegant touch that must have been quite a challenge for the designers.

Outside of the images in this chapter, if you want to see the exhibit in person before the latter part of 2008, you'll have to catch it on the road, or buy the exhibit book, *Samuel Colt: Arms, Art and Invention* written by noted historian Herbert G. Houze.[1]

[1] The book is available from Man at Arms Bookshelf, 54 E. School St., Woonsocket, R.I. 02895 for $65 plus shipping and handling. Order on line at www.manatarmsbooks.com or call 800 999-4697.

A young man and an idea. Sam Colt carved the cylinder, arbor and hammer for his future invention while serving as a seaman aboard the cargo ship Corvo during its 1830 voyage to Calcutta. He was 16 years old.

The exhibit is cleverly broken up by doorways leading to other doorways as the displays flow around an open room. It keeps visitors moving in no particular direction yet no atter which waya you go everything seems to fall into place.

n inventor and an entrepreneur,
illiterate, a profligate libertine,
ere is a kernel of truth to some
Colt, most reports were

re the Civil War, Colt was a
oal was to sell firearms, which
als. The press followed Colt's
a man of international
d in sensational stories of his
ions.

ritics. He viewed the mention
as advertising, and he viewed
-mindedness in promoting
life from 1830 until his death
ition.
on and its accompanying
Colt's achievements as a
rican industrial pioneer thrust
the world stage, and
dustry.
e in the permanent collection
um of Art.

Straight ahead a display of early revolving arms built prior to Colt's patent. Seen prominently in the display is a Collier revolving flintlock pistol. At far left a display board of Colt's revolvers and longarms.

Elizabeth Hart Jarvis Colt and her son Caldwell in a portrait painted by Charles Loring Elliott in 1865.

Swords and awards combine to make this display case a very interesting exhibit. The magnificent Two-St

This wall display exhibits a variety of Colt's models from the 1850s and 1860s including Roots revolving rifles, Roots pistols, and Colt revolvers ranging from the 1851 Navy to 1862 Police and Pocket Models of Navy Caliber.

A display of prototypes and early production models explains the evolution of Colt designs.

A display of production rifles and pistols
including a very rare 1862 Trapper Model
(lower left) of which fewer than 50 were built

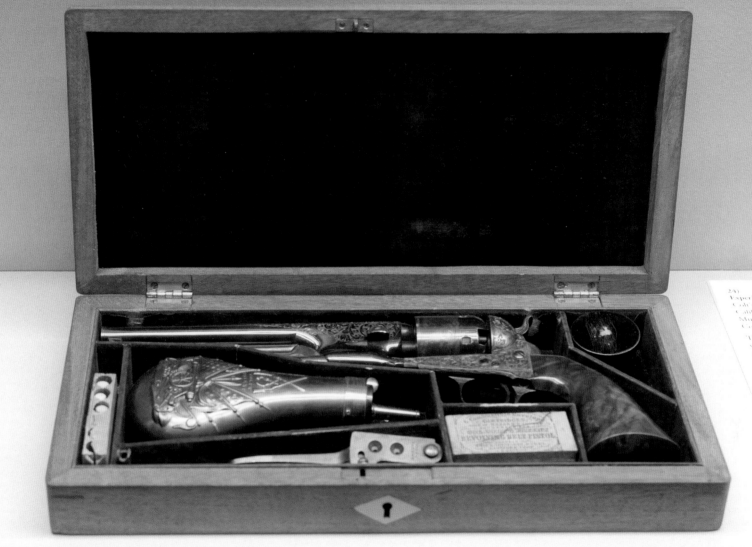

Leading the way into another section of the display are these marble busts of Samuel and Elizabeth Colt sculpted by Edward Sheffield Bartholomew, c.1857.

A display of art commissioned by Samuel Colt, many of which were turned into promotional prints for the company, as they featured Colt's firearms in one way or another. The works shown were all done by the renowned painter of Indians George Catlin.

A case of its own. A gun worthy of a singular display, this is one of the finest Texas Patersons in the world.

Samuel and Elizabeth Colt had their portraits painted by two different artists in 1856; his by
Gerald S. Hayward, and hers by Richard Morrell Staigg. Both are watercolor on ivory in a gold
locket case with hair work on reverse under a glass window.

The great portrait of Samuel Colt was actually painted in 1865, three years after his death. Artist Charles Loring Elliott was commissioned by Elizabeth Colt to do the piece as a portrait of her husband was never done on a grand scale. The oil on canvas painting measures 84 x 64 inches (7x5 feet). Elliott depicted Colt as a much younger and thinner man than he appeared at the time of his death in 1862. He used several portraits of Colt provided by Elizabeth including one from their wedding in 1856.

One of Samuel Colt's great successes, the 1851 Navy, shown here disassembled.

this vase to Colt in 1859. It appears in *Colonel Samuel Colt*, the posthumous portrait painted by Charles Loring Elliott.

17

Samuel Colt received many awards and presents from foreign dignitaries during his career, some of which are shown in this display, including the Turkish Order of Mejidie, 1861 (center left with ribbon), and an ornate Buehl Box made in Vienna of Rosewood, ivory, mother-of-pearl, brass, and silver.

Buehl Box, 1849
Vienna, Austria
Rosewood, ivory, mother-of-pearl, brass, and silver
Bequest of Elizabeth Hart Jarvis Colt, 1905.1256

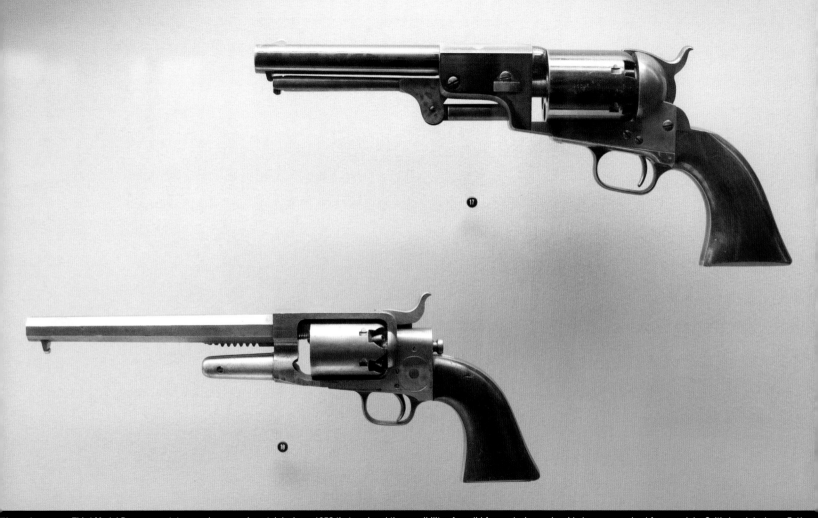

Shown here are a Third Model Dragoon prototype and an experimental design c.1852 that explored the possibility of a solid frame design and a side hammer evolved from work by Colt's head designer E. K. Root. Obviously a loading lever would have been attached to the extension on the frame and used a toothed ratchet to drive the rammer. A variation of this idea appeared on the 1860 Army which was fitted with a new loading lever known as a "creeping" type, which used a toothed design. The solid frame also appeared in 1855 on the Roots pistols.

The Buehl Box is filled with medals awarded to Samuel Colt.

A long view of the portrait wall in the Wadsworth exhibit shows the portraits of Samuel Colt and Elizabeth and Caldwell Colt.

Photographer Unknown
American
Colonel Samuel Colt, 1851-52
Daguerreotype
Gift of Mrs. Henry K.W. Welch, 1944.13

Presentation Snuffbox, 1859
Swiss
Gold, diamonds, and enamel
...Jarvis Colt, 1905.1535.

Another famous portrait of Samuel Colt, a photograph taken in 1851 or 1852. The display also contains a variety of diamond rings presented to Colt by various foreign dignitaries, including (right and left of the center ring) a ring with eight diamonds surrounding the imperial crown of Czar Nicholas I, a gift in 1854, and a ring presented to Colt in 1856 or 1858 Czar Alexander II.

The ivory fire screen features spectacular carving of the Rampant Colt on a shield, with the Connecticut River fronting the Colt factory at top, Colt pistols to the left and rifles to the right, and the America eagle and shield, all in individual oval panels. Samuel Colt chartered the steamboat depicted, for his wedding on June 5, 1856. The framework around the fire screen was carved from the famous Charter Oak.

A close-up of the Rampant Colt displayed at the entrance to the exhibit.

Index

(Illustration captions marked with italics)

Models by year of manufacture